PROFESSIONAL
MAIL
MANAGEMENT

A Guide To Cutting Costs In The 90's

Herbert W. Akers

Published by
Akers Marketing
P.O. Box 10693
Rockville, Maryland 20849-0693
(301) 294-2305

Library of Congress Catalog Card Number: 91-91868

International Standard Book Number 0-9629096-0-2

Copyright Acknowledgements are on Page 286

The editor for this book was Lola B. Akers
Front cover design by Robert T. Akers

Printed by
St. Anthony Press
3431 Carlin Springs Road
Bailey's Crossroads, VA 22041-2802
A Division of St. Anthony Publishing

Printed and bound in the United States of America

CONTENTS

PREFACE

Like my first book, this book is intended for managers. Those who aspire to be managers, those who are managers, and those who manage managers. It is designed to teach, to remind, and to explain how to provide any organization with the best mail service at the least cost. The hundreds of money saving ideas that it contains are not necessarily either new or original, but many are all the more valuable because they have withstood the test of time. They represent over 35 years of total involvement in mail, mail processing, mailroom equipment, and mail personnel.

This book was written to be especially easy to read and interesting as it suggests how to improve mail preparation and processing. It was also written with the firm conviction that it would become an important ally in your daily battle with mail costs.

It is intended to be used as a daily reference. As your mail center and your organization grow, this book will continue to provide ideas to help fight inflation and improve mail service. It offers new approaches for the professional mail manager with many years of experience, and it can help the novice of only a few months' experience understand most of the pitfalls of mail center management. It will help a big corporation with very large mail installations, and fledgling mail operations that have only part-time help. Any organization that considers its mail important enough to warrant the use of a postage meter can be assured of even better mail service by applying the suggestions contained in this book.

That should give you some idea of what this book *is,* but it is equally important that you understand what it is *not.* It isn't intended as an interpretation of the *Domestic Mail Manual*; there is a Rates and Classification Center in every region for just that purpose. But it does offer ideas about mail classification that will prove helpful, and it does remind you when and where to ask questions. It also explains how you can be sure that you get everything you are entitled to when you buy any postal service. In addition, although this book isn't a consumer's guide, it does provide extensive background information about most kinds of equipment that are available to help solve mail center problems. Every attempt has been made to offer unbiased information, to include every known source for each product, and to make the coverage as comprehensive and helpful as possible.

The names and addresses of various publications and organizations that can help you solve problems are listed throughout the book. These include specialists who will survey your packaging needs, magazines you should be reading, business shows that you can attend to learn more about mail equipment, and many other sources of information.

Finally, we come to the subject of prices. Every book with a price quoted in it seems to go out of date rapidly in view of continuing inflation. Yet, without some range of price, the relative worth of a service is difficult to evaluate. Therefore, prices are often mentioned so that you will learn the relative cost as compared to other costs. In addition, mail rates are discussed throughout the book, not to teach you how to rate a piece of mail, but to teach you how to compare one rate with another class of mail. The importance of comparing costs will continue regardless of the current rates.

Professional Mail Management will teach you to be *effective* in mail management, *to do the right things.* At the same time it will teach you to be efficient in mail management, *to do things right.*

Herb Akers

March 1991

ACKNOWLEDGEMENTS

I am indebted to many people who assisted me in writing and publishing this book. I especially appreciate my son, Bob, taking the time from his busy advertising world to design the front cover for this book. I had no idea what he was preparing for me and I was thrilled with the outcome.

Most of all I am indebted (again!) to my best friend, Lola, my bride of 42 years. Without her encouragement all these years I would be a likely candidate for skid row. This book would have been impossible without her help and guidance.

I greatly appreciate the enthusiasm, information and advice from my printer, St. Anthony Press. By the time Van Seagraves sent me to them I really needed a St. Anthony.

I still must thank the thousands of Pitney Bowes customers in the Tidewater Virginia area, Atlanta, and Washington, DC, who always took time to answer my questions and explain their methods to me over the 18 years I was connected with that organization. I appreciate the help of hundreds of sales representatives in one business show after another who still take the time to show me how their equipment operates. I am also grateful to so many Postal Service employees for always being so helpful in answering my never-ending questions. Without the kindness and help of all of those people, this book would not have been possible.

CHAPTER 1

THE FUTURE OF THE UNITED STATES POSTAL SERVICE

The United States Postal Service will slowly have its mail volume eroded by various electronic methods of transferring data, and by alternate methods of distribution, until it self-destructs. That's what various writers have been predicting for the past 15 or 20 years, but *it is not going to happen!* The doom and gloom experts say that UPS has all of the parcel business, Federal Express has the largest share of the overnight business, and that soon the Postal Service will lose its other business. Baloney! The Postal Service is here to stay.

The Electronic Age

In the 70's and the 80's the big buzz words were "Electronic Mail." Everyone who had ever had a letter delayed or stood in line in a post office immediately began to tout its virtues as the solution for all of the world's postal ills. But now suddenly it is a different story. One question arises over and over again whenever E-mail is discussed; *What about privacy?* Of course, there isn't any.

Only the Postal Service provides *absolute* privacy. Most overnight carriers reserve the right to open *everything*. But, the Postal Service has to obtain a Federal court order or a search warrant to even open First-Class, Priority Mail, or Express Mail. Now that's privacy!

The fax machines and E-mail are superlative methods of communicating, if you do not mind everyone else reading the message. If you are in Dallas and need to send an urgent purchase order to a supplier in Chicago or Los Angeles, you can't beat a fax machine. If you have a report to send to your home office, and it is due today, the fax may save your life. But don't send a branch office any payroll information unless you wish it to be all over the branch five minutes after it arrives. (In some cases fax messages have even been copied before being delivered to the actual addressee.) Don't send any confidential information via fax if you value its security. In addition to the loss of privacy, even the thermal paper used by some fax machines leaves a great deal to be desired if sent as a permanent record.

As for E-mail, it may be ideal to leave a message on another personal computer without leaving your chair, specially if you are in a large corporation located in a multistory building. But don't do it if the message contains confidential corporate or personnel information. PC workers often take a break from their own tasks and "roam" or "browse" through their computer's mailboxes. It's true that passwords retard such activity, but passwords are not foolproof either.

A secretary was recently chastised in a Federal agency for simply typing an eight item grocery list in an idle file on her terminal. She discovered her senior department manager routinely read all of the secretary's computer files. Perhaps she acted in an unbusiness-like manner, but it illustrates the total lack of privacy in E-mail and in open computer files.

In addition, there have been a number of court cases where employees charged that the computer manager printed their E-mail and maintained files on their activities, in a sort of Big Brother operation. Whether it is snooping or a "right" of an employer is not the issue, only that there is absolutely no privacy with either fax mail or E-mail.

In spite of electronic direct deposits by both commercial banks and the Federal Government; in spite of all kinds of electronic mail handled by ever more complex computer systems; and in spite of the newest fad, the facsimile or fax machine; mail volume handled by the Postal Service has consistently and continuously grown by leaps and bounds. It is highly unlikely to slow down, much less stop. Because there is no substitute for hard copy, delivered directly to your door, *with absolute privacy*. Can you imagine sending a past due notice via *fax*! "Oh, I'm sorry, I had my machine unplugged!" Or, "Gee, it was in the shop."

What's in the Future?

First of all, the customers continue to multiply. The population growth in the U.S. may have slowed down somewhat after the baby boom, but from 1970 to 1990 we added 46 million new Americans. And what grandma can resist sending the new grandchild six or eight cards even the first year? Then as soon as those children are 18 they start accumulating credit cards which translate into a minimum of 12 pieces of mail annually. But one card will rarely suffice, and the average family will undoubtedly have several, with each one constantly generating bills (and perhaps some past due notices!). There are many other examples of how the American life-style isn't likely to change from its constant generation of mail.

One only needs to look at the statistics of the Postal Service to see proof of these concepts. In Fiscal Year (FY) 1986 it processed a total of 147.4 billion pieces of mail which increased to 166.3 billion in 1990, for a gain of almost 19 billion pieces in just 48 months. Of particular interest to the mail manager is the fact that most of the growth was in First-Class Mail. In FY '86 First-Class Mail totaled slightly over 76 billion pieces, leaping to over 89 billion pieces in FY '90, a growth of *13 billion pieces* in 48 months. At the same time, third-class (advertising) mail grew over eight billion pieces. Certainly not a track record of an organization that is likely to disappear any time soon.

That should prove one point beyond refute, if you are to manage mail efficiently, that is to do things right, you simply must learn to work well (sometimes, cope!) with the Postal Service. For all practical purposes, with some exceptions, of course, it is the only game in town.

The second point is also beyond refute, postal rates will continue to go up!

Historians point to the past as some indication of what the future may bring. This is certainly true of postal rates. But it is equally true today of the cost of a newspaper, a gallon of gasoline, or a loaf of bread. Look at the chart in Figure 1 showing the history of First-Class postage rates.

INFLATION'S IMPACT ON POSTAGE COSTS

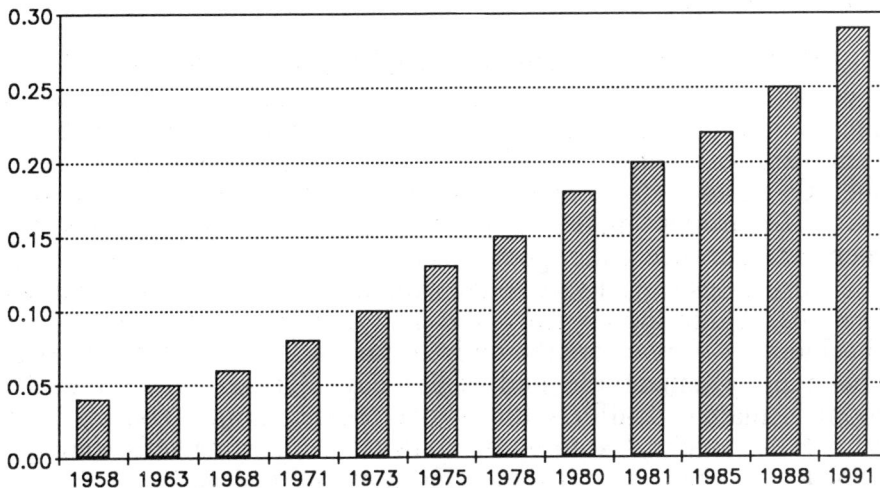

Figure 1 The history of First-Class postage rates.

Now, do you think First-Class Mail rates will go up in the nineties? There is no question about it. The only real question is, once, twice, or three times? Although the Postmaster General has vowed to keep postage increases below the rate of inflation, the perceptive mail manager will realize that cost reduction programs initiated in the early nineties will produce double, triple, or even quadruple benefits by the year 2000.

In addition to inflation, there is also a new type of pressure on Postal Service rates. The Omnibus Budget Reconciliation Act of 1990 requires up to $4.7 *billion* in additional payments by the Postal Service through FY 1995. The USPS payments will fund the cost-of-living adjustments for postal retirees and survivors who have retired since 1971. The payments will also fund the employer's share of health benefit premiums for postal annuitants since the reorganization of the USPS.

That law impacted the 1990 rate case by $562 million, and the Postal Rate Commission *did* include the financial impact in its cost and revenue projections and its final recommendations. And listen to what Postmaster General Frank said recently: "In terms of postage rates paid by the American people, this law means *more, sooner*." And, "Of course, were it not for the additional costs assessed by Congress, future postage increases would be smaller with longer intervals between them."

Thus, you are left with these facts. Postage rates will go up, the Postal Service will be around a long, long time, and the volume will get larger and larger. Therefore, if your organization sends only a moderate amount of First-Class Mail, you must strive to get the best possible service from the Postal Service, at the least cost. But whatever you do to reduce costs is likely to bring repeated benefits throughout the next decade. And yesterday's knowledge doesn't usually solve tomorrow's problems.

EFFICIENT MAILROOM MANAGEMENT IS ESSENTIAL

Many companies today depend on their incoming mail for their very existence. They may utilize advertisements in periodicals or direct mail to occupant lists to produce all of their sales, and therefore all of their revenue. Other organizations may be just the opposite. They may utilize other types of business methods to generate sales but until the invoice, or statement or insurance policy goes into the mail no revenue is generated.

Few businesses can survive today without some degree of dependency on the mails. Quite the contrary, the mail operation is the very heart of most businesses. Very often, the entire effort of all of the employees goes into the mail system at the end of the day. Therefore, how well the mailroom is managed affects the whole organization. You could well paraphrase that cliche, "Nothing happens until someone sells something" to say "Nothing happens until something goes into the mail!"

Service to the customer is on the lips of every person in business today. But just imagine the impact of missent or delayed mail, arriving with an improper address or not securely sealed, and you will understand how mailroom management affects relations with those important customers.

Or imagine irresponsible (read underpaid and/or untrained) mail clerks overpaying postage with that old mailroom adage, "Hey, put some more postage on it, then it'll never come back!" Or a crew that constantly uses overnight service, regardless of the sender's intentions. Then you will be able to visualize the tremendous potential for waste in a mailroom without efficient management.

But it is not easy. In fact, it is more complex than ever. The classification of mail changes, cost-saving work-sharing programs become commonplace, personnel management becomes more complicated and competitive, and tons of new equipment enter the marketplace. All of these factors make mailroom management more complicated and serve to emphasize more than ever the importance of *efficient* mail center management.

SETTING YOUR MAIL MANAGEMENT OBJECTIVES

If you expect to attain any goal, whether it be personal or business, it is generally agreed that to succeed you need to establish the actual objectives you wish to reach. The goal of efficient and professional mail center management is certainly no exception. You obviously wish to eliminate waste and reduce postage costs, so those two items might lead the list. Of course you need to understand the importance of developing sound productive relations with the Postal Service and to realize that cooperation is a two-way street. In addition, you should know that you can never overemphasize the importance of a well-educated mailroom staff, one that is kept up-to-date with a series of ongoing training sessions covering all kinds of rates and regulations.

In addition to those objectives, you should believe that modern, well-cared for equipment in a mailroom that successfully utilizes all of its allotted space is a vital ingredient in any efficient mail operation.

And last, but surely not least, you should strive to effectively utilize the skills and full potential of your staff.

Perhaps a check list of these major objectives will serve as a reminder:

- Eliminate postage and shipping cost waste
- Reduce operating, shipping, and postage costs
- Develop a close working relationship with the Postal Service
- Provide detailed and current postal information to employees
- Effectively utilize up-to-date mailroom equipment
- Effectively utilize all of your available space
- Effectively utilize and develop mail center personnel
- Understand management's concepts of the mail operation
- Understand how mail impacts other departments

Remember, some of your greatest challenges may be in trying to convince your top management of the importance of their mail operations in relation to the overall success of the organization. This book will give you many tools and ideas that will help you sell yourself and your mail operation to upper management, and help you to reach your objectives.

CHAPTER 2

HOW THE POSTAL SERVICE FUNCTIONS

It's 4:40 p.m. on Friday in one of the twenty largest cities in the U.S. when you discover that your mailing machine operator forgot to change the date on your postage meter. Now you have 3,500 statements with yesterday's date on them, and you have already received two warnings about "stale" dates on your meter stamps. And, the manager of the billing department may physically attack you if those statements are delayed for any reason whatsoever. Maybe you can telephone someone at the post office and find out if there is anything you can do to assure that the statements will not be delayed. That's when you remember you haven't the slightest idea who to call, or even where to call!

That's not too exaggerated a situation for the newcomer to mail management, and it should emphasize the necessity of understanding the organization of the United States Postal Service (USPS). There are over 760,000 career employees in the USPS and over 28,000 post offices. Just imagine trying to get an intelligent solution out of that maze of people and places unless you have some understanding of how such a large organization functions. That is exactly the purpose of this chapter, *to aid you in problem solving.*

THE ORGANIZATION OF THE USPS

In Washington, DC, at Postal Service Headquarters, about 2200 people guide the organization toward the swift completion of its appointed rounds. Few organizations of anywhere near the size and scope of the Postal Service can boast of fewer people at its home office. That serves to emphasize how a large majority of the operating authority and responsibility has been delegated to the regional postmasters general and the division general managers (who also wear a hat marked *postmaster*).

While some of the departments at USPS Headquarters serve in a staff (or advisory) capacity, there is one line of authority that is especially important to those having complex and far-reaching involvement with the USPS. This authority flows from the deputy postmaster general, through the operations department at Headquarters, to the regional postmasters general, and down to the division general managers/postmasters. That line of authority continues from the division general manager to all of the managers of the mail factories designated as *management sectional centers (MSCs)* and on to the postmasters in the smaller post offices (which are designated as *associate* offices).

Regional Offices

The five regional offices of the Postal Service are located in Windsor, CT, Philadelphia, Memphis, Chicago, and San Bruno, CA. With a staff of about 400 in each region, headed by the regional postmaster general, each of these offices is responsible for the collection, transportation and delivery of all mail in nine or ten states. Each region manages those processing operations for an average of 110 million pieces six nights a week, every week, week in and week out.

Divisional Offices

Reporting to the five regional offices are 73 divisions strategically located throughout the U.S. in the major centers of population. It is at this level that the majority of operating finesse (and headaches) takes place because the people in the divisions have the responsibility to physically move the mail and are also responsible for managing the MSCs and the smaller associate offices. The division is the uppermost level of management that works directly with USPS customers. So it is somewhat a court of last resort if you have mail problems to solve in a MSC or associate office. At the same time the division is a complex operating facility, another *mail factory*, and its function is not only managerial, it is operational as well.

Management Sectional Centers

There are currently 136 MSCs, a little less than two per division. They are no different in their operational scope than the divisions, except that they may be smaller facilities and may process a smaller volume of mail from the surrounding associate post offices. The MSC postmaster not only must manage all of the mail processing operations but may oversee a smaller sectional center facility operation as well. In addition, approximately 100 associate postmasters will generally report to the MSC manager.

Sectional Center Facilities

The smallest "factories" are the some 264 sectional center facilities (SCFs). They do not differ much in overall *kinds* of work, they are simply smaller than the divisions and MSCs and consequently process a smaller volume of mail from the surrounding associate post offices.

Associate Offices

While they represent the smallest post offices in size and scope of operation, the *associate offices* make up the largest portion of the approximately 28,000 post offices. They serve the small communities throughout the U.S. which often have less than 5,000 residents. These are the post offices clustered around every SCF. They feed all of their mail into the nearest SCF for processing, except for some local mail which they may trap for local delivery to post office boxes. You may hear postal managers and seasoned mail managers refer to them simply as "AOs."

Stations and Branches

In addition to the 28,000 post offices, there are about 5,000 additional postal facilities designated as stations or branches. A *station* is located within the corporate limits or delivery area of the city, town, or village in which the main post office is located. A *branch* is a post office that is outside the corporate limits or city delivery area of the city, town, or village in which the main post office is located. Branches have their own community identities and defined ZIP Code boundaries which may be used as the last line of the delivery address.

There are also almost 4,400 *contract* stations and branches which, instead of being staffed by career postal employees as in the regular stations and branches, are operated under a contractual agreement between the USPS and an individual contractor.

Bulk Mail Centers

There are 21 Bulk Mail Centers (BMCs) located throughout the U.S. that process magazines, bulk third-class mail, and parcels. The New Jersey BMC, at Seacaucus, also processes most of the international surface mail, magazines, and parcels. There are also seven smaller Auxiliary Service Facilities (ASFs) that help take the load off of the larger BMCs.

The BMCs function under the guidance of a general manager who reports to the nearest divisional general manager/postmaster. There are all kinds of people at the BMCs who can assist the customer in the complicated intricacies of bulk second- and third-class mail, including a customer engineer who serves as liaison between the customer and the various operational managers at the BMC.

To provide some idea of the functions of the BMCs it should be noted that in FY 1990 there were 75 *billion* pieces of second-, third- and fourth-class mail processed, a great majority of it through one or more BMCs. And, while it is true that UPS has siphoned off most of the parcel shipping done by commercial shippers, the general public still depends to a great extent on the USPS for parcel delivery. Parcel volume alone in FY 1990 was almost 128 *million* pieces.

Staying Up-To-Date

All of these figures are subject to change from time to time as the USPS adjusts its field management organization. But the current list of divisions, with their corresponding MSCs, their street addresses, and the first three digits of the ZIP Codes they serve, is updated periodically in the *Postal Bulletin*. That list is also shown in the *National ZIP Code Directory* (which is published annually) along with a list of the location of each SCF, its mailing ZIP Code, and the three digit ZIP codes it serves. If you have any doubt of the nature of your local post office, and where it fits into the scheme of the USPS organization, the *National ZIP Code Directory* can provide the answer.

In addition to the *National Zip Code Directory* and the *Postal Bulletin*, the summer issue of the USPS' *Memo To Mailers* is usually published as a mailer's guide to the organization of the Postal Service. It has a wealth of information. It contains maps of each state showing the division and MSC boundaries and the names and titles of key USPS personnel along with their telephone numbers. It also contains the names, addresses and telephone numbers of the managers of the *Transportation Management Service Centers* and the *Rates and Classification Centers*. The address for requesting a free subscription to the *Memo To Mailers* is listed in *Chapter 18*. The *Postal Directory* described in *Chapter 18* may also help you keep in touch with USPS employees all over the U.S.

Problem Solving

Problem solving with the Postal Service is simple, *if you can reach the right person*. If you have continual delivery problems, for example, in a small post office you should certainly give that postmaster an opportunity to fix the problem. But if it continues, then you simply work your way up the chain of command until you get the action you deserve, or an explanation of what's wrong. Above all you must remember that, like most large institutions, the USPS is strictly "paper oriented," and you should *always* write a letter to the appropriate level of management explaining in detail the exact nature of your problem. Then scatter copies around to every office involved!

To help business mailers better understand the services offered and to aid business customers in resolving problems, there is a group of *account representatives* assigned to all of the divisions and most of the MSCs. If you are a major business mailer, you really should be in contact with your account rep. They can serve as a sort of liaison between customers and all of the operating groups in a postal facility. They are well versed in all phases of mail preparation and can be of great benefit to any mailer.

Also, at the division level, there is a Field Director of Marketing who should be your contact for serious mail problems. But you must remember to solve problems where the action is. If you write to General Motors about a problem, it is likely that the letter will be sent right back to the local car dealer, because that's where the action is. If you have a problem in a small post office near an MSC there's not much sense in writing to only the division. You should direct your letter to the small post office and then send *copies* to the division (to the attention of the Field Director of Marketing) and to the MSC manager. If you will remember to solve local problems locally, you can't go far wrong.

HOW MAIL MOVES

By now you should understand where to turn within the USPS when you have a postal problem. But you only have half the story. Now you need to comprehend *how* the Postal Service actually moves your mail. Think of the entire mail operation within the U.S. as a huge transportation system. The only way all of your mail will receive the best possible service at the least cost is to coordinate it with the system as a whole. You have to know when and where is the best place to get into the transportation system. You have to understand the things that may impact it en route. Then you have to know the best way to get off the system at the correct address and have your mail delivered.

The system for First-Class Mail (FCM) is not nearly as complex as you may imagine. If you learn about some ten or twelve basic cautions, you can achieve exactly the mail service you desire with a minimum of problems. On the other hand if you ignore some very basic ground rules you can extend the delivery time for letters going across town by 24 to 48 hours and those going across the U.S. by two or three days.

Beware The Street Collection Box

The first thing you should understand about how your mail moves is that it is all based on *schedules*. Everything must move on a schedule. Remember there are millions of pieces of FCM processed every night, so without strict schedules it would be chaos. All you have to do is meet those schedules, and your mail will be well on its way. And the best way to meet those schedules is to deposit your evening mail directly into a post office rather than a street or lobby collection box, because the first thing those schedules affect are the street boxes.

There simply are not enough people and trucks to collect mail late in the day from every street box and every lobby building box and still meet other processing schedules. Collection boxes in the center of the business districts *may* have a pickup as late as 5:00 or 5:15 p.m., but many do not. So if you really want the best postal service, you should always avoid a street or lobby collection box unless it is a real hardship to take it to a post office <u>and</u> your people are absolutely positive of the time of the last pickup. Of course, an even greater warning is appropriate when one of the 10 three-day-long holiday weekends is approaching. Then the USPS does not pickup from business boxes and buildings are locked up. Your mail can spend **four nights** right in that collection box or lobby!

If collection boxes *must* be utilized by your organization, or whenever you utilize drive-by boxes in front of a post office, you should always be sure to follow the separation of mail designated by the different kinds of boxes. Some business areas, and lobby boxes, will be especially marked for metered mail. These separations are important in preserving one of the primary benefits of metered mail, eliminating the need for cancelling. The separation of local (often defined by ZIP Codes on the collection box) and out of town is equally important in smaller cities where the nearest SCF is out of town.

Whenever possible, remember to take all mail from your office directly to a post office. In addition to avoiding possible pickup delays, your mail will bypass the collection boxes and lobby boxes completely and avoid that extra and unnecessary step in moving your mail toward its destination.

Sunday Mail Processing

In December of 1987, the Office of Management and Budget advised the Postal Service that it would be assessed about $800 million during 1988 and 1989, as its share toward reducing the deficit budget. The Postal Service conducted special meetings with its customers and hurriedly revised its budgets, especially those involving new postal facilities that were being stretched to the breaking point by increased mail volume.

Other budget cuts were in the area of mail collection and processing, and it was decided that it was necessary to curtail all collections from street boxes on Sunday. At the same time, all mail processing on Sunday evening was drastically curtailed or eliminated altogether.

The business world has apparently learned to live with this cutback and considering the ongoing financial pressures on the USPS is it not likely to resume Sunday collections and processing. This is no great burden, but wise mail managers will let their staffs know of this restriction so that someone doesn't rush around preparing some kind of important mail over the weekend only to have it sit in a collection box or a post office.

Your Local Processing Plant

Unless you live in one of the smaller cities, when you take your mail to the nearest post office it will probably be a station or branch of your main processing plant. That local mail factory may be one of the divisions, a management sectional center (MSC), or one of the smaller sectional center facilities (SCF). (And, since the functions of each of those kinds of facilities are so similar, we will use the term SCF to designate *all* of those different size operations.) That station or branch post office has a strict schedule and will prepare mail to be trucked to your local SCF perhaps several times during the afternoon and evening. The mail handlers will adhere to a *cutoff* time to assemble and package the mail and then follow *dispatch times* for vehicles to actually depart for your nearest SCF. These times are available to you as a guide for you to know the latest time you can deposit your mail and still receive prompt processing. These times often change, to adjust to other changing transportation conditions, and an alert mail manager will check on those schedules periodically if last minute deposits of mail are desired. Obviously, if your nearest SCF is out of town, these schedules are even more critical.

Except for some very small SCFs, where installations are still pending, the USPS will process your mail on optical character readers (OCRs). These machines will read the address at speeds up to 36,000 pieces per hour and spray a bar code representing the complete address on the lower 5/8 inch of your envelope. Later on, at its destination SCF, your letter will be sorted to a small associate office or the delivering carrier by this same bar code.

If it is destined to any one of the cities and ZIP Codes served by your local SCF it will be ready for delivery the next day anywhere in an area of approximately 100 miles. This varies with the quality (read congestion!) of the transportation in the area but includes the approximate 100 smaller post offices clustered around your SCF. (They are listed in the back portion of the *National ZIP Code Directory*.)

From Your SCF to Delivery SCF

If your mail is addressed to a ZIP Code served by another SCF more schedules rear their ugly heads. And it is these out of town destinations that can delay your mail unless you make a practice of mailing early and often during the day.

If your mail is going to another SCF within approximately 200 miles it will travel by truck. Those schedules are somewhat less demanding, perhaps more flexible, but are still vital because of potential congestion problems en route and the critical need to arrive early in the morning for final sorting to the carriers.

If your mail is destined for another SCF beyond that area where highways are practical then the real schedules take hold, airline schedules. All FCM beyond about 200 miles usually travels by commercial airline, and you likely know all about those changing schedules. Flights are added or cancelled often, plus changes are made every spring and fall as daylight savings time comes and goes.

At its destination, the airline will turn your mail over to a truck from the delivering SCF (another schedule) and then into town for the processing necessary (by reading the bar code sprayed on at its origin) to sort your mail to its delivering associate office, station, or branch post office and carrier. More schedules.

WHAT IMPACTS MAIL SERVICE

It is no wonder that you have to be so careful about the things that *you* do that affect mail service because there are so many other things over which you haven't the slightest control. Yet if you are aware of their impact you can often circumvent the negative influence they may have on your mail service. While some are unusual, when they do occur you can often start a new routing process for your mail, send backup material or stop mailing altogether until the problem has been cleared up.

You should be alert to large *fires* or *floods* in areas where you will be directing your mail or in major mail facilities or airports. Postal employees are forbidden to strike, but you should respond to *strikes* that may affect other processes such as United Parcel Service, airline, and rail employees, or other methods of transportation or delivery services. And sometimes the entire postal system in foreign countries (such as England and Canada) will go out on strike. An unusually heavy *snowfall*, one that makes the evening news, is proof there are likely to be delivery problems tomorrow. Some years ago, snow followed by *icy roads* closed down mail delivery in Boston for four days! *Tornadoes* and *earthquakes* disrupt Postal Service property and its employees so much that they often are simply unable to function. Routine mail, such as monthly statements, should immediately be suspended from such areas.

Air disasters are terrifying to see on TV newscasts. Nevertheless you should remember that, almost without exception, every airliner has a considerable amount of mail on board. And in the event of a fire the mail is often destroyed. The question to ask is whether or not your mail was headed in the same direction as the unfortunate aircraft.

Hurricanes always disrupt mail service, particularly a storm that hovers off the east cost for several days or causes the devastation experienced during 1989 in South Carolina. Really serious hurricanes wreck post offices along with everything else in their path. Even a smaller one may cancel all activity in airports along its path or cause unusually high water to cancel mail deliveries in a wide area for a day or more.

International incidents such as the 1991 Persian Gulf War or the dispute between England and Argentina over the Falkland Islands can, of course, disrupt all service to the affected countries. If you have international customers or correspondents, you should be very conscious of alternative methods of communication when such problems occur.

Even an *interstate highway accident* can cause such a traffic tie-up that both commercial courier service and USPS trucks will miss every flight that evening. In perhaps the thirty largest cities in the U.S., this can be a weekly occurrence. There is no alternative route to choose when this happens but at least you should be aware of the problem as it affects special documents or items being sent from one coast to the other.

Here is a convenient check list of what impacts mail service:

■ Fires	■ Strikes
■ Floods	■ Snowfall and Icy Roads
■ Tornadoes	■ Earthquakes
■ Air Disasters	■ Hurricanes
■ International Incidents	■ Interstate Accidents

AND YOU!

HOW YOU IMPACT MAIL SERVICE

There are so many things that affect your mail service, over which you have no control, you really need to pay special attention to those factors which you *can* control. Some of these items may seem trivial but they are quite important if you want to obtain the best possible service.

How You Prepare Mail

You cannot expect to overstuff a typical 6 3/4 inch statement envelope or #10 business envelope and have it pass through the processing designed for ordinary business mail without either injury (tearing or bursting) or delays caused by the need for hand processing. You will need the correct envelope for bulky contents or 9 x 12 inch envelopes so that the pages may be mailed flat, if you expect to receive the best mail service. And whenever you use kraft envelopes you should clearly mark on them whether they are being sent third-class, First-Class, or Priority Mail.

You cannot expect improperly sealed mail to avoid opening and tearing on high speed equipment. Nor can you expect the USPS to accept envelopes with meter stamps that are so faint they are becoming illegible. To prevent such problems you must have someone continually monitor your mailing machines to inspect both the quality of your meter stamp imprints and the sealing of your mail.

How You Address Mail

Every single piece of mail the Postal Service handles is processed by ZIP Code. If your addresses do not contain up-to-date, accurate ZIP Codes you can not expect to receive the best possible service. Nor will you receive the best service when you need a new ribbon on your typewriter or computer and provide addresses that are almost too faint to read either by humans or machines. In addition, you cannot expect the best whenever you do not format your address properly. The last line should contain only the city, state and Zip Code and anything else on that line, *or below it*, makes it difficult for both postal people and machines to decipher the destination. It is very important that computer programmers understand the importance of not having account numbers or other numbers anywhere near this last line in an address.

If you do not include apartment numbers and suite numbers in your addresses you can expect less than the best. Geographical designations such as "NE" and "SW" in an address are also absolutely essential for good delivery service.

Perhaps the most common problem found in addressing business mail is having a folded insert which contains the name and address, slip up, down or sideways in a window envelope so that the full address is no longer visible. Such mail may be set aside until the evening rush is over so that the envelopes can all be tapped by hand to bring the addresses back into view, a very time-consuming process. In sufficient quantities, the mail may simply be refused. A simple adjustment of the folding machine will allow the folds to exactly fit into the envelope, usually with no more than 1/16 inch clearance to prevent slippage in any direction. Well-designed forms will have folding marks printed directly on the edges of the forms as a folding guide.

If you expect your mail to receive the benefits of greater speed and accuracy offered by the automation program of the USPS, there are even more stringent requirements you need to review in *Chapter 5*.

Where You Deposit Mail

The earlier sections should have convinced you to avoid street and lobby collection boxes whenever you can, but if you are in one of the so-called industrial parks you may need to use a collection box whether you like it or not. If so, pay special attention to mail deposited on *Friday afternoon*.

Here is a typical example of the problem. There is a group of four or five two-story office buildings clustered together in an area near Interstate 90, about eight miles from a major city in the midwest. There is a collection box on a corner near these buildings with the last weekday collection shown as 4:45 or 5:00 p.m. The next collection is scheduled for about 5 p.m. on Saturday. An examination of that collection box at 8 p.m. one Friday showed that *it was stuffed to the very top with mail!* It is unlikely that the collection was skipped that afternoon, such things are not tolerated in the Postal Service. Evidently most of the businesses near that box simply deposit mail without paying any attention to the collection schedule. Depending on its destination, that mail was delayed at least 24 hours and perhaps more.

What Time You Deposit Mail

In mid-afternoon the larger postal facilities such as the divisions, MSCs and SCFs have been compared to one of the superdomes, *before the game!* There is a full staff ready to handle the onslaught of the evening mail and all of the equipment is humming, but *there isn't any mail*. For years and years, the postal people have been preaching the virtues of mailing early, but only the real pros seem to take heed. Some post offices have even agreed to pick up mail from customers if they have 3,000 pieces in trays ready by 3:00 p.m. If you deposit your mail early enough to reach the processing floor ahead of the 7 o'clock rush you can always count on catching earlier trucks and planes. It is as if you receive preferential treatment when you mail early in the day.

If your organization has a need to deposit mail later in the evening than usual you should contact an account representative at your nearest SCF. Then you can learn exactly how late you can deposit mail *at the SCF* and still have it dispatched that night. In many cases it may be accepted as late as 10 o'clock in the evening. If this would expedite your accounts receivable a whole day, for example, it might be worthwhile for you to employ a courier to take your mail from your office to the SCF.

This may be as good a time as any to urge you to visit these mail factories for yourself. The Postal Service is always happy to provide tours of their facilities but they especially welcome business mailers. Try to arrange to visit around 7 p.m. to really understand what your own mail is competing with during the initial processing. You will not believe it until you see it!

Remember, *all* of these things impact your mail service:

- How you prepare your mail

- How you address your mail

- Where you deposit your mail

- What time you deposit your mail

CHAPTER 3

IMPACT OF USPS AUTOMATION PROGRAM

Grocery store managers and the management of the Postal Service came to the same conclusions about the same time. They began to realize that people keying numbers into machines make mistakes, and the more products to be read the more people are needed. The solution was bar codes. Aided and abetted by the advances in optical reading technology and the computer sciences, there were incredible changes in a relatively short time. It is somewhat amazing today to see a Universal Product Code on *every* product in a grocery store from Jello to the *Washington Post*. It is equally amazing to see a bar code on practically every single piece of letter-size First-Class Mail. Few changes in the eighties have had an impact on more people than these two have.

The impact of automation within the USPS has been very significant and beneficial, especially in two key areas. Mail processing in general is far more accurate than it could ever be without automation. And although there have been rate increases, they would have been larger without the labor savings made possible through automation.

HISTORY OF INSTALLATIONS

Mail volume jumped from 56.4 *billion* pieces in 1956 to 89.8 *billion* pieces in 1976, an increase of 59.2 percent! It generally decreased during recessions and immediately after rate increases, but, as usual following such events, the volume soon began to climb again.

This growth did not go unnoticed at USPS Headquarters. (It is well it did not go unnoticed. From 1976 through Fiscal Year 1990, overall volume skyrocketed *another 85 percent* to 166.3 billion pieces.) In 1978, efforts began to expand the current five-digit ZIP Code to include an additional four digits which would exactly identify the delivery point.

Some degree of automation was achieved as early as 1965, when the first optical character reader (OCR) was installed in Detroit. But real progress began with the multi-position letter sorting machines that were the backbone of mail processing in the '60s and '70s along with the facer-canceller machines. Both helped speed up processing, but the letter sorters could only process 1,750 pieces of mail per work hour.

In preparation for the expanded ZIP Code the first computer driven OCR machine, capable of spraying a bar code on the lower portion of an envelope, was installed in the Los Angeles post office along with less expensive bar code sorters to interpret the bar codes down stream. Then the expanded code was born in 1983, and christened *ZIP+4 Code*. Now the Postal Service points with pride to its accomplishments and reports that it has saved $800 million in labor costs since 1981.

By the end of 1984, 252 OCR channel sorters had been installed in 118 major processing centers along with bar code sorters for subsequent mail distribution. The earlier OCR machines could interpret only the last "city, state, and ZIP Code" line of the address on an envelope. These machines were retrofitted to read the last two lines of an address as technology improved, and were then able to spray a nine-digit bar code on the bottom of an envelope. That code included the ZIP+4 Code, regardless of whether the mailer had it printed as part of the address.

Major customers began to realize that they could benefit by eliminating the OCR reading and encoding process at the originating post office and applying it themselves. It soon became apparent that the location of the bar code on the envelope (a 5/8 inch strip across the bottom) was not the ideal location. Customers found it difficult to code inserts and have the bar code appear in the proper position in a window envelope.

Once again technology came to the rescue. Tests on 29 machines in the Tampa area post offices indicated that it was practical to convert the two line bar code readers to read a much larger area, one measuring 4 x 10½ inches, and the *wide area* bar code reader became a reality.

STATUS OF INSTALLATIONS

Any status report on automation within the USPS will probably change in 30 days. Nevertheless, to understand the far-reaching impact of automation on business mailers you should be interested in the sheer magnitude of the overall picture.

In early '90, the USPS reported that there were more than 2,000 optical character readers and bar code sorters in service. There are, of course, a number of post offices with more than one OCR, but the significance of so many installations is that automation is alive and well and growing every day.

By late 1991, the Postal Service reports, all of the current 1,369 bar code sorters will be capable of wide area bar code reading, as will the additional 5,226 bar code sorters expected to be installed by 1995. Recent USPS reports also state that, since about 47 percent of the carrier's time is spent in hand sorting mail in the office, wide area bar code readers are expected to save $2 billion annually by 1995.

The newest technology, remote video encoding, lifts the image of the mail piece from non-OCR readable and handwritten addresses and processes it with more powerful computers with enhanced software programs. These in turn decipher the address into the necessary nine-digit code which is then sprayed onto the envelope. In extremely difficult situations, operators view the address on a video screen to determine the correct address and aid the machine to encode the nine-digit code.

PERCENT OF MAIL BEING PROCESSED

You only need to shuffle your morning's First-Class letter mail (looking for the bar codes sprayed on the lower edge of envelopes) to see for yourself the percentage of mail being processed through automation. It is an ever growing volume of mail. A record 42 percent of all letter mail was processed on automated equipment in FY '89, and 49 percent was processed in FY '90.

The Postmaster General has stated that it is the intention of the Postal Service to have 100 percent of all letter mail barcoded by 1995. He expects the USPS to apply 40 percent of the codes, industry to apply 40 percent of the coding, and have the balance of 20 percent applied through the remote video encoding systems.

ADVANCED BAR CODE

In addition to the plans of the Postal Service to have 100 percent of the letter mail barcoded by 1995 and to have all bar code readers equipped with wide area reading technology, the USPS has another bar or two up its sleeve. By 1992 it expects to have modified all optical character readers to apply an additional 10 bars to the barcode. Already nick-named *ABC* for *Advanced Bar Code*, it will add the last two numerals of the street address number to an existing ZIP+4 Code. An *ABC* may be applied by a mailer, a service bureau, or the USPS, and plans call for an added incentive for the ultimate in a machine-readable delivery address.

The purpose of the ABC is to reduce the office time of the carriers. At the delivery post office or sectional facility less expensive bar code sorters will read the Advanced Bar Code and arrange the letter mail into carrier delivery sequence. The USPS estimates this will allow the carrier up to two additional hours of actual delivery time on the street.

The implementation of the Advanced Bar Code only involves software programming for the optical character readers, not hardware or special technology. The USPS expects to have that phase completed by 1992. In September of 1990, at the National Postal Forum, the Postmaster General announced that mailers who were considering purchasing software to barcode their mail should be sure it also had the capability of adding the ABC.

BENEFITS OF AUTOMATION TO MAILERS

All of these impressive statistics should convince any mail manager that the automation process and its corresponding discount programs are here to stay. No logical manager can choose to continue to ignore the benefits of the automation programs taking place within the Postal Service. The benefits of adding ZIP+4 to addresses (as discussed in *Chapter 4*) are considerable, and the USPS raised the stakes further in the '91 rate change. So the Postal Service will reward you well for either adding the ZIP+4 codes to your addresses or prebarcoding your mail.

There has been a discount for showing the ZIP+4 Code on your mail (and following some simple procedures) since 1983. But early in '91, the discount was increased to a significant 1.4¢. This is a 55 percent increase in the discount and is just short of a 5 percent discount on the FCM letter rate.

After mid-'91, even without a ZIP+4 Code, if you add a bar code before you mail it you can save 2¢, a 6.9 percent discount on the regular letter rate for FCM. Or take the next step and presort that mail and receive a 5.1¢ discount for 3-digit prebarcoded mail or a 5.7 cent discount for 5-digit prebarcoded FCM. That last classification is a 19.7 *percent discount*! (See chart in *Chapter 7, First Class Mail Discounts*).

With potential savings of almost 20 percent, it is impossible to ignore either the ZIP+4 Codes or the prebarcoding discount program.

EVALUATING PRESORT PROGRAMS

The Postal Service has put together a special computer-oriented program that helps provide an orientation to postal automation and how it affects the business mailer. It is called the *Mail Flow Planning System* and consists of a single 5¼-inch diskette which should be available at your nearest USPS division office. It is designed to help you, "learn about the automation that will be sorting your mail; how the USPS will share its savings with you if you share its work; and just how much savings are involved."

You can run the program directly from the diskette on any IBM or compatible personal computer, or install it on a hard disk. Its seven-line menu allows you to select the area about which you wish to learn, and a nearby window explains what that subject covers. Its unique program allows you to select various ways to address your mail, to pay the postage, and to select the degree of presort or work sharing. Then you can view animated flow lines as the type of mail you have designated flows through a diagram of a typical postal facility. It is no substitute for a visit to your nearest mail processing facility but it is a valuable foundation for those who have never been behind the scenes in a sectional center. By changing the variables, you can clearly see the effect that preparation and automation have on your mail. (It could be an excellent self-training tool as well.)

In the section on *Worksharing Incentives,* you select whether you will be mailing cards or letters, the quantity, the weight, and the number of mailings per month. After you set those parameters you simply press [ENTER] and the screen displays the cost per mailing, per month, and per year for each of the seven programs *along with the annual savings.* Therefore, it provides a quick, easy guide to the amount you can save with each of the various worksharing programs.

Aware that you may have more questions after viewing this diskette, the Postal Service reminds the mailer that it has a professional support staff available to serve you.

■The *Account Representative* is the main point-of-contact and will be able to answer most of your questions.

■The *Automation Readability Specialist* can answer your detailed questions about making sure the OCR machines can read your addresses.

■The *Technical Service Representative* can answer your questions involving the use of computers to help your mailing operation.

The program's diskette is designed to be mailed to postal customers, so it is easy to obtain, even if you live some distance from a divisional office. It is also likely that any postmaster can obtain one for a customer.

PRESORT SERVICE BUREAUS

All of that information and all of those people are available to help you set up your own "on premise" presort program. Your needs might range anywhere from a $250,000 OCR machine, which will barcode and presort your mail at speeds up to 30,000 pieces per hour, to a single clerk who manually presorts into bins divided into 20 or 30 ZIP Codes. Either may be financially rewarding, depending on your volume. But your volume is more likely to be somewhere in between those extremes. Perhaps you have too little First-Class Mail for the OCR machine and too much for your own clerks to handle. There is a solution designed precisely for such organizations.

All you need do is obtain a "slug" to fit in your postage meter so that "PRESORTED FIRST CLASS" is printed on your mail along with the current presort discount rate. Then a representative of a *presort service bureau* will pickup your mail, presort it at a central location, and deliver your mail to the post office. That's all you need to do to obtain approximately 50 percent of the total discount. Your actual benefit will depend on the volume of mail you release to the service bureau and how much competition there is for your business. If you live in a smaller city where there is perhaps only one presort service bureau you will probably split the savings with the presorter. But in larger metropolitan areas, such as Los Angeles or Chicago, it has been reported that the mailer may receive 75 percent of the savings because there is so much competition for his or her business.

While it will vary with the presorter, the point at which it becomes financially rewarding for the presort bureau to pick up your mail is around 1,000 pieces of First-Class Mail. The presort service may schedule more than one pickup for you if you are churning out mail all day. The latest practical pickup is usually about 7 p.m., to allow the presorter time to sort all of the mail. But the last pickup can be later if there is still time to meet the USPS schedules and dispatch times.

There is one other point you may want to consider if you are just beginning to get into one of the presort programs. All of the discounts offered recently by the Postal Service have been in *tenths of a cent*. Thus the amount of postage you will need to print on each piece after the discount includes a fraction of a cent, expressed *in tenths*. But not all postage meters are capable of printing, and keeping records of postage spent, in *tenths of a cent*. Therefore, although reports indicate that they are in short supply, you will want to attempt to obtain a postage meter which will print postage in fractional tenths. You can overcome this problem through a special payment of additional postage when submitting a presort mailing, but that is not as quick and simple as having the correct postage meter.

If you are looking for a presort service bureau, check the *Yellow Pages*. You can also inquire at the back dock of your nearest postal facility, because the USPS employees will usually be aware of any presorter operating in the vicinity. If all else fails, write or call the National Association of Presort Mailers, 3906 Butternut Court, Brandon, FL 33511-7961, telephone 813-684-4118, for the names of the nearest presort service bureaus. Incidentally, that association's 90 members presorted 10 *billion* pieces in 1990, or about 40 percent of all the presorted mail the USPS received. So, if you choose to use a service bureau to presort your mail, you will be joining forces with thousands of other mailers who think it is an excellent way to take advantage of the presort programs.

EXPECTATIONS

In deciding whether or not to reap the benefits of either the ZIP+4 discount or the prebarcode discount, you should review the benefits of applying ZIP+4 Codes to your files (in *Chapter 4*), and you should realize two other important things.

First, remember that after all of your addresses are coded, and you have installed a process to code *new* addresses, your troubles are over, and the maintenance of your ZIP+4 files will be minimal. And second, the Postal Service is dedicated to and heavily involved in worksharing programs throughout every class of mail. It is unlikely to reduce any incentives for any kind of worksharing. Quite the contrary, the incentives have been increased in the past and are likely to be increased in the future. If you believe the ZIP+4 and prebarcoding programs offer considerable savings in postage at the present time, with First-Class Mail at 29¢ an ounce, think of the potential savings for your organization *in the next decade*: for inflation is likely to bring on at least two or perhaps three additional rate increases by the year 2000!

CHAPTER 4

THE IMPORTANCE OF ZIP CODES

The need to mark mail with some sort of code to aid in its processing was first realized by the Federal German Post Office in 1961, and the U.S. Post Office Department followed other nations in adopting such a code in July of 1963. In the U.S., ZIP (Zoning Improvement Plan) Code became mandatory on second- and third-class mail in 1967, but it is still not mandatory on First-Class Mail. Yet almost 100 percent of all mail is ZIP Coded, and those who do not code their mail almost always find it delayed or misdirected.

Not a single piece of any kind of mail moves in the United States unless a ZIP Code is involved. It guides every action in the USPS. The names of cities and SCFs have no real meaning in the Postal Service because everything goes by the first three digits of the ZIP Code. If you do visit one of the SCFs, you will see that every bin, tray and sign contains the three-digit code for wherever the mail is destined. A typical sign will read "TOLEDO, OH MSC 434-435-436." That tells mail handlers that the Toledo, Ohio, Management Sectional Center processes all mail with the first three digits of ZIP Codes 434, 435, and 436.

Inaccurate ZIP Codes invariably mean missent mail; an error of just one digit can mean a thousand mile error during processing. That usually translates to a two- or three-day delay. Mail passing through the letter sorting machines, where 12 operators read the ZIP Code and push keys to direct the mail to some 277 bins, is "riffled" to spot-check inconsistencies between the written city destination and the ZIP Code on the envelope. But that only catches a few of the errors. If you use the correct ZIP Code on your letter and type "Toledo, OH 43606" you will have no problems. But make a mistake and type "Toledo, OH 33606," and your letter will probably end up in TAMPA! When you consider an annual volume of over 89 billion pieces of FCM (in FY '90) you can understand why there isn't much time to examine each envelope to see if the city and the ZIP Code match. (But, as you will discover later, that is one of the benefits of the automation program, for the OCR machines do exactly that.)

HOW FIVE-DIGIT ZIP CODES ARE DESIGNATED

The United States is divided into ten national areas which determine the first digit of the ZIP Code. The codes do not necessarily adhere to boundaries of cities, counties, states, or other jurisdictions but they do generally follow state lines. Yet that first digit is really not significant for it is always used with the second and third digits to form the "*3-digit ZIP Code*" so often referred to in sorting requirements for different classes of mail. The second and third digits of a ZIP Code designate either a sectional center facility or a multi-coded city--that is a city so large that it has many individual ZIP Codes assigned to its borders. Some cities, such as New York, Houston, Los Angeles, and Dallas, are so large they have TWO 3-digit ZIP Codes assigned.

The last two digits designate either a delivery area, such as a station or branch, or an associate post office. Occasionally, when cost beneficial for the USPS, the last two digits will be assigned to a company, a Federal agency, a college or university, or other entity with *sufficient mail volume*, based on the average daily volume of letter-size pieces received. When used with the 3-digit ZIP Code it becomes an *unique* Zip Code. Administrative people who often work with ZIP Codes should understand unique codes. Otherwise, they may disregard a correct unique ZIP Code as an error and assign the ZIP Code for the surrounding area. This may happen, for example, in the case of a very large building when a tenant has a unique ZIP Code but the last two digits for the balance of the building are totally different. For further study both national and state maps are contained in the *Zip Code Directory*.

ZIP PLUS FOUR CODES

If you understand that the first three digits of a ZIP Code identifies an SCF or a large city, and that the last two only identify the delivering *post office*, then you can understand the need for additional numbers to identify the actual point of delivery. That is exactly what the four additional numbers, known as the *ZIP + 4 Code*, do for the USPS.

ZIP + 4 is a logical step into the future. It is like the technology in a modern grocery store. The Universal Product Code is read by a scanner and automatically totals up your grocery bill. With ZIP + 4, an optical character reader scans your envelope and translates the ZIP + 4 Code into an actual point of delivery.

The first two numbers of the ZIP + 4 Code designate a *sector* of the delivering area in the destination post office, and the second two digits break a sector down to *segments*. *Every* delivery point in the United States has been coded by the USPS with its own individual 5-digit and ZIP + 4 Code. Whether it is a rural route box, a post office box, a residence, a high-rise apartment, an office building, or a factory, it has a five-digit and ZIP + 4 code that completely identifies the point of delivery.

You can understand that the sheer volume of First-Class Mail growth really demanded that the Postal Service find a way to automate its processing. Later you will see how the ZIP+4 Code was essential to the development of the automation program.

SOURCES OF INFORMATION FOR ZIP CODES

There is such an incredible amount of information in the *National Five-Digit Zip Code and Post Office Directory* (*Publication 65*) that just the table of contents would fill two or three of these smaller pages. Published at the beginning of every year, it is available at most medium size and larger post offices or it may be ordered by mail. It cost $12 (in 1991), but that's only $2 a pound, it weighs six pounds! In addition, there is a coupon inside the front cover of the 1990 edition that is worth a dollar toward the purchase of a new directory. But whatever the cost, it is a real bargain. Here's a sample of its contents:

- State list of post offices and
     post offices with street listings
- Post office delivery statistics and
     location of main post office by county and state
- Alphabetical list of post offices
- Numerical list of post offices
     by ZIP Code and three-digit service areas
- Definition and technical detail of mail services
- Service improvement programs
- USPS Headquarters and regional offices
- Inspection service regions and divisions
- Management sectional center areas
- Division office areas
- Bulk mail centers and auxiliary service facilities
- Sectional center facilities
- Rates and classification centers
- Area distribution centers
- Army, Navy, Air Force, FPOs and APOs

And that is only a partial list!

Another source for maintaining accurate ZIP Codes in your files is the smaller booklets often published by individual divisions located in multi-coded cities. These are particularly helpful if the majority of your customer base is within one or two major metropolitan areas.

The Postal Service licenses several printers to publish ZIP Code directories about the size of a thick pocket novel. While they often have smaller type they may be more convenient for a secretary's occasional reference use.

As soon as you enter the world of electronics you can become besieged with methods to zap your addresses, either en masse or one by one as you enter each one into your electronic files. For example, some computer software will allow a typist to enter an address into the files, and, using a continually updated data base, the system will automatically look up and verify or change the ZIP Code if it is not correct. Others will verify the accuracy of ZIP Codes that customers provide. If you would like more information about such software, one source of supply is the Melissa Data Company, 32118 Paseo Adelanto #8, San Juan Capistrano, CA 92675-3606, or telephone 800-443-8834 to request their free catalog.

In an effort to encourage and support business mailers wishing to convert their files to ZIP+4 Codes, the Postal Service offers postage discounts to mailers who add ZIP+4 Codes to their present addresses. In addition, the USPS offers a number of programs to help with the matching or coding process. Mailers who store their addresses in computers, who can write their own matching software, can utilize the USPS's *ZIP+4 Code National File Directory* computer tapes. This data base tape consists of 26 million address records plus monthly or quarterly updates. A national tape may be requested, or individual states may be selected. For mailers that maintain address files on diskette, the USPS will change five-digit ZIP coded addresses to ZIP+4 coded addresses at no charge, usually with a 21-day turn around. Request forms for both the *ZIP+4 Code National File Directory* tapes and diskette processing are in the back of the *National Five-Digit ZIP Code Directory*, or are available at your local post office.

If the addresses in your files are concentrated in a relatively small area you may find that *printed* ZIP+4 Code state directories are adequate. The are 35 different versions of the *ZIP+4 State Directory* (*Publication 66-#1/35*). Each directory covers a specific state or combination of states and may consist of more than one volume. For example, Texas has three volumes and Washington, DC, has two, which include the neighboring states of Maryland and Virginia. Your post office lobby is supposed to have a copy available for public use in the event you wish to see it before you order a copy. They are available for purchase at a nominal cost ($12 in 1991) and the order form is--where else? in the *National Five-Digit ZIP Code Directory*. You may also order them on *Form 4242*, which is available at MSCs and division offices. Or, you may write to the National Address Information Center, 6060 Primacy Parkway, Suite 101, Memphis, TN 38188-0001, or telephone 1-800-238-3150, Ext. 40.

All kinds of order forms are in the National Directory, but, if you have questions about any of those services, you should contact your postmaster or account representative. They can also provide you with a list of commercial firms who will convert your files to include the correct

ZIP+4 Codes. The Postal Service has even gone to the trouble to "certify" the accuracy of those firms (but does not endorse any organization). These commercial firms are part of the Coding Accuracy Support System (CASS) and have met USPS matching accuracy standards to provide five-digit ZIP Code, ZIP+4 Code, and/or Carrier Route Information System matching services to potential clients. A complete list of those organizations is published periodically in the *Postal Bulletin.*

There are also service bureaus that will take copies of your addresses on magnetic tape and match your present files with ZIP+4 Codes. Still other firms offer microfilm and microfiche for manual use in smaller offices. A more extensive list of the kinds of ZIP Code services that are available from the USPS and industry is in *Chapter 5.*

ADDRESS LIST PRIVACY

Depending on the nature of your business, you should be sure to consider the issue of *privacy* whenever you contemplate using any type of "outside" service that refines, manipulates, or ZIP Codes any of your address lists. Names and addresses are a valuable commodity, and there is always the chance that unscrupulous persons may have an interest in *your* organization's customer or membership list. This shouldn't be a concern if you are dealing with well-known, reputable, national or regional organizations. But you should be cautious of dealing with local organizations with whom you are not familiar. In such cases you should ask for business references and other indications of reliability and honesty. In addition, you should ask for solid evidence of the technological capabilities of the organization to complete the task the way you want it.

Concerns about privacy are another reason you may find it advantageous to purchase software that will accomplish the desired result without your address files ever leaving the premises.

BENEFITS OF ZIP+4 CODES

Since it was necessary to explain how and why the USPS found it essential to add four additional numbers to the five-digit ZIP Code, it seems appropriate to explain the advantages and benefits of participating in the ZIP+4 program. In addition to the 1.4¢ discount (in 1991) provided for mailing as few as 250 pieces of properly prepared ZIP+4 mail there are other distinct advantages.

Regardless of which method you choose, when you add the ZIP+4 codes to your address files the processing *identifies duplicates* and *identifies wrong addresses.* The "wrong" addresses are those having inaccurate descriptions such as corner designations ("West and Baker Streets") rather than the correct street number, or other incorrect formats. All of the data processing methods standardize the spelling and format of the delivery address line and the city and state line. All five-digit ZIP Codes are validated and corrected where necessary.

The ZIP+4 program requires that the mail be *machineable* so that it can be processed on the optical character readers. That means your mail will receive *improved delivery consistency and reliability*. The OCRs are about 99 percent accurate in interpreting the address and sending it to the correct bin for dispatch. Few humans can match that accuracy, so you receive better consistency and reliability from the point of origin to the destination.

The ability to process your mail on the high-speed OCRs saves the Postal Service money and helps it cope with the high cost of its labor-intensive operation. In the long run, this should help provide future rate stability, increase sorting accuracy (meaning less missent mail) and improve service.

In addition, with sufficient incoming mail, the Postal Service will assign your organization a series of ZIP+4 numbers which you can assign to specific departments. While the USPS is not prepared at this time to separate that mail for you, incoming mail ZIP+4 coded for your various departments or operations may be a great help to your operation.

The requirements for a ZIP+4 mailing are not very complicated and are spelled out in detail in the *DMM (Sec. 324.21)*. Basically, it must consist of a minimum of 250 pieces, each must bear a ZIP+4 Code, be OCR readable, and meet letter mail dimensional standards. Postage must be paid by meter stamp, permit imprint, or precanceled stamp. However, your address lists must conform to CASS standards as explained in *Postal Bulletin 21781B*, of January 28, 1991, and detailed in *Chapter 5* of the *DMM*.

In addition, Presorted First-Class Mail may be combined with ZIP+4 qualified mail to obtain an additional .6¢ discount (in 1991). There are two distinct areas that affect the quality of accuracy in your 5-digit ZIP Codes and your ZIP+4 Codes, and you should devote equal effort to both areas. One is the effort you and your organization make to collect the correct codes from individuals *outside* your organization, such as customers, clients, etc. The other is the effort you make to assure correct codes are applied by people *inside* your organization, such as salesmen, counter sales clerks, telephone sales people, and all administration and data processing personnel. You cannot neglect one without reducing the effectiveness of the other.

CHAPTER 5

ADDRESSING FOR AUTOMATION

The previous chapter should have convinced you that automatic mechanized mail processing with electronic enhancement is here to stay and that any alert mail manager should make every effort to have his organization's mail conform to the requirements of that automation. Business mailers who do not conform are only kidding themselves, for their organization's will surely lose. It really is something like a contest. The best mail wins!

The contestants will be shuffled in with those 89 *billion* pieces of First-Class Mail; you will be competing with about 334,316,613 pieces *every evening*. Sloppy addressing habits and out-of-date addresses with poor address formats will continue to provide less than winning results. Duplicates and stale addresses will lose out to letters correctly addressed and properly coded. And all of these causes will result in a continual loss of postage and printing costs, as well as delays in the delivery of your mail.

OBJECTIVES FOR MAILERS

Take a tour, any tour, in any processing center (such as a division, an MSC, or an SCF). Then you will see for yourself. *Everything* is mechanized. Machines "face" the mail so that all of the addresses are facing the same way; machines cancel the stamps; machines separate heavier envelopes from machineable ones; machines read the addresses; machines initially sort the mail toward its destination; and then machines sort the mail down to the carrier. So you must conform. Your mail must meet all of the specifications of these machines, in both size and shape, if you expect your mail to be speeded on its way with no interruptions.

The Postal Service has standardized the endorsements you place on each class of mail so you must provide up-to-date notations if you expect to receive the service you really want. Your mail should clearly indicate exactly how you expect it to be handled if it is undeliverable, and the return address should be the exact location where returns will be processed, not some location that will require transhipping.

You must "clean-up" your computer-originated addresses. Nonessential codes and file numbers must be *above* the address rather than on the last line of the address where an OCR can mistake it for some type of ZIP Code. So you must teach data processing managers and programmers the elements of good address hygiene and then do the same with others who create or compile addresses, such as outside sales people, administration personnel, and even advertising agency people who design coupons, etc.

Above all, you must make sure that the *contrast* of your address is satisfactory for OCR machines to decipher the address; this means good maintenance on all kinds of printing devices. This is especially true of old fading ribbons which can cause inaccurate reading by machine and mail handlers alike.

In summary, if you expect to reap the benefits of automation your objective should be to be sure that your mail conforms to all automation dimensions; has good contrast and is easily read; has accurate, uncluttered addresses; and is endorsed to assure proper handling.

AUTOMATION DIMENSIONAL STANDARDS

As the Postal Service began work toward coding every address with its assigned ZIP+4 Code, its engineers were warning the operation people that there would simply have to be some restrictions on the size limitations of letter mail if it was to be rapidly processed through OCR readers. So you can easily see how the USPS *dimensional standards* became a reality in 1978.

The dimensional standards are simple. They practically match the specifications of the facer-canceller machines, the multi-position letter sorting machines, and all the rest of the high-speed processors.

Any piece of mail smaller than 3½ x 5 inches is impossible to control very well on any machine with lots of moving belts that process mail at 20,000 to 36,000 pieces per hour. The metal frames that are necessary to hold all of that machinery together will not allow anything to pass through that is larger than 6 1/8 x 11½ inches or thicker than ¼ inch. And post cards less than .007 inch thick are difficult to feed at high speeds and often jam the equipment. In addition, the machines cannot find the stamp (and the address lines below it) when the piece of mail is *square*.

So, while the equipment actually establishes the dimensions the *Domestic Mail Manual (Sec. 352.21* and *Sec. 353)* dictates the following standards:

Minimum: *All* mail ¼ inch thick or less:
                            must be rectangular
                            must be at least 3½ inches high
                            must be at least 5 inches long
(Exceptions: Keys and identification devices.)

Maximum: First-Class Mail and single piece third-class
mail weighing *one ounce or less*:
> must not exceed ¼ inch in thickness
> must not exceed 6 1/8 inches in height
> must not exceed 11½ inches in length

Postcards must be between .007 and .0095 inches in thickness (*DMM, Sec. 322.2c*).

In addition, the aspect ratio (the ratio of the height to the length) must fall within a ratio of 1.0 to 1.3 and 1.0 to 2.5 inclusive.

Envelopes that do not meet the *minimum* standards are not mailable, while those that exceed the *maximum* standards will incur a surcharge of 10¢ per piece or 5¢ per piece if presorted (in 1991).

One other note, the USPS prefers and suggests that letter mail designed for automation be slightly shorter so as not to exceed 10½ inches, but larger mail will not incur a surcharge until it exceeds 11½ inches.

The dimensional standards are not a great problem. Most of the scrutiny is done for you by the envelope manufacturers. Also, the average 9 x 12 inch kraft envelope weighs about three quarters of an ounce so it is difficult for a piece of First-Class Mail to exceed 6 1/8 x 11½ inches, weigh less than one ounce, and incur the surcharge. And later on you will see a suggestion that you not use third-class mail at all until it exceeds five ounces (because the FCM rates are identical through five ounces). However, if special mailings or new forms are created without checking with a knowledgeable mail manager, literally thousands of pieces of mail may be subject to the unnecessary surcharge (at a cost of from $50 to $100 per thousand!) or even be non-mailable.

COMMON AUTOMATION PROBLEMS

In any situation involving problem solving it is usually helpful to be sure to separate the causes from the effects. If you can understand where the problems exist, you have a good start toward searching out the solutions.

The USPS has a very helpful brochure entitled *Addressing for Success* (*Notice 221*) which reviews the various "do's and don't's" of preparing mail for the OCR to successfully read the addresses on your mail. You may want to review that publication along with the following checklist:

<u>Common Problems</u>	<u>Usual Solution</u>
Characters in address touch	Change font on typewriter or printer
Script type font used	Replace font on typewriter or printer

Common Problems (Con't.)	**Usual Solution** (Con't.)
Not enough contrast or printing too light	Replace ribbons on regular basis and maintain quality of ink
Address not visible through window	Adjust folding machine to prevent insert from moving within envelope
Address slanted because label applied crooked	Instruct people affixing labels or switch to machine to apply labels
Printing on envelope in line with address	Arrange for mail manager to approve envelope layouts prior to printing
Non-address information below city-state-zip line	Coordinate all address formats with mail manager

You might consider having a supervisor, or "OCR specialist", spot check your mail every day to identify any of these common problems. A more in-depth discussion of the problems and other suggestions for developing OCR readable mail is available in the USPS publication, *A Guide to Business Mail Preparation* (*Publication 25*).

IMPORTANCE OF ACCURATE LIST MAINTENANCE

The computer has revolutionized filing and maintaining lists of customers and their addresses. Today any business with only a few hundred accounts or clients is likely to have some sort of data processing system to prepare statements and invoices. And, if smaller businesses do not have electronic data processing (EDP) facilities located in their offices they will have a computer service prepare their statements. This makes the whole process easier but brings up a common problem, the computer will print the stale or inaccurate address over and over and over. Then too, in the jargon of the EDP professionals, GIGO (*garbage in - garbage out*) persists in the address area too! Put in an incorrect ZIP Code and it will always be an incorrect ZIP Code. Put in a sloppy address, such as an intersection of two streets instead of a street number, and it will always be a sloppy address. So great caution should be exerted by every organization to see that the addresses in their files are indeed accurate and have correct 5-digit and ZIP+4 Codes.

Every organization should take a lesson from the professional marketeers who sell billions of dollars worth of merchandise and services through their direct mail efforts. You don't find them using inaccurate street addresses, incomplete street designations, or wrong ZIP Codes. They even know the number of the carrier assigned to your house or business! To them, proper addressing is a necessity simply because they know that otherwise they will not reach their prospects and they will waste printing and postage costs. They make sure the original input is correct; they run their EDP tapes against others to verify the ZIP Codes and then run merge and purge programs to remove addresses that are no longer valid. They know that a bad address invariably results in wasted money, because the mail cannot be delivered by the Postal Service.

Benefits of Clean and Accurate Addresses

The extra effort necessary to collect and maintain accurate, well-coded addresses pays big dividends. Whatever the cost of manuals and EDP tapes necessary to protect the validity of addresses, whatever the cost of training personnel to protect the accuracy of the addresses, there are many benefits in return. Clean and accurate addresses:

- Save on material costs
- Provide consistent service
- Add to customer satisfaction
- Save on postage costs
- Reduce undeliverable mail
- Increase direct mail sales

How to Improve Address Accuracy

The single greatest impact on those responsible for transcribing addresses into a computer file might be a memorandum from an officer of the organization listing the cost of postage in a previous year and emphasizing the need to maintain accuracy on all address and customer systems. An example of a recent specific problem resulting from an incorrect or stale address will add an impact to the memo.

The next step might be to study every single way that an address is collected or originated. One of the most accurate sources for address formats is the printed envelope or letterhead of business organizations. But special diligence is necessary when accepting addresses from individuals. Those addresses should be screened carefully, especially for full and complete street identification and the ZIP and ZIP+4 Codes. The *National Five-Digit ZIP Code Directory* does not contain ZIP+4 Codes but it is a great source for verifying an individual's home address as are the corresponding computerized versions.

Outside sales people are notorious for their lack of concern about mundane things such as addresses; they have a tendency to concentrate, perhaps rightly so, only on selling techniques. If that is so in your organization, someone should be carefully screening every sales order.

Still another area of concern should be the process by which your organization collects changes of addresses from your customers. If your organization deals primarily with other business firms, your problems are less because businesses usually notify their correspondents when they move. However, a screening process may still be necessary when a change of address is received showing a post office box *and* a street address, for mail should be directed to the post office box. You will likely find it worthwhile to continually remind your administration people that post office boxes often have different ZIP Codes than the street addresses that people show on moving notices.

If you deal mostly with individuals at their homes your problems are often compounded. It is hard to understand why so many people move and do not inform others of a new address. So every effort must be made to constantly remind individuals of the need to advise you of their intention to move.

Many national and local firms use courtesy envelopes to remind their customers to send in new addresses with "*Has Your Address Changed?*" printed prominently on the back. Similar notices are often found on the return portion of all kinds of statements. Still others request moving notices (and old address labels) six weeks prior to a move by printing reminders on the outside wrappers of magazines or on inserts enclosed inside of plastic bags. Similar notices can appear in space ads that you print in your own publications and even on the faces of envelopes with postage meter ad plates.

And there are other ways. When the *Americana* magazine receives a new subscriber its welcome letter includes: "Would you take a moment now to check your name and address as they appear on the enclosed copy of your bill? If house numbers or or other spelling is incorrect (except for necessary abbreviations), please make corrections on the bill and return it in the enclosed reply envelope." And it must work well, they have been using it for at least 12 years! The notice goes on to say that sending a change-of-address six weeks prior to moving can prevent delays in receiving their magazine, so they get it right to start with and solicit change notices at the same time.

In addition to knowing if people have moved, you may occasionally need to know if they are still interested in what you mail to them. There are several methods to check on that type of distribution list. One common way is to send out a double postcard requesting confirmation that the recipient still wishes to receive whatever you distribute. This is particularly suitable for those kinds of publications or newsletters that are distributed free. Other organizations send out a letter-type questionnaire to verify continued interest in a publication, as well as to verify the name and title of the individual receiving the issues.

Computerized Address Updating

The Postal Service and the mailing industry offer such a wide array of products and services which can improve the accuracy of your address files in any type of computer that describing them all in detail could fill an entire chapter. However, the Postal Service has established the *National Address Information Center* in Memphis to consolidate all types of addressing products and services. These can help you qualify for presort and ZIP+4 coding postage discounts. They can also help lower basic production and postage costs by reducing the percentage of *undeliverable-as-addressed* mail. The following is a list of the types of services and products available from the National Address Information Center along with a brief description of what the product or service provides to the mailer.

■*Address Change Service:* This service allows the automatic update of address files for customers who have moved. It provides mail forwarding information in days, rather than weeks, after the change becomes effective. The changes are forwarded to participants on magnetic tape or on-line, and a small fee is charged for each address record.

■*Address List Correction Service*: Deletes names that cannot be delivered or forwarded; corrects ZIP Codes, house, rural or post office boxes, etc.; furnishes addresses for customers who have moved; adds building apartment, suite, or room numbers, when known; indicates business (B) or rural route (R) addresses.

■*Address List Sequencing Service:* This service will arrange your addresses in the order that they are delivered. Three levels of address card sequencing for resident, business, or combination lists are available: address card sequencing; address card sequencing showing total possible deliveries; and address card sequencing with missing and new addresses added (with some restrictions).

■*Carrier Route Information System (CRIS):* This is a standardized format list of carrier route schemes for all city and non-city delivery post offices. This national file, with over four million records, contains city, rural, highway contract route, and post office box schemes. The system helps mailers take advantage of substantial presort postage discounts. Available on cartridges, tape, or microfilm. Hard copy is also available by 3- or 5-digit ZIP Codes.

■*City State File*: This comprehensive list contains ZIP Codes, and the city, post office, and county names associated with those ZIP Codes. It helps with: ZIP Code validation and assignment; city place name validation; and county code/county name identification. Available on tape or cartridge.

■*Computerized Labelling Address Sequence Service (CLASS):* This provides computerized delivery sequencing of addresses, eliminating the need for mailers to submit cards. Some of the benefits are: 100 percent sequencing of all deliverable addresses; accurate sequence information; fully standardized and ZIP+4 Coded addresses; faster notification and implementation of route and zone changes; and a reduction of undeliverable mail.

■*County-Cross File:* This file allows users who assigned the ZIP+4 Code to their address files to obtain county data at the ZIP+4 Code level. Available on tape or cartridge as a national file only.

■*CRIS/CROSS File*: Produced for ZIP+4 Code presorters, this file contains every ZIP+4 Code and the corresponding carrier identification service for that code. CRIS/CROSS is used by computerized sorters to facilitate carrier coding of address lists containing ZIP + 4 Codes. Available on tape or cartridge.

■*Delivery Statistics File*: This file contains information on the number of deliveries by carrier route and post office box sections. Using this file, mailers can determine the number of post office boxes in any post office, as well as the number of residential and business deliveries for every city, rural, and highway contract route in the country. Available on tape, cartridge, or microfiche. Hard copy is available by 3- and 5-digit ZIP Code.

■*DIME File*: This file tape matches the Census Geographic Base File/Dual Independent Map Encoding (GBF/DIME) file with the ZIP + 4 National File. Demographers, market researchers, and others can relate ZIP + 4 Coded address lists with Census Bureau demographic data without having to first match addresses with the GBF/DIME File. Available by subscription.

■*Five-Digit ZIP Code File*: This file, along with the *City State File*, enables mailers to add a 5-digit ZIP Code to add addresses in their files and to validate existing 5-digit ZIP Code assignments. The file contains detailed street data only for cities with more than one 5-digit ZIP Code (multi-coded cities). Available on tape, cartridge or microfilm.

■*Operation MAIL*: This unique program offers you a thorough evaluation of your mailing operation, from preparation to delivery. Particular attention is directed to the quality of your mailing lists. The aim is to improve the address quality of your mail before it enters the mailstream, helping you increase the number of mail pieces reaching your customers.

■*ZIP + 4 Diskette Coding*: Submit your mailing list on personal computer diskette and the National Address Information Center will correct the street and city names, state abbreviations, and 5-digit ZIP Codes. It will also assign ZIP + 4 Codes, and carrier route numbers (optional), and standardize address formats. The service can process most formats of 3½-, 5¼-, and 8-inch diskettes. The usual turnaround is 21 days.

■*ZIP + 4 National File:* Primarily for mailers having in-house capability to write their own software, this file contains 27 million address range records and ZIP + 4 Codes for all delivery points. Available on tape or cartridge.

In addition to these products and services supplied by the Postal Service the following products and services are provided by commercial vendors licensed by the USPS.

■*CD-ROM Retrieval System*: Many vendors offer addressing and presorting maintenance capabilities for personal computer users. The compact disk, read-only-memory (CD-ROM) can code your addresses with the carrier route codes and add ZIP+4 Codes. One single CD-ROM can hold 27 million address records.

■*Coding Accuracy Support System (CASS)*: This system allows mailers, service bureaus, and software vendors to verify the accuracy of ZIP+4 Coding accuracy, CRIS, and 5-digit coding. USPS CASS certification is a measure of coding accuracy. Beginning September 1, 1991, all addresses on mail claimed as qualifying for an automation discount *must* have been verified by a CASS certified system.

■*National Change of Address (NCOA)*: This system keeps track of current change of address information from across the nation. Through licensees, the system offers: address change updates before a mailing, address change data on tape or disk, standardization of all input addresses, ZIP+4 encoding on all processed addresses, and improved mail deliverability on a frequency that can be determined by the mailer.

■*National Deliverability Index:* This is a process developed by the mailing industry and the Postal Service that verifies six factors of the address and the 5-digit and ZIP+4 codes. It allows the purchaser of a mailing list to determine the deliverability of every address.

In addition to those products and services previously mentioned, the USPS will accept typewritten sheets, cards, or continuous forms listing business and resident addresses and will correct ZIP Codes and delete invalid addresses. There is a minimal charge for this service and it can be arranged at your local post office.

As you can see from these lists, there are many programs from both the Postal Service and commercial vendors that can clean up your address files and verify or correct both 5-digit ZIP Codes and ZIP+4 Codes. You can contact your local postmaster or account representative to discuss exactly which of the products or services would best suit your particular organization. If you live in a smaller city, your postmaster may be able to have a USPS account representative from the nearest MSC visit your office to provide you with additional information.

For more information about any of the USPS products or services you can write to the National Address Information Center, 660 Primacy Parkway, Suite 101, Memphis, TN 38188-0001, or telephone 1-800-238-3150 (in TN, 1-800-233-0453).

Recommended Address Formats

USPS publications, *A Guide to Business Mail Preparation* and the *National Five-Digit ZIP Code Directory*, along with many other USPS booklets, show the various address formats that are recommended. They also list the two-letter abbreviations for the 50 states which will save space in a computer file and speed up the typing or data input process.

The rules are not complicated. All computer codes, subscription expiration dates, file numbers, etc. should always be *on the top line* of an address, never below the city, state, and ZIP line. If a specific person in a company is to be addressed, his or her name should be on the line *above* the organization's name. "Attention Accounting Department" and other kinds of notations should go on that line as well. Any room or suite number should appear *after* the street address. The street address should always include any directional notations, which should be abbreviated without any punctuation as shown in the USPS publications. Figure 2 indicates how your business envelope should look.

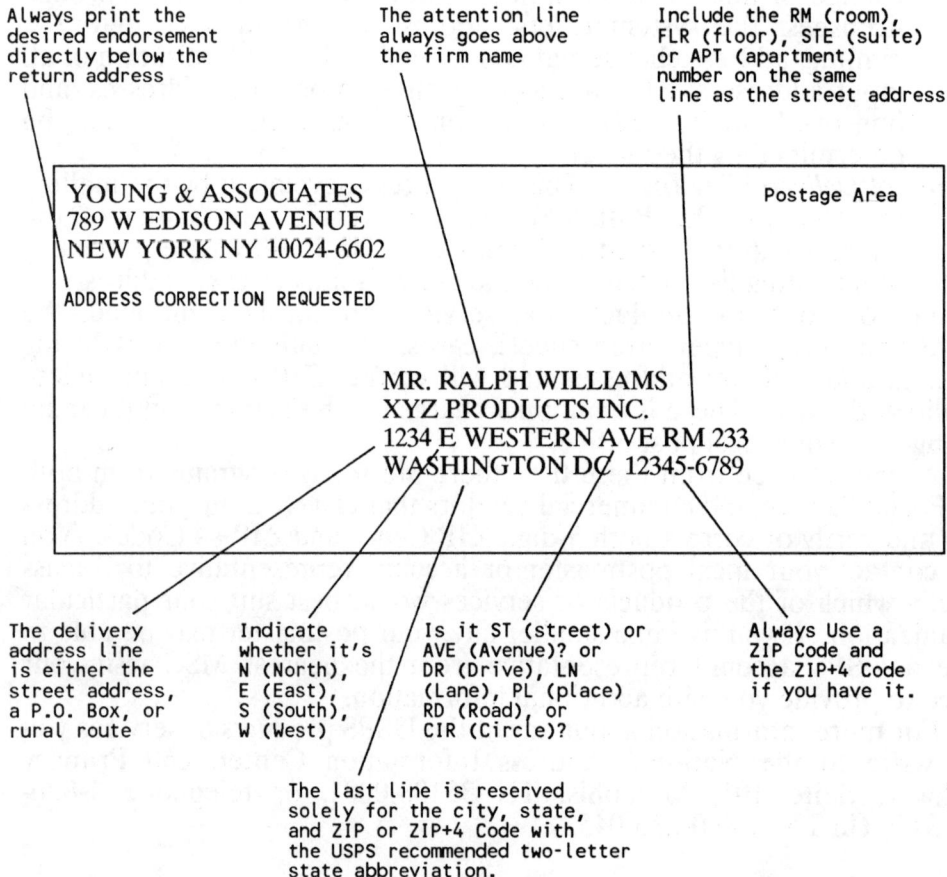

Always print the
desired endorsement
directly below the
return address

The attention line
always goes above
the firm name

Include the RM (room),
FLR (floor), STE (suite)
or APT (apartment)
number on the same
line as the street address

YOUNG & ASSOCIATES
789 W EDISON AVENUE
NEW YORK NY 10024-6602

ADDRESS CORRECTION REQUESTED

Postage Area

MR. RALPH WILLIAMS
XYZ PRODUCTS INC.
1234 E WESTERN AVE RM 233
WASHINGTON DC 12345-6789

The delivery
address line
is either the
street address,
a P.O. Box, or
rural route

Indicate
whether it's
N (North),
E (East),
S (South),
W (West)

Is it ST (street) or
AVE (Avenue)? or
DR (Drive), LN
(Lane), PL (place)
RD (Road), or
CIR (Circle)?

Always Use a
ZIP Code and
the ZIP+4 Code
if you have it.

The last line is reserved
solely for the city, state,
and ZIP or ZIP+4 Code with
the USPS recommended two-letter
state abbreviation.

Figure 2 Correct format for business envelopes.

In addition, it may be necessary to dispatch someone to service a customer on the premises but be able to mail the invoice for service to a *post office box.* The Postal Service will permit this convenient format if you remember to put the post office box on the line directly above the city, state, ZIP line, and the street address *above* that line. Figure 3 illustrates how that format should appear on a business envelope. Known as "dual addressing," it is authorized by the Postal Service *(DMM Sec.122.22)*, and the mail will be delivered to the post office box.

SERVICE ASSOCIATES
435 NW INDUSTRY DRIVE
ATLANTA GA 30309-3456

ADDRESS CORRECTION REQUESTED

Postage Area

GRAND PRODUCTS INC
100 DRUID STREET
P O BOX 4123
ATLANTA GA 30361-4123

Figure 3 Example of dual addressing.

Maintaining Small In-House Lists

Most organizations have a need to maintain several small internal mail lists for distribution to other departments, branches, or plant locations outside of a central location. Other types of lists would include the media, special VIP customers, or labor organizations. All of the cautions about maintaining up-to-date addresses for these groups are equally important and sometimes more difficult to maintain because they seem less important than customers.

It is not difficult to set up a relatively simple system to control and update those lists, since most often the changing process is performed at a central location. Utilize sheets with headings that identify the list involved and two columns with "*Add To List*" and "*Delete From List.*" Then require that the person performing the adding and deleting process on the computer provide the originator of the changes with a printout of the new list. This will allow the originator to verify the accuracy of each addition and deletion while retaining a current hardcopy list for reference purposes. But the absence of the list printout and checking process will soon completely invalidate the accuracy of the list.

Changing Your Own Address

Whenever your organization is moving you should make sure that the address you give to your customers and other associates is in the exact format that you wish to have on your incoming mail. You should apply the same address hygiene rules to your new address as you do to your outgoing mail. It will be helpful to everyone if you include your telephone number in the notice and, of course, the specific date that the new address is to become effective. Many organizations also put their new address on their postage meter ad plate for a period of three or four months.

UNDERSTANDING COMPUTER FORWARDING

Hand in hand with accurate, well-formatted addresses is understanding exactly what happens when your mail cannot reach its destination or, as the USPS labels it, is *Undeliverable As Addressed (UAA)*. The Postmaster General recently reported that the USPS forwards 2.3 *billion* pieces of mail annually because 40 million Americans relocate every year. The cost of that forwarding impacts everyone's postage rates so whenever you minimize the opportunity for your mail to be forwarded you help contribute to more stable rates. More important, your mail reaches the party you sent it to whether it be a bid, an invoice, or some other vital communication. If you do not understand how to have your mail mesh with the forwarding system, that can greatly reduce your chances of your mail being delivered in a timely manner, or even cause the mail to be returned to you.

How It Works

The USPS has installed the second generation of its *Computerized Forwarding System (CFS)* and is now processing 100 percent of the mail that requires forwarding on this new system. When the carrier identifies a piece of mail that is undeliverable-as-addressed (UAA), he or she forwards it to another section within the mail facility, or to the nearest SCF or MSC with such a system. The operators of the CFS will then search the computerized list of address changes looking for a new address for the individual or organization on the UAA piece of mail. That electronic process searches with great accuracy. In the past, when a new address was located the computer automatically printed a yellow, pressure-sensitive label about 1 x 3 inches with the new address. The operators stuck the label over the old address (but not over either the name or any identification numbers appearing above the name), and the piece was on its way to the new address. CFS II provides a more efficient means of processing letter mail by eliminating the manual label application and providing a new barcoded address for subsequent mail processing.

Sources for New Addresses

The Postal Service has campaigned for many years to have people file changes of addresses whenever they move. Two cards are available at your post office. The *Change of Address Order (Form 3575)* directs the Postal Service to change your address, and *Form 3576* is available for notification of magazine publishers and other personal correspondents.

The Change of Address Order has previously been the only source of information accepted by the USPS as input to the memory banks of the Computerized Forwarding System. In the past no other source has been accepted. Now a machine similar to an automatic teller machine is being tested; it will encourage a postal customer to simply enter his or her name along with the old and new addresses on a standard keyboard and a user-friendly color screen. This new system, *Postal Buddy*, is being tested as a commercial venture operated under contract to the USPS and provides many benefits.

The Postal Buddy terminal is available 24 hours a day, has many security checks, and reduces chances of errors due to illegible handwriting or misread addresses. It also automatically inserts the five-digit ZIP Code and the ZIP+4 Code into the new address. During the test over one hundred national publishers, department stores, and catalog merchants subscribed to the electronic service and received the new addresses the same day they were filed. It appears to be one of the rare instances where everyone benefits.

Address Retention Period

At one time the Postal Service maintained computerized address files for a period of two years covering everyone who moved. But as these files grew larger and larger, requiring greater computer storage capacity, it became economically prohibitive. While there was some grumbling from the larger business mailers, an improved CFS helped relieve anxiety about address changes, and the Postal Service announced that new addresses would only be retained in their CFS *for a period of one year*. In a moment you will see how this is very important to the endorsements you place on First-Class Mail.

Forwarding First-Class Mail

Every organization, and especially one that extends credit to individuals, should be concerned about its First-Class Mail being forwarded. It seems unclear to many businesses exactly what happens to their FCM when their customers move. Actually, all First-Class Mail is forwarded *free*, but with no notice to the sender, and that can make strange things happen.

Examine this scenario. A customer purchases something and agrees to pay for it in 24 payments. You send monthly statements to the customer, and payments are received on time for nine months. Then the payments start arriving later and later. The customer pays the twelfth payment 60 days late, and you send a past-due notice via FCM. To your dismay the past-due notice is returned by the Postal Service marked, *Not Deliverable as Addressed, Unable to Forward*. Now you have to lose half of the balance when you get a collection agency to chase the customer or have one of your employees spend half a morning trying in vain to get a lead on where the person moved.

What happened? The customer moved the second month and filed a change of address card with the local post office, but failed to notify your office. Since your statements were sent as FCM they were forwarded free to the customer's new address, but you had no way to know that. Then his or her finances had a major set-back, and it became impossible to make payments on time. By the time your past-due notice arrived at the delivering post office the 12-month period had expired and the post office simply returned the notice.

Address Correction Requested

None of that aggravation is necessary, and you do not have to risk having customers move away without your knowing it. The cost is far less then chasing after customers, and you will save postage, time, and the cost of mailing materials. All you need do is have the notation, *Address Correction Requested* printed on all of your envelopes directly below your return address.

Whenever you print *Address Correction Requested* (directly below the return address) on your Express Mail, First-Class Mail, Priority Mail, or postal or post cards the Postal Service will *not* forward the piece. The USPS will provide address correction or reason for nondelivery directly on the mail piece, and return it to you at no charge (see *DMM, Exhibit 159.151a*). If you prefer the endorsement, *Do Not Forward*, the piece will be handled in the same manner. The cost for the address correction service is only 35¢ (in 1991), but it is not charged unless a separate address correction notice is provided to the mailer when the piece is forwarded. That is a real bargain, and it is harmless until someone moves. If you doubt the value of that endorsement you should make it a point to inspect incoming mail both at the office and at your home to see that most large business mailers are already using it.

Over 600 second- and third-class mailers participate in a program offered by the Postal Service and periodically receive a computer tape of all address changes and a charge of only 20¢ for each correction. Mailers with a high volume of address changes should call the USPS *Address Information Center* in Memphis, 1-800-238-3150, for additional information.

Understanding Envelope Endorsements

Section 159.151a/f in the *Domestic Mail Manual* pertaining to endorsements shows every endorsement for each class of mail and then describes in detail exactly what will happen to *undeliverable-as-addressed* mail when it carries such an endorsement. There are about eight pages of details about endorsements in the DMM, so the amount of study you devote to those endorsements should be proportional to the size and scope of the mailing you are planning. Any time you are planning a significant mailing, of a different class than you usually use, you should discuss the proper endorsement with your postmaster or USPS account representative before your envelopes are printed. In addition, if you order printed envelopes in large quantities, it is always a good habit to check with your local postal people before you place your order to be sure there have not been any recent changes in endorsements.

CHAPTER 6

THE CHARACTERISTICS OF MAIL

Managing the mail in the 90's can be a complex and confusing world because of the wide varieties of knowledge needed to be successful. Problems occur first in one area and then in another. You stamp out one fire and another starts somewhere else. One moment you are coping with personnel problems, next a machine problem, and then you must interpret some USPS regulation. Of all of these areas, one of the more important ones is an understanding of the characteristics of mail, that is the actual physical properties of mail. The physical makeup of all kinds of mail can greatly influence the kind of mail service you can expect to receive and what it will cost.

Planning an open house? Print extra large invitations and they will incur a surcharge, be processed by hand, and perhaps be received too late by your expected guests. Or print giant postcards and pay First-Class letter postage when a smaller card would have been equally suitable. Reply cards can be so large that every single one received back from customers or prospects can be at the letter rate instead of the card rate. Or fail to stock several types and sizes of shipping bags and expect someone to stuff one so full it rips open or bursts en route.

These are not farfetched examples. You can walk into any post office and see every one of them almost any evening. Understanding the characteristics of mail is part of good mailroom management as it is often the basic groundwork and key to surviving the various transportation systems.

You can help overcome some of the mystery of good mail preparation by establishing an envelope file. Collect every single envelope used anywhere in your organization. Examine each one for deficiencies. Speak with the users in each department to determine if it *exactly* fulfills their requirements. Ask about any problems with every size and type of envelope, make notes on the envelope itself, and then set up a file for review in six months or a year. Next review each type of box, padded envelope, or other container that you stock in the mailroom. Determine if there is a sufficient assortment of each of those containers or if some kinds are not being used at all.   Then you will have a grasp of exactly what is going on in your entire organization and what areas may need further investigation.

ENVELOPE SELECTION OBJECTIVES

Many factors that affect the selection of the right envelope or container, and effective mail management should include an extensive knowledge of the preferred qualities of each type. Each envelope that you stock in your organization should:

- Be as economical as possible and still meet management's needs
- Provide ease in preparation and inserting
- Be easy to seal securely against damage or pilferage
- Be compatible with printing and USPS requirements
- Be strong enough to survive any transportation system
- Be large enough to prevent bursting
- Be available in a variety of sizes

If your organization utilizes inserting machines, all of the envelopes you stock must be suitable for your particular inserting machine and match its specifications. When you order envelopes for mechanical inserting, be sure to notify your supplier that they will be used for mechanical inserting. In addition, if you will order 9 x 12 inch envelopes with the flap on the *long* side you will be able to seal and stamp them on your mailing machine.

SELECTING THE CORRECT ENVELOPE

Day in and day out, envelopes probably cause more distress in mailrooms across the country than any other single irritation. They can cause all kinds of problems. They can jam the sealer in the mailing machine, and they can disrupt the inserting machines. But with a little care you don't have to put up with those problems.

Whenever you need an envelope for a newly created piece of mail you only need to ask yourself these five questions to eliminate those headaches:

■*What do I want to send?* Your answers might be any of these items. A single page from the computer or a folded printed sheet. One enclosure, or several, or a check. An insert with an address on it, or the envelope must be addressed. A reply or courtesy envelope must be included. It is a confidential letter. It's small. It's oversize. It's delicate. It can't be folded.

■*How do I want to send it?* Some answers and conclusions. First-Class Mail, so I want it to meet automation requirements. Bulk third-class mail, so I need advertising copy on face of envelope. International mail, so we must verify size requirements.

■*How will I insert it?* Casual labor will do inserting, will need ample clearance. Machine will insert, must meet specifications and end clearance. Contract printer will insert, not my problem.

■*How will I pay postage?* Will use postage meter, flap must be machine sealable. Will use permit imprint, need to print with advertising copy. Want to personalize it with adhesive postage stamp.

■*How will USPS process it?* It's bulky, it will go through the bulk mail centers, I'll need reinforced envelopes. Those stamps will need cancelling, can't enclose the promotional lapel pin. I'll want benefits of automation, must double check size.

If you have already established an envelope file, now is the time to review it for it will tell you exactly what kinds of envelopes you have on hand. If nothing on hand really suits your needs then you will have to call on your envelope sales representative.

With such a wide variety of paper types, weights, textures, and colors, the sales rep for an envelope company becomes an engineer as he or she starts to build an envelope that exactly fits your needs. The answers to the questions above will allow the envelope engineer to create that perfect fit.

Humidity

Any printer will tell you that one of their greatest enemies is humidity. Paper is very sensitive to the *surrounding humidity*. Paper is made up of millions of tiny hollow fibers that absorb moisture when the paper is drier than the surrounding air, and this moisture exchange adjusts itself to balance with the air. Such changes in the amount of moisture in paper, especially envelopes, can result in dimensional changes and distortion. Edges curl and become wavy, and this can cause two problems. First, the envelope warps and if laid flat on a table will have one corner 1/4 inch to 1/3 inch off of the surface of the table. Such an envelope can drive an inserter operator crazy. The other problem is the gum on the flap of the envelope. If envelopes are left with their flaps extended open for any length of time, especially overnight, the gum is quick to absorb any moisture that is in the air. The edge of the flap then curls, which in turn causes poor sealing and can cause a jam in the mailing machine. Along with all that aggravation, complete sealing on envelopes is essential to your overall efficiency. Customers become quite upset when they receive bills in unsealed envelopes or even enraged if an envelope arrives with a check missing. Items can fall out of poorly sealed envelopes, and the flaps can catch on all of those moving belts and rollers.

If a project requires a group of people to perform manual inserting of many envelopes, or if you have a small inserter that requires the flap to be extended prior to insertion, every effort should be made to seal *all* flaps at the end of the day. In areas where unusually high humidity is experienced during the summer months, efforts should be made to seal the inserted envelopes as the work progresses, for even a few hours can cause problems.

IMPACT OF USPS DIMENSIONAL STANDARDS

The dimensional standards that developed during the automation program are explained in *Chapter 5* and should not be a problem. That is, unless some demanding person comes running into the mailroom saying, "I need an envelope for this right away," and someone else orders a special envelope that does not fit within the dimensional standards. Otherwise the envelope manufacturers will guide you through the maze and not even stock an envelope that is too small or the wrong shape.

However, they will sell you an envelope that can cause problems. Because plastic envelopes that exceed the acceptable dimensional standards weigh less than half an ounce, you can put one or two sheets of letter size paper in them and the envelope and its insert will still weigh less than an ounce and cost 10¢ extra (in 1991) or 5¢ extra if presorted. If it is a certificate of some sort, or a photo, and absolutely cannot be folded, then you should add a sheet of cardboard to protect it from folding. But if it is a two page letter to a branch manager it becomes an extravagant waste of postage. With the growth of the use of plastic envelopes and the maximum size for *one ounce or less* of First- or third-class mail at only 6 1/8 inches in height, any envelope taller or higher than that dimension will trigger that 10¢ surcharge (See *DMM Sec. 353*).

Postal and Postcards

A *postal* card is one that is printed and sold by the Postal Service and measures 3½ x 5½ inches. It has the postage stamp embossed or printed on the face of the card and is available as a single card or as a perforated double card. The double card is extremely convenient when you want to notify people of an event and have them respond immediately by detaching and mailing the second card, which is usually pre-addressed for their convenience. Used in conjunction with computer printed pressure-sensitive labels which may be removed and then applied to the second card, the double card becomes a great tool for a quick reply while providing the full address and file references of the recipient. Postal cards are also available in sheets of forty for use by printers, and are cut to size after printing.

One word of caution, however. If you begin to use postal cards in your operation, be careful when you hear that the USPS has filed a new rate case. Don't get caught with a bunch of printed cards that have the wrong amount of postage on them.

A *postcard* is a card that is printed privately, conforms to certain size limitations, and must have postage applied by postage stamp, permit imprint, or postage meter. A postcard may be as small as 3½ x 5 inches in the domestic U.S. mail (but must be 5½ inches long if entered into the international mails). A postcard may be as large as 4¼ x 6 inches and still retain its identity as a postcard and be mailed at the postcard rate. If it exceeds either of those dimensions, postage must be paid on the card at the current letter rate for one ounce or less. Furthermore, a postcard with a height greater than 6 1/8 inches, which would normally weigh less than one ounce, *will* incur the current surcharge. If you want the impact of a giant postcard be prepared to pay the surcharge. But don't design the extra large postcard and then be surprised when you take it to be mailed.

Postal Bulletin 21781B, dated January 28, 1991, established eligibility for automated rate categories, and it has a definite impact on *postcards* in *Section 525* of the newly activated *Chapter 5* of the *DMM*.

All postcards must be at least .007 of an inch thick (*Sec. 352.21a*) but they *must also* meet an industry basis weight of 75 pounds (the weight of 500 sheets measuring 25 x 38 inches) if you expect to claim a discount for First-Class non-presorted ZIP+4, ZIP+4 presort, and ZIP+4 barcoded mail; and third-class basic ZIP+4, 5-digit ZIP+4, or ZIP+4 barcoded mail.

The same *Postal Bulletin* also *recommended* 90 pound index stock for larger cards and states that double postcards *must* be secured with one tab to receive automated rates.

Postcards Versus Envelopes

Before a comparison of postcards and envelopes is made it would be well that you understood why rates are discussed in this text at all.

As soon as an author begins comparing any kind of costs that change from time to time it seems to shorten the useful life of the publication, because new costs make the publication appear to be outdated. However, this should not happen when using this book. Throughout this book you will see comparisons of costs in order to emphasize that certain kinds of things should be compared. The important thing to remember is *what is being compared and the result of the comparison*, not the current cost.

For example, in 1978 it was good business to compare the cost of postage on a postcard with that of a envelope weighing one ounce. The envelope required 15¢ postage and the postcard only 10¢, a savings of 5¢ or 33 percent. In 1991, an envelope required 29¢ postage and the postcard only required 19¢, a savings of 10¢, and *still* 33 percent.

The actual rates are unimportant. What is important is that you examine the postage rate of envelopes with that of postcards, *regardless of the current rates*. This was part of smart mail management in 1978, again in 1991, and it will be just as smart in the year 2000. You should try to keep these comparisons in mind when you see references to rates elsewhere in this book.

Now, back to the comparisons. With the postcard requiring 33 percent less postage, and saving a big dime, it is a most frugal endeavor to examine all of your mailing pieces to see if it is practical to convert some of your present letter mail to postcards. Your savings could well exceed the current rate of interest!

Attractive printing on light colored card stock can be quite an inexpensive method to send notices to customers or for internal organizational messages. Meter readings, utility billings, newspaper bills, and special sale notices are all likely candidates for postcard use. They are also excellent as coupons saying, for example, "Bring this card in and receive...." High quality photographs, of homes or luxury automobiles for example, on a 4 x 6 inch card can have quite an impact on a prospect. If you are a retailer, you will find that many manufacturers often provide attractive postcards at very little cost.

Another advantage of postcards is that they require no folding or inserting. They are easy to feed through a mailing machine to apply a meter stamp, or a permit may be printed on the card at the same time the text of the card is printed. Forms manufacturers can provide you with cards in a continuous form for computer printing variable data and the address at the same time. And, of course, they are excellent as business reply cards, as discussed in *Chapter 9*.

There are a few disadvantages. You should be aware of the obvious loss of privacy, the fact that neither business reply nor courtesy envelopes may be sent along with your message or statement, and that you cannot, under Federal law, "communicate with consumers regarding a debt by postcard."

One other important point about postcards. You should review the regulations covering postcards in the *Domestic Mail Manual* (*Sec. 159.47c*) because without some sort of endorsement, or a return address, a postcard will be destroyed if it is undeliverable. Once again you need to rely on *Address Correction Requested*, and be sure to have your return address on postcards.

Self-Mailers

A self-mailer is a sale notice, a church bulletin, or other piece of paper or card stock which is folded (usually) to approximately the size of a #10 legal size envelope and mailed without any type of envelope. The *DMM* allows the printing of a permit indicia by the stencil or offset process for inexpensive printing in an office. After proper printing and folding, the permit imprint is in the upper right corner, and the piece is ready to be addressed and mailed. This is in widespread use by churches and smaller organizations. Some well-designed advertising self-mailers printed on card stock have detachable perforated cards on the lower portion that meet the *DMM* requirements for business reply cards.

Section 352.22 of the *DMM* states that to insure prompt and efficient processing of First-Class Mail it is *recommended* that self-mailers "be sealed or secured on all four edges so that they can be handled by *machines.*" Furthermore, since the rate for First-Class Mail and single-piece third-class mail is identical for over 4 but not exceeding 5 ounces (in 1991), a self-mailer should be sent as First-Class Mail unless it weighs over 5 ounces, or unless you want to prepare the self-mailers as bulk third-class mail. However, remember if the *DMM* states it is *recommended* or you *should* do something you have some leeway. If it states you *must* do something you have no alternative.

To further complicate your choices, *Postal Bulletin 21781B* of January 28, 1991, established the heretofore reserved *Chapter 5* of the *DMM* as *Automation Compatible Mail,* and *Section 523* is entirely devoted to *Folded Self-Mailers.* It establishes the minimum weight of paper mailed as either a single or multiple sheet self-mailer if *one* tab is used to seal the unfolded edge. If two tabs are used, one on each end of the unfolded edge, a lighter weight paper may be used. (Until February, 2, 1992, self-mailers may be constructed of the lighter weight paper and mailed with only *one* tab to seal the open edge.)

All of these requirements apply only to mail pieces that are eligible for automated rate categories. *If* you are mailing self-mailers as ordinary First-Class Mail or bulk third-class mail you do *not* have to obey these requirements. But your mail will not be processed on automated equipment and consequently may be delayed. You *must* prepare self-mailers to conform to *Section 523* if you expect to claim a discount for First-Class non-presorted ZIP+4, ZIP+4 presort, and ZIP+4 barcoded mail, and third-class basic ZIP+4, 5-digit ZIP+4, or ZIP+4 barcoded mail.

It may be easier and simpler just to insert your self-mailer into an envelope. If you must send a small quantity and do not care whether they receive automated processing, you can obtain round pressure-sensitive disks from your stationery store. Staples should not be used for they often cut the hands of postal workers, and the recipient is very likely to tear the self-mailer trying to get it open or, worse, throw it away in disgust.

If you have a high volume of self-mailers or booklets to mail at automated rates you might investigate equipment that can attach two seals in one pass through a machine. But be prepared for sticker shock, they start in the mid-$50's.

Fisher Technologies   TapeMark
P.O. Box 1366   150 E. Marie Avenue
Cedar Rapids, IA 52406-1366   West St. Paul, MN 55118-4000
1-800-397-0112   1-800-328-0135

TYPICAL TYPES OF ENVELOPES

The Envelope Manufacturers Association of America (1600 Duke Street, Suite 440, Alexandria, VA 22314-3421, telephone 703-739-2200) reports that there were 165 billion envelopes manufactured in 1989 by 81 manufacturers operating 155 plants. Therefore you can easily see that a few pages here cannot begin to cover all of the varieties of available envelopes or who manufactures them. But the following information may help you sort out *some* of the major types of envelopes that are available. There are many more.

Envelopes for First-Class Mail

You should pay special attention to the envelopes you stock for First-Class Mail. You should be sure to keep an assortment of sizes on hand to help you meet small emergencies. Even blank envelopes can be rubber stamped with a return address when you are in a bind, or you might keep an ad plate for your postage meter handy to imprint the return address with your mailing machine.

This is probably an appropriate place to emphasize the value and importance of having green "diamonds" printed around the border of larger size or *catalog* envelopes. It is another factor that you ought to see for yourself while on a tour of your local postal facility. You will see thousands of 9 x 12 inch envelopes, picked up from collection boxes and office lobbies, dumped on a moving belt so that the mail handlers can *try* to sort out the First-Class Mail from the third-class (read *slower)* mail. In the larger installations, there may be twenty people trying to keep up with all of the mail as the evening crunch starts. There are all kinds of mail, and it is everywhere. Then you will see an envelope go quietly by these people with a little pica-size typed legend above the address that meekly whispers *First-Class.* It is soon obvious that the notice is too small to be noticed as the envelope continues on with the third-class envelopes. And the sender will complain later when it takes eight or nine days to get from one coast to the other.

You only get one chance, miss that separation in the beginning and it will be swept into the river of third-class mail. Then it will be processed as third-class mail, transported as third-class mail, and delivered long after First-Class Mail to the same destination has been received.

That same evening those same people will quickly spot green diamond bordered envelopes, move the envelopes into the First-Class Mail processing line where the envelopes will go out on the earliest trucks and planes. It is just as if you receive some sort of preferential service for your green diamonds; they are a great investment. Some of the associations based in Washington, DC, are so conscious of the need to get information to their members as fast as possible, they even have green diamonds printed on their #10 size envelopes.

In addition to green diamond envelopes, be sure to stock some #9 envelopes. Your administrative people will occasionally want an envelope to enclose inside of a #10 envelope to insure a prompt reply and one #10 envelope inside another is not a good solution. In *Chapter 9* you can review what kind of postage you wish to use on the return envelope.

Another area often overlooked is a standard check envelope. It is somewhat smaller than a #9 envelope but with a window that can eliminate the addressing of check envelopes simply by having the full address on the "pay to" line of the check. You may also want to order a printed design *inside* the check envelope to make it opaque for complete privacy.

Years ago, the Post Office Department required that envelopes with third-class postage affixed had to be capable of being opened for postal inspection. Someone thought it would be a great idea to put a double tang metal clasp on large catalog envelopes to hold them shut but let them be opened for postal inspection when necessary. Then (*at least* 12 years ago) the USPS ruled that third-class mail could be sealed but apparently no one told the envelope manufacturers! The metal clasp envelope is more expensive than a plain flap on an envelope, can hang up on processing equipment and other mail, must be sealed manually, and serves no useful purpose. Maybe there should be a bumper sticker: Help Stamp Out Clasp Envelopes!

Continuous Form Mailers

You should be aware that an impact computer printer can print both ordinary envelopes and one-piece sealed mailing pieces designed as continuous forms. While the new addressing machines capable of simultaneously printing a barcode (and thereby qualifying the mail for a substantial discount) may soon make them obsolete, there may be a time when they can solve a problem for you.

A pre-packaged mailer, complete with a business reply envelope and two or three other printed inserts, can be designed in a continuous form to be mailed either as First-Class permit or bulk third-class mail. They only require computer printing and bursting (or detaching from each other), and they are ready to go into the mail. A sales rep from any forms manufacturer should be able to help you design a continuous form mailer but make sure the final size meets the dimensional mail standards.

In addition, you may wish to contact Performance Dataforms, 1545 White Oak Road, Suite 100, Lake Forest, IL 60045-3653, or telephone 708-234-0140. They specialize in the manufacture of forms that are designed to be folded and sealed after a pass through an impact computer printer. Mailers can be designed that contain an outbound envelope, billing message inserts, top flap return envelope, and piggy-back advertising panels.

Piggyback Envelopes

If your organization has an important printed report weighing six or seven ounces, and your management wants a personal letter to accompany each one, you need not send the whole package as First-Class Mail. You may obtain a catalog envelope for the report which has a #10 envelope affixed to the front of the larger envelope. In this manner the report can go as either single-piece or bulk third-class mail, while you simply pay the FCM rate on the letter in the #10 size envelope. To evaluate whether or not the piggyback envelope would be more economical, add the cost of either single-piece or bulk third-class mail to the cost of one ounce of FCM plus the cost differential for the piggyback envelope. Then compare that postage to mailing the entire report and the letter via First-Class Mail in an ordinary 9 x 12 FCM envelope, and remember that in the latter case you receive forwarding and return at no extra cost. If you choose the combination envelope, check on the *current* forwarding regulations on such packets, as it usually will be forwarded under the conditions for forwarding the contents of the larger envelope (as second-, third-, or fourth-class mail, not as FCM).

Reinforced Envelopes

Sears, Penneys and L. L. Bean all utilize reinforced envelopes (that are almost bags) to ship so-called "soft goods" from their catalog departments via both the Postal Service and United Parcel Service. These are excellent for unbreakable material where tear and burst strength is the deciding factor. Usually constructed of resin-laminated, two-ply kraft and glass fiber reinforcement, they are water and stain resistant, puncture and tear resistant, and simple to close and seal. In a pinch, if you are very frugal, they are even reusable. They would be a good choice for a computer printout several inches thick. Some manufacturers make the same type of envelope, or bag, with *gusseted* sides that expand to receive unusually thick items. Most manufacturers can provide reinforced envelopes in any size from 4 x 8 inches to 14½ x 20 inches.

Padded Envelopes or Bags

One of the most common shipping containers is the padded bag, which has built-in cushioning that acts as a shock absorber, is easy to close on scored folds, and has a unique tear-tape for neat, convenient opening by the addressee.

These cushioned bags are available in about 15 different sizes from several manufacturers. If your organization has need for a *padded* or *cushioned* bag (in contrast to one that is only *reinforced)* you should carefully research how many different sized items need the cushioning. If you do not stock a variety of sizes, employees are likely to waste both the cost of the more costly bag and additional postage by shipping small items in oversized bags. If you have six or seven different sized items that are shipped then you should stock bags in six or seven different sizes.

Some cushioned bags are heat sealable. If you use staples to seal cushioned bags you should always cover the staples with some kind of tape. It provides greater security, protects the hands of the mail handlers, and prevents the staples from catching on other mail.

Air Bubble Envelopes

You will have to do some of your own investigative work to decide whether you should be using padded cushioned envelopes or envelopes of kraft paper with an inner lining of polyethylene or polypropylene bubbles. Available in either self-seal or heat-seal, the air bubble cushioned bag is lighter then the traditional padded bag, although some appear to be more prone to puncture than padded envelopes. Yet the postage savings, for some items, may be considerable. These too are available in a wide range of sizes, and you should realize that your organization could require several sizes of padded envelopes sitting on a shelf right beside several sizes of bubble envelopes.

Plastic Envelopes

There are two types of plastic envelopes that are virtually tear proof, waterproof, and tamperproof. In addition, they are the lightest envelopes available and an excellent choice when you need added protection but do not require cushioning or padding. The most well known brands are *Tyvek* spunbonded olefin manufactured by the DuPont Company and *Rigur*, manufactured by Poly Pak America, Inc. Both types of envelopes are sold by various dealers throughout the U.S.

Polyethylene Foam

Several manufacturers provide envelopes with a 1/16-inch or 1/8-inch lining of polyethylene foam that are very light but do provide additional cushioning protection. They are generally available in the usual wide range of cushioned or padded envelopes, and some may be heat sealed.

One organization, The Crowell Corporation, manufacturers a unique product consisting of 1/6-inch, 3/32-inch, and 1/8-inch closed-cell foam combined with a heavy kraft paper base. Provided in either sheets or rolls the *Cro-nel* is self-sealing but will not stick to other products. The manufacturer claims it is excellent for packaging books, catalogs, and other products and is accepted by both the USPS and UPS.

Reusable Pouches and Bags

Approved by the Post Office Department in 1960, reusable 200-denier nylon pouches have been going back and forth between home offices and branches for over thirty years. Color coded for instant recognition, they save postage by consolidating mail while providing maximum strength. A reversible address tag provides quick, effortless turn-around time, and a tamper-proof plastic tie provides ample security. Costing as little as $4.50 (for a 9 x 12 inch bag) in small quantities, they are almost half that cost in lots of 120 or more. They have a terrific reputation and are probably in use in well over half of the Fortune 500 companies. Several companies sell them and provide customized silk-screen printing on the bags.

Floppy Disk Mailers

As more and more people begin to work out of their homes with personal computers there is likely to be an increased number of 5¼-inch floppy disks and 3½-inch diskettes sent through the mails or via overnight express. You will want to provide extra protection to diskettes to prevent any damage in transit.

The Microsoft Corporation uses heavy-duty cardboard mailers almost a millimeter thick to mail its floppy disks, and you may be able to find similar mailers (by Dennison Manufacturing Company) at your stationery store.

Another unique product is a tough, reusable plastic case with security pins, that fit either size of diskette. Designed so that you can be absolutely positive that your important data arrives intact, they are available from Evans Speciality Company, Inc., P.O. Box 24189, Richmond, VA 23224-0189, telephone 1-800-368-3061.

Sources of Supply

When shopping for a particular type of envelope or bag do not overlook the advantages of visiting business shows and the National Postal Forums where you can see samples of the products and discuss the merits of each with knowledgeable sales representatives. In addition, most of the larger manufacturers have customer engineers that will come to your office or plant and analyze your problems.

When ordering any of the special containers be sure to specify *green diamonds* on the borders if you send First-Class Mail in flats weighing under 11 ounces. You should also order some envelopes with *Priority Mail* in conspicuous lettering if you frequently have First-Class material weighing over 11 ounces. At the same time, remember the *free* envelope available from the USPS for *flat rate* Priority Mail. The rate is $2.90 (in 1991) for *any weight* up to whatever you can stuff into the envelope.

Whenever you need envelopes, check the *Yellow Pages* first to see what supplier may be nearby, or contact the following:

American Envelope Company
222 North LaSalle Street
Chicago, IL 60601-1002
1-800-232-6861

Astro-Valcour, Inc.
100 Thomas Road North
Hawthorne, NJ 07507-0495
1-800-334-1417

Bagmasters
6430 Dale Street
Buena Park, CA 90621-3115
1-800-843-2247
In CA 1-800-558-2247

The Crowell Corporation
P.O. Box 3227
Newport, DE 19804-0227
302-998-0557

Curtis 1000, Inc.
2100 RiverEdge Parkway
Atlanta, GA 30328-1056
1-800-241-0224

DuPont Company, Tyvek Marketing
1007 Market Street, Room 2N47-B
Wilmington, DE 19880-0705
1-800-44-TYVEK

Poly Pak America, Inc.
2939 East Washington Boulevard
Los Angeles, CA 90023-4277
1-800-826-4000
In PA 1-800-358-7300

A. Rifkin Company
P.O. Box 878
Wilkes-Barre, PA 18703-0878
1-800-458-7300

Sealed Air Corporation
19-01 State Highway 208
Fair Lawn, NJ 07410-2805
201-703-5500

Shuford Mills
P.O. Drawer 2228
Hickory, NC 28603-2228
1-800-334-3525

Tension Envelope
819 East 19th Street
Kansas City, MO 64108-1781
816-471-3800

Westvaco
P.O. Box 3300
Springfield, MA 01101-3300
1-800-628-9265

Remember, 1-800-555-1212 provides information on all 800 numbers.

PROPER PARCEL PREPARATION

It would be difficult to overemphasize the importance of packaging of shipments that takes place in a medium size mailroom. The large merchandise shippers that daily pack and ship several hundred different items are likely to have already gone through the agony of selecting packing and boxing material best suited to their own particular merchandise. It is the smaller mailrooms that need to examine their practices, those that have a medium amount of packaging but it is not their entire mission in life.

Improper and inadequate packaging is expensive. It costs in good will, in replacement merchandise, and in wasted clerical time. Therefore the packing of small parcels should be an area of serious concern to any mailroom manager who is interested in providing the best service at the lowest cost. Often, the "we've always done it that way" syndrome can be one of the biggest stumbling blocks. But it will prove very rewarding to review every method of packing on a regular basis; otherwise, it will be difficult to stay up-to-date in technical changes affecting the packaging industry.

Packaging Requirements

To a great extent, with the exception of hazardous materials, the proper packaging for any article will depend on six basic packaging factors:

- Fragility
- Density
- Weight
- Shape
- Volume
- Value

When these six factors are taken into consideration, they should automatically prescribe the proper packaging necessary at the lowest cost.

For example, a heavy piece of machinery that has a high density must be packed in a carton that is strong enough to prevent it from smashing its way out and damaging other parcels. If a product is very fragile or very expensive, then special precautions must be taken to ensure that the carton can take a few bumps without damaging the contents. On the other hand, all a wool shirt needs is a mailing bag that is tough enough not to tear en route.

If you examine all of your packaging with these factors in mind, you will be able to provide better packaging and perhaps at less cost. But the subject of packaging is very broad and exacting. There are two kinds of packaging engineers or designers. One deals with eye appeal is involved in designing cartons and packages with market appeal. The other involves survival, survival in a rather hostile atmosphere, all of the moving belts, rollers, and slides of the Postal Service and United Parcel Service plus the overnight carriers. It is this survival with which you should be very concerned. If you first consider the inner cushioning or packing, then the container, and how to seal it well and label it properly, your packages will survive *all* of the transportation systems.

United Parcel goes one step further to identify three other factors that affect how well your package will survive: shock, vibration, and compression.

■*Shock* occurs when a moving package strikes a stationary surface, such as the sides of a sorting chute or another package. You can prevent shock damage by adequate and appropriate cushioning.

■*Vibration,* a rapid back and forth movement, often occurs during over-the-road transportation of packages in trucks, and the solution lies in the damping effect of cushioning material. The key is to prevent the contents from shaking inside the package, and to prevent or reduce the transmission of vibration from a moving vehicle to your product.

■*Compression* occurs when other packages are stacked on top of your package, and the carton fails to withstand the weight of the other packages. UPS recommends a carton with a minimum 200-pound burst test rating (for up to 40 pounds), a rating you can check by looking at the round manufacturer's certificate printed on the bottom of the carton. Heavier articles must be packed in 275-pound rated cartons.

UPS also suggests that when selecting new packaging material it is a good practice to have a sample pack tested before ordering production quantities. United Parcel Service maintains fully equipped package testing laboratories that can evaluate packages according to National Safe Transit Association standards, which simulate actual road conditions of a 1,000 mile journey. They offer a free evaluation through their customer service offices (which are listed in the *white* pages).

Both the USPS and UPS operate re-wrap sections in their major facilities to repair poorly prepared packages. Obviously, every effort is made to match wrappers and contents, so while you hope to prevent *your* merchandise from falling into the hands of the re-wrap sections, it is still a good idea to enclose some sort of label for identification of your products in the unlikely event they do burst out of their packages.

In addition to other mailroom records, you will find it a good practice to keep a record of your damage rates so that you will be able to identify any really serious problem with your packing or packages.

Packing and Cushioning Methods

The following is only a brief overview of the different types of cushioning material, but it may serve to guide you in the right direction in your quest for adequate protection at the least cost. As you work your way through the packing maze you should consider four packing elements. First, the inner cushioning or packing (with identification of some sort); second, the container; then the sealing methods; and, last, the outside label.

Several manufacturers provide plastic foam that may be "foamed" directly around a product to completely surround any very delicate or expensive instrument. It completely immobilizes the item and provides complete protection during shipment.

Other types of form fitting plastic are available from manufacturers who will take your product and design a mold to exactly fit it. This is a common everyday product that you often see on such items such as cameras, radios, or other electronic devices. It would be the type of packing to choose when you have a great many identical products to pack as they come off of a manufacturing line.

One of the most common packing and cushioning products is the familiar foam polystyrene pellet, commonly referred to as "peanuts." These are light weight; vermin proof, and relatively inexpensive. They surround a product well as they can be "poured" much like a granular product. They surround, suspend, and cushion the product very well, and for interoffice use are even reusable. You can purchase as little as a bag the size of a large trash container or keep 80 or 90 cubic feet of the peanuts in plastic storage hoppers mounted above your packing tables and fill containers as needed with convenient spouts.

Rolls and sheets of polyethylene foam or polyethylene bubbles are excellent choices when you wish to wrap a product and simply place it into a shipping carton. Various thicknesses of foam and various sizes of bubbles allow you to select the exact type best suited to your product. One large Texas catalog shipper utilizes double thicknesses of foam sealed on three sides to form a protective envelope for delicate china. Bubble wrap is also available with a layer of nylon between two layers of polyethylene for greater resistance to air leaking from the bubbles and thus losing some of its protection and cushioning. Again, these products are available in small dispenser boxes, or the manufacturers can provide relatively large rolls for constant use.

There are paper packaging materials consisting of heavy kraft papers and an inner cushion of cellulose wadding. These too are available in sheets or in more convenient rolls for larger and more convenient usage.

And still another method to protect your products in-transit is to shrink wrap them directly onto heavy corrugated boards. This makes the product completely immobile. This process is often used when there are several parts or pieces which need to be held in place and prevented from banging into each other.

A more recent need has been brought about by the proliferation of many types of sensitive electronic devices, especially computer boards. These not only must be protected very well, but the packing, which is most often polyethylene bubble wrap, must be free of static electricity. Several manufacturers can provide you with this added protection for electronic devices.

Fiberboard Cartons

There is a real science to the corrugated and solid fiberboard used for shipping cartons. To make such boxes, several sheets are glued together to form solid fiberboard with facings or outer walls of jute or kraft paper and a layer of similar material or chipboard in the center. Corrugated fiberboard has walls of a varying number of layers with flutes of corrugating between each wall. In addition, there are various interior coatings available and many other special characteristics. The industry has grown tremendously as fiberboard has been used to ship items that were previously shipped in wooden boxes. You need only to peek inside a UPS truck or check out the pile of empty boxes outside a grocery store to see that this is true.

The design and construction of such cartons involve professional package engineering and it would be quite presumptuous for an amateur to offer advice in that area. But there are well over a hundred major fibreboard carton manufacturers, so you shouldn't have a problem finding someone who is knowledgeable to help you.

If you only need a few hundred cartons from time to time, and you are located in or near one of the major metropolitan areas of the country, you may be able to find a box store. That's right, a retailer that deals only in boxes and perhaps bubble wrap and plastic "peanuts." Some of these retailers stock as many as thirty different size boxes, and you can purchase ten or a hundred. Most are listed in the *Yellow Pages*.

You may also find perhaps ten sizes of fiberboard boxes available in the small establishments, known in the east as Mail Boxes, Etc., which feature UPS shipping for individuals, rental mail boxes, copy machines, and Western Union money orders.

Either of those choices would be preferable to the practice of cutting up your old incoming cartons and using use them to fashion a box to contain something totally different from what the original carton was intended to hold. A rush trip to one of those shops may be better than the wasted time cutting up old cartons, and it will cost less than the potential expensive damage or loss resulting from a poorly fitting box.

Checks on several sets of metropolitan area *Yellow Pages* reveal from 20 to 30 listings for "*Boxes, Corrugated*," so you should have no problem finding someone interested in your packaging problems. But, if you live in a smaller city, a visit to your library will surely solve your problems. In the reference area, look for the *Thomas Register of American Manufacturers, Product and Services Section*, the big bright green set of a dozen volumes, each four inches thick. Under the same heading, "*Boxes, Corrugated*," there are over 500 companies that provide shipping boxes.

While you are there, you might also look at "*Packaging Materials*"; there are 16 pages of manufacturers and suppliers listed!

Carton Sealing Cautions

You can use all the substantial packing in the industry and the strongest carton, but if it doesn't stay sealed while in-transit to its destination all of your efforts will be wasted. If you walk into any mailroom that receives a dozen parcels a day, you will quickly see at least one box with its sealing tape beginning to curl up slightly. Walk over to the box, grab the tape, and 90 percent of it will come right off of the box. All of the glue will be nice and shiny, never moistened at all when it was shipped. It will make you wonder how it survived the trip.

The glue on reinforced tape is quite thick. It takes a relatively large amount of water to thoroughly wet the glue, and if it isn't wet it simply will not stick properly.

That is one problem. The other is string or twine. Admittedly, this usually has come from an individual rather than a business, but there are a few offenders in smaller offices. The average parcel going from one major city to another will probably pass over two dozen belts and rollers, all anxious to snag a parcel tied with string. You should never use string on *any* parcel moving through the Postal Service, and UPS will not even accept a parcel tied with string or twine.

Hot Melt Adhesives

If you visit a plant where shipping cartons are being sealed, one after another, all day long, you are likely to see large expensive equipment applying a melted adhesive to the carton flaps. Packing authorities generally agree that hot melt adhesives are usually a preferred method for an assembly line type of carton sealing. But that is hardly a solution to sealing 10 or 12 cartons a day.

But now 3M can provide the same quality of seal for a low initial equipment investment and minimal maintenance. Their various models of the *3M Polygun* use a wide variety of adhesive cartridges to economically speed the sealing of cartons. The adhesive protects against loss due to pilferage since, depending on the sealing technique, the carton must be literally destroyed before it can be opened.

If you store several sizes of flat cartons which you construct as needed, the *Jet-melt System* may be an ideal way to speed up the process.

This 3M system is sold through distributors and can be located in the *Yellow Pages* under *Shipping Room Supplies*. If you are unable to locate a local source, write to 3M Adhesives, Coatings and Sealers Division, Building 220-7E-01, 3M Center, St. Paul, MN 55144-1000.

Gummed Sealing Tape

United Parcel Service and other authorities all state that you should not use ordinary gummed paper tape to seal parcels. Heavier gummed paper of 60- and 90-pound stock is available in various widths from 1½ inches up to 4 inches. This tape is stronger and, when properly moistened and applied, gives far more protection against handling en route.

Experienced shippers also emphasize that in the long run, it is better to use *reinforced* paper tape, even though it is more expensive, for it gives a better, stronger seal at less cost per package. Reinforced tape consists of fibers that are laminated between two layers of heavy paper and that may be imbedded into either a clear resin or an asphalt base. Three different patterns are generally available, each varying in strength and cost.

Reinforced paper tape requires some special attention to be sure of a positive seal, but it has the advantage of being available with all kinds of printing and color coding. For example, a branch office may receive packages from a wide variety of departments at the home office, but when a parcel is received with dark green tape on it, everyone knows it contains stationery supplies. Reinforced tape is generally available in 2-, 2½-, and 3-inch widths and approximately 375-foot rolls.

Gummed paper tape dispensers are a vital part of parcel sealing for two reasons. They are "programmable" in that you may push a button or pull a lever and get the exact length required to seal a specific carton. Therefore they reduce tape consumption by dispensing the correct length, no more, no less. The other distinct advantage is that some models keep the water warm by a heating element built into the water tank area. This heated water provides greater depth penetration of water into the glue. The heat makes the tape more flexible and easier to form to the box, and this is particularly true of reinforced tape. The heated water also allows the tape to stick more quickly with less pressure and thus provide a better seal. Of course, the sealing brushes are the key to the quality of the sealing you may expect, for when they accumulate glue and need washing, they simply won't do a good job.

For sales literature showing five different models of Better Packages' gummed tape dispensers, contact International Mailing Systems, Inc., 19 Forest Parkway, Shelton, CT 06484-0903, or telephone 203-926-1087.

Pressure-Sensitive Tape

While ordinary masking tape should not be used in the mailroom because it simply cannot withstand handling by either the USPS or UPS, the use of stronger pressure-sensitive tape has grown tremendously in the past 10 or 12 years. Shippers now use plastic and fiberglass filament reinforced pressure-sensitive tape for both sealing and reinforcing cartons because it is economical, easy to use, strong, and dependable.

The packing industry uses L clips and C clips to close cartons. The L clip is a relatively short strip of tape placed across a corner with equal lengths adhering to each surface. In the case of C clips, the tape simply starts on one side about 3 inches from a corner, runs across the entire length of an adjoining face, and completes the closure with a short length on the following side, hence the C.

Several manufacturers supply pressure-sensitive polyvinyl chloride tape, which is super strong, unaffected by moisture or temperature changes, and available in 2 inch wide rolls. A hand applicator for such tape is available at most stationery stores for about $10.

Parcel Label Tips

The principles of proper addressing discussed in *Chapter 5* are perhaps more important for parcel labels than for letters. After you have carefully cushioned your product, selected the proper carton, and sealed it well, it would be unfortunate to have it lost en route because of a poorly designed, inadequate, hard-to-read label that will smear at the first hint of moisture.

A poorly designed label is one that concentrates too much on who the parcel is *from*. What you really want to do is emphasize the *recipient* of the parcel. You want to stress where the parcel is *going*, not where it came from. Remember, the easier the address is to read, the more accurately it can be processed by any system whether it be UPS, RPS, or the Postal Service.

An equally important aspect of the label is the size of the type used for the address. Today a great many labels are produced as a by-product of some type of computerized order/entry system which has the capacity to produce larger-than-pica address labels. The larger type on a parcel label can be very beneficial for prompt and accurate processing on its way to its destination. Many organizations take advantage of this fact by providing pre-printed labels with half-inch letters for mail and parcels destined to its branches. Similar cards can be printed if you intend to use the reusable nylon bags for branch office mail.

If you ship to the same addresses over and over again, and your parcel labels are computer generated, they should include the zone number in the upper right corner of the address. Special methods of forwarding and the identification of specific carriers can also be coded into the upper right corner of the address. Such information will increase the postage rating consistency and accuracy in your mailroom.

Label Protection

Your well-cushioned, securely sealed carton may have a clean address label when it leaves your mailroom, but by the time the package slides across a truck floor or a sorting slide that label might not be so easy to read. You can prevent such problems by applying 3M's *Scotch Brand Labelgard*, a tough, abrasion-resistant, pressure-sensitive tape, available in 4-inch wide rolls. It meets USPS requirements for label protection because it accepts most inks from pens, markers, and soft pencils for all kinds of notations. The matte-finished surface makes labels easier to read and may reduce delivery errors. 3M can also provide a heavy-duty tape which offers even greater adhesion and resistance to abrasion plus a bright clear yellow protection tape for maximum identification on corrugated boxes.

3M offers a label protection tape dispenser which simplifies the application of its *Labelgard*. You simply place your label face down on the tape, pull out and tear off the tape, and apply the tape (with the label already in place) to your package.

In addition to the rolls of label protection tape, 3M provides both grades of *Labelgard* in convenient *pads*. The pads are pre-cut to 4 x 6 inches, are portable, and require no dispenser. One edge of the tape has a ¾ inch protective peel-off strip so that the individual pieces of tape are easy to handle and apply.

For affixing packing lists or other documents to any package, 3M provides *Scotch Pouch Tape Pads*. Available in either 5 x 6 or 6 x 10 inch size, the pouches have adhesive only on a ½-inch strip around the edge, which allows your documents to be inserted. A peel-off strip allows adhering the pouch securely on all four sides.

All of the 3M products are usually available from distributors listed under *Shipping Room Supplies* in your *Yellow Pages*, or you may write to the 3M Packaging Systems Division, Building 220-8W-01, 3M Center, St. Paul, MN 55144-1000.

Environmental Concerns

Whether opening packages at home or in the office, polystyrene "peanuts" and other plastic nuggets can scatter everywhere in seconds. No one seems to like them, in spite of the outstanding protection they offer in packing fragile items, and they are even non-biodegradable.

Business Week reports that a Chicago firm, American Excelsior Company, is attacking the problem of disposal with *Eco-Foam*. A cylindrical pellet which looks like polystyrene, but consisting of 95 percent cornstarch, *Eco-Foam* disintegrates before your eyes when added to water. With polystyrene peanuts priced at about 65¢ per cubic foot, *Eco-Foam* is considerably more expensive at $1.50 per cubic foot. Nevertheless, sales are said to be soaring, and these new pellets may appeal to some dedicated environmentalists regardless of the price.

Other shippers have reported good results with another biodegradable product for packaging, pop corn! But cost comparisons are not available, and its use may be detrimental to rodent and insect control in the basements of older buildings.

There have been reports of the availability of cushioning pads of crumpled-paper which are made of paper which may be recycled and offer substantial protection while meeting environmental concerns, but such products do not seem to be well advertised.

Poly Pak America, Inc., manufactures *Rigur* plastic envelopes and operates a Poly Pak Recycling Center for its used envelopes, and Astro-Valcour, Inc., manufacturers *Astro-Green* air bubble cushioning made from recycled material. Both are listed in the preceding *Sources of Supply* and both have 800 numbers. You might also contact the organizations listed in the next section for further information about biodegradable packaging material.

Sources of Information on Packaging

If your parcel problems appear greater than the information presented here, you should be quick to seek more professional assistance for the packaging industry is truly a science, and one that often changes.

Perhaps your faithful *Yellow Pages* can provide a source for more information on packaging and for packaging supplies. If you look under *Packaging Machinery* you will usually find "shrink-wrap, hot melt sealing, tying machines, and strapping machines." Under *Packaging Materials* you are likely to see listed "bubble wrap, custom-made and corrugated boxes, carton sealers, tapes, peanuts, jiffy bags, and cushioning materials" in the various display ads. The *Tapes, Industrial* pages indicate sources for "pressure sensitive and gummed tapes, strapping tapes, 3-M tapes, and polypropylene packing tape." And, under the heading *Shipping Room Supplies* you can find a variety of material and most 3M supplies. You may not be able to find what you are seeking in your particular area, so remember that most public libraries have out-of-town *Yellow Pages* in the reference section.

If all else fails, the following organizations may provide you with additional resources:

Fibre Box Association
Ten Gould Center, #412
Rolling Meadows, IL 60008-4040

Gummed Industries Association
Five Darrow Court
Greenlawn, NY 11740-2931

Parcel Shippers Association
1211 Connecticut Avenue, NW, Suite 406
Washington, DC 20036-2701

Packaging Institute International
20 Summer Street
Stamford, CT 06901-2304

Pressure-Sensitive Tape Council
The Breeden Company
104 Wilmot Road
Deerfield, IL 60015-5107

Technical Association of the
Pulp and Paper Industry
P.O. Box 105113
Atlanta, GA 30348-5113

CHAPTER 7

SIMPLIFIED MAIL CLASSIFICATION

Mail classification is a very important part of efficient mail management and forms the very foundation of *reducing costs* and *eliminating waste.* A great deal of time can be lost in a mail center while four or five clerks discuss all of the possibilities of classifying a single piece of mail. And because the class of mail determines the service it will receive, the wrong decision can cause many headaches. Worse still, the wrong decision when preparing a large mailing can waste many printing dollars and even result in the mailing being refused. *Therefore*, if one of your primary objectives is *to obtain the best mail service at the least cost*, you and your staff must become familiar with at least the basics of mail classification.

Mail classification is not as complicated as it may seem at first glance. To a great extent it breaks down to either a very simple classification, such as a typewritten letter or a statement, or some piece of mail that completely defies classification and must be submitted to the Postal Service for 100 percent accuracy. A great majority of classification questions come up when evaluating whether or not a publication qualifies as second-class mail. However, that is not something which should concern most mail center employees.

There is an established path for mailers to follow in matters concerning classification. Requests for a classification ruling should be submitted in writing to your local postal official, usually the postmaster. If you disagree with a classification decision made by your postmaster, you may appeal the decision in writing to the postmaster within 30 days.

The postmaster will refer the appeal to the *Rates and Classification Center* assigned to your post office, and you may again appeal that ruling within 15 days to the Director of the Office of Classification and Rates Administration at Headquarters in Washington. (While the Rates and Classification Centers were established primarily to aid postmasters, their addresses are listed in both the *Domestic Mail Manual* (*DMM*) and the *National Five-Digit ZIP Code Directory.*)

But it is desirable and helpful that your staff have a working knowledge of the classification of mail. It is an orderly and progressive grouping of mail that is more or less a process of elimination. You simply need to pass that attitude on to your clerks and take some of the mystery out of it for them. When listed one after the other, each class of mail becomes quite logical, especially when you remember that the entire classification structure tends to favor the dissemination of information to the public in the form of newspapers, plays, books, printed or recorded music, and other educational materials.

To provide you with an overall picture, here is a simplified list of each class of mail:

■**First-Class Mail**: Postal and postcards, handwritten material, typewritten material, bills, statements, invoices, and computer-printed material having the character of actual and personal correspondence. Also any matter sealed against inspection weighing up to 11 ounces. (First-Class Mail becomes *Priority Mail* when it weighs over 11 ounces and anything mailable, weighing not more than 70 pounds, may be sent as Priority Mail.)

■**Second-Class Mail**:   Newspapers, magazines, or other periodicals.

■**Third-Class Mail**: Anything not *required* to be mailed as First-Class Mail; circulars, printed matter, or merchandise weighing less than 16 ounces.

■**Fourth-Class Mail**: *Everything* that is not included in First-, second-, or third-class mail.

There are, of course, some minor exceptions or additions to these classifications, such as various weight books, but those are the basic ground rules. When examined in that manner, they help to simplify the whole process of mail classification. Those interested in becoming more proficient should refer to the *Domestic Mail Manual*.

Understanding Zone Charts

In any discussion of the classes of mail, as well as small package ground services, you need to understand *zones*. When parcel post was inaugurated in 1913 it soon became obvious that the farther the distance the greater the cost to transport packages. So, in spite of the fact that letters had been carried anywhere in the U.S. for the same fee since 1863, the former Post Office Department soon developed a system of zones. The zones were based on the number of miles from the point of origin to the destination. Then, as the five-digit ZIP Code and sectional center plan was established in 1963, it became easier to more accurately define each of the eight zones in the continental U.S. Now the Postal Service maintains a series of charts for each mail processing center, whether it is a sectional center facility (SCF), a management sectional center (MSC), or a division office. The three-digit ZIP Codes assigned to each one of those processing facilities form the basis for each zone chart, and each zone chart lists a range of numbers for every other three-digit ZIP Code in the 50 states.

One of the blessings of electronic scales is that you can key in the destination ZIP Code, and the scales will automatically determine the correct zone. If you do not have the good fortune to have an electronic scale you will need a printed zone chart to manually determine the correct zone. They are available at no charge from your post office.

Manufacturers of scales use computer tapes which the Postal Service sells for $35 (in 1991) covering the entire data base of zone charts. In addition, if you need zone charts for a large number of originating points and do not want to rely on your own people to obtain current charts, you may order a printed set of the entire data base for $15 (in 1991). These may be ordered from the Zone Chart Data Order Center, U.S. Postal Service, 1250 Broadway, New York, NY 10095-9599. For more information, telephone 212-613-8576.

If you do not have an electronic scale, do not underestimate the importance of up-to-date zone charts. You may not use parcel post but *Priority Mail* weighing over 5 pounds must be zone rated as well.

Nonmailable Matter and Hazardous Material

You and your staff should also realize that there are many things that you *cannot mail at all*, and still others that can only be mailed when certain precautions are taken. *Section 123* of the *DMM* describes *written, printed, and graphic matter* that is nonmailable, and *Section 124* identifies nonmailable *articles and substances*, along with special mailing rules. The latter section covers articles which may be generally harmful or dangerous, such as flammable material, poisons, or perishable matter. Both sections specifically state that it is the *mailer's* responsibility to know what is nonmailable, therefore questionable items should be cleared with your local postal people prior to mailing.

Particular attention should be paid to any type of hazardous material, for the *DMM* is quite specific about such items. It has over 12 pages of text devoted to the various types of hazardous material. The USPS's *Publication 52* can provide additional information on the acceptance of hazardous material. (Also see *Chapters 10 and 11* for additional information on hazardous material).

Customized Classification

Depending on the nature of your organization and what it mails, you should devise some type of process to check on what is being put into the mail. There are several ways to accomplish this. Depending on the numbers involved, you may attempt to alert the secretarial staff to the basics of hazardous material and have them call you or a member of your staff for questionable items. If your organization mails a wide variety of products, not just papers of one kind or another, you may develop a customized list of the various items and how they should be shipped. In addition, if your outgoing mail warrants it, you may find it helpful to talk with department heads and other managers in your organization to alert them to the potential problems of hazardous material in the mails.

NOTE: The general mail classification discussed in this book was accurate at the time it was published but be sure to refer to a current copy of the *DMM*, or consult with your local post office, if you have a more complicated classification task.

ORGANIZATION OF THE DOMESTIC MAIL MANUAL

In the past decade the Postal Service has made monumental strides toward becoming one of the most customer-oriented Federal, or actually quasi-Federal, agencies in Washington. It has put into practice more and more of the major mailers' input. Simpler rules make it easier to do business with the USPS yet it still protects its revenue. It works closely with all of the major business mailers in the U.S. through a committee that meets quarterly with USPS management in Washington, through *National Postal Forums*, and through the localized forums sponsored by the Postal Service known as the *Postal Customer Councils*.

Yet an even greater stride has been made in the most important publication published by the USPS. The old loose-leaf rule book, each issue of which became a filing nightmare, and which was published on an erratic schedule, is long gone. In its place is an easy to read, well-indexed *Domestic Mail Manual*. It is an inexpensive manual published through the Government Printing Office with pre-announced quarterly publication dates. Each issue is distributed *before* its effective date, and you use the previous issue until that date. For added convenience, you can even fax your subscription order, charge it to Visa or MasterCard, and the charge for a one-year subscription (in 1991) is only $19.

To make it easier for both the public and postal employees, a description of changes made since the last issue is published in the front of each issue. Also, a change bar (a heavy black vertical line in the margin) signals that the adjacent text has been revised and that a description of the change is in the summary of changes.

Subscriptions may be sent to the *Superintendent of Documents, Government Printing Office, Washington, DC 20402-9371*, or the *DMM* may be ordered over the telephone by calling 202-783-3238. Fax orders may be sent to 202-275-0019. In addition to the charge cards, they will accept checks made payable to the Superintendent of Documents, or, if you purchase other publications on a regular basis, you may keep a *GPO Deposit Account* to simplify ordering. The *DMM* is also available on magnetic tape and diskettes, which may be ordered via 202-275-3329.

The *DMM* should be considered an essential part of professional mail management in all but the very smallest mailroom. The Postal Service has worked hard to purge it of governmental gobbledygook and to write the regulations so you can understand their intent. Perhaps more important, it not only states what you cannot do, *it clearly states what you <u>can</u> do.*

Contents of the DMM

Each of the classes of mail is assigned to a *chapter* in the *DMM*, and each major topic of a chapter is identified as a *section* and has a numerical designation. While there are some variations, because of the nature of each class of mail, there is substantial uniformity throughout each of the chapters covering the classes of mail. The chart in Figure 4 may be helpful as an introduction to the DMM and as a training aid.

DOMESTIC MAIL MANUAL CONTENTS					
	SECTION NUMBERS:				
	EXPRESS MAIL	FIRST CLASS	SECOND CLASS	THIRD CLASS	FOURTH CLASS
SECTION TITLE:					
RATES & FEES	210	310	410	610	710
CLASSIFICATION	220	320	420	620	720
SERVICE OBJECTIVES	230	330	430	630	730
AUTHORIZATIONS & PERMITS	240	340	n/a	n/a	740
PHYSICAL LIMITATIONS	250	350	n/a	n/a	750
PREPARATION REQUIREMENTS	260	360	440	640	760
MAILING	270	370	450	650	770
PAYMENT OF POSTAGE	280	380	460	660	780
ANCILLARY SERVICES	290	390	470	690	790

Figure 4 Comparison of similar sections of DMM in each class of mail.

Now you can see the similarity between each chapter and the orderly manner in which each chapter is arranged. The actual titles of a few sections vary just a little from those shown in the chart. Express Mail *Section 230* shown as *Service Objectives* is actually *Service Guarantee*; Second Class *Section 440* shown as *Preparation Requirements* is actually *Getting the Publication Ready for Mailing, Presorting*; and Third Class *Section 640* also shown as *Preparation Requirements* is actually *Bulk Mail Presort Requirements*. But the meanings of those sections are approximately the same as the others in the chart, and it makes the whole arrangement of chapters and sections easier to work with and to remember. To further support the arrangement of subjects, this chapter will follow the same order of classes of mail as the *DMM* does. You should challenge your staff from time to time to find their way around the *DMM*.

When a question arises let them study the *DMM* a few times until they find the solution (even if you or others know the correct answer). Then when they really need to solve a problem they will know how to do it accurately. There has been a widespread change in attitude about the *DMM* among mail managers in the past 10 years. More and more people are finding it easier to understand than they believed possible. That has been the result of Postal Service people telling the mailers to "Try it, you'll like it!", plus the improvement in the text. So attitudes do make a difference, and it will make a difference in your mail center as well. You may as well read the book because, as one of the USPS mail managers in New York always says, "Steven Spielberg will never make a movie of this one!"

EXPRESS MAIL

The former Post Office Department originated Express Mail in 1970 to assist the Federal National Mortgage Association in providing next day service to its regional offices. It was expanded to 36 cities that October and became a full-fledged class of mail on October 9, 1977.

Today, Express Mail has strong competition from several over-night delivery carriers. But it is a highly respected service and can provide a number of beneficial features which no other carrier can provide. A testimony of its value to businesses can be shown in the USPS figures for FY-1990, 58,582,000 pieces and $630,707,000 in revenue, an increase over the previous year of 10 percent!

For additional information about Express Mail see *Chapters 11* and *12*.

FIRST-CLASS MAIL

The classification of matter that *must* be sent as First-Class Mail (FCM) has remained basically the same for over 50 years. There are few changes in this basic classification. It largely narrows down to one thing, if it sends a *message*, if it has "the character of actual and personal correspondence," then it becomes First-Class Mail.

The other prime factor is whether or not it is "sealed against postal inspection." (The quotes are from the *DMM*.) FCM *cannot* be opened by the Postal Service, it takes a Federal court order or a search warrant, so whenever you seal an envelope it becomes FCM (unless you carefully mark it third-class).

These two ingredients then form a natural classification for First-Class Mail, and the *DMM* states it simply as:

1. Matter in writing or typewriting
2. Matter closed against postal inspection
3. Bills and statements of accounts

It does go on to list some examples, such as computer-prepared material which has the character of actual and personal correspondence, either cancelled or uncancelled checks, and postcards and double postcards. In addition, a separate section states that all *Business Reply Mail* is First-Class Mail.

It is not complicated to use those simple rules to classify mail, but if you are unsure about computer sheets you wish to mail, check with your USPS account representative or your postmaster. It is possible to save considerable postage if they need not be expedited as First-Class Mail.

Size Restrictions and Markings

There are two factors that govern the size of First-Class Mail: the *dimensional standards* discussed in *Chapter 5*, and the fact that when FCM weighs more than 11 ounces it is classified as *Priority Mail* and must be zone-rated if it weighs over 5 pounds.

To reiterate the dimensional standards, all mail *must* be rectangular and measure at least 3½ inches high and 5 inches long, if it is *less* than ¼ inch thick. And FCM weighing less than *one ounce* must not exceed ¼ inch in thickness, 6 1/8 inches in height, nor 11½ inches in length or it will incur a surcharge of 10¢ (in 1991).

No special marking is *required*, but you will consistently receive better FCM service if you utilize *green diamonds* on your 9 x 12 inch kraft envelopes, known as "flats" in the Postal Service.

Getting Your Money's Worth

Your organization is not getting its money's worth unless FCM sent to customers contains at least some sort of advertising, promotional material, or public relations information. There are literally hundreds of items that can be added to envelopes for a *free* trip to your customer's home or office. In billing operations that have enough volume to use inserting machines, the inserts can be added at practically no cost. If your organization is a retailer that sends statements, there are thousands of sales folders available from manufacturers that are suitable for inserting into 6¾-inch envelopes. Many can even be imprinted with the name of your organization. *Every* organization can benefit from inserts. Mail originating from a home office might often include all kinds of notices about the employee benefits of the organization, with new notices monthly. An association can remind its members of all of the services it offers to its members and include monthly information to promote its programs. Since you may add three sheets of letter-size paper to an envelope containing a single letter and still mail it for the same rate, this is simply another way to get more value for every postage dollar.

First-Class Mail Discounts

As the Postal Service has worked toward coping with the growth of mail volume and providing some relief to business mailers on FCM rates, it has added more and more work-sharing programs. In return for more detailed preparation in the address area and for performing some of the necessary sorting that a piece of mail requires en route toward its destination, the USPS allows a number of discounts of the First-Class Mail rate.

It is not the intention of this book to provide itemized rules and regulations about participating in any of the USPS discount programs. The requirements are changed or adjusted from time to time so that any listing would be unreliable until verified and compared with current USPS requirements. Nevertheless, if you are to appreciate the rewards of participating in such programs you do need a barometer of the values as shown in Figure 5.

TYPE OF PRESORT	POSTAGE	SAVINGS	DISCOUNT
Non-presorted FCM	29¢	---	---
Non-presorted ZIP+4	27.6¢	1.4¢	4.8%
Prebarcoded*	27¢	2¢	6.9%
Presorted 3&5 Digit-Basic	24.8¢	4.2¢	14.5%
Presorted Basic & ZIP+4	24.2¢	4.8¢	16.6%
Presorted 3-Digit, Prebarcoded	23.9¢	5.1¢	17.6%
Presorted 5-digit, Prebarcoded	23.3¢	5.7¢	19.7%
Presorted Carrier Route	23¢	6¢	20.7%

* Scheduled for implementation in mid-'91.

Figure 5 Comparison of First-Class Mail Discounts

There is another barometer that may assist you in determining how far you want to go in the barcode and ZIP Code area, and in presorting. The utilities, the telephone, gas and electric companies, have consistently been the leaders in obtaining the maximum discounts on their monthly statements. If a new work-sharing program is announced, look to the utilities; if they start participating you can bet it will be worthwhile and economically profitable for your organization too.

If you have a relatively large amount of First-Class Mail and want to investigate any of those discount programs you need only call your postmaster or account representative. If you have a smaller amount of FCM, call and ask for a brochure listing the requirements and exactly what steps you must take to qualify. To aid you further, each discount program is carefully spelled out in *Chapter 3* of the *DMM*.

First-Class Service Standards
After an 18-month in-depth examination of FCM delivery service, the Postal Service announced the beginning of the revision of *overnight delivery standards* of FCM on July 28, 1990, and completed the changes in October.

The USPS stated that the *"realignment"* provided the Postal Service with an opportunity to improve postal service and to improve the *"consistency of overnight service."* The Postmaster General (PMG) testified before a Congressional committee in September that the change in New York had achieved that objective and also reduced the number of complaints about local delivery. At the same time that service was improving, the PMG said that the USPS had realized solid operational benefits by increasing the percentage of mail being handled with automation, which in turn reduced overtime.

These changes reportedly only affected about 5 percent of the FCM. If you will telephone your nearest division, MSC, or SCF, the marketing people will provide you with a schedule showing the FCM delivery standards between your 3-digit ZIP Code and other 3-digit areas.

These delivery standards are important. If you do not know how long it usually takes for FCM to reach the cities to which you frequently mail, you will be unable to make intelligent decisions about when you must send documents via overnight couriers. In addition to the data the USPS will provide, you and your supervisors should frequently read the postmarks on incoming mail to build a mental reference about the average transit time for a First-Class letter from major areas in the U.S. or, at a minimum, from any of the cities with which you do business.

PRIORITY MAIL

First-Class Mail is unique in that its name and classification changes whenever it weighs over 11 ounces. If it weighs over 11 ounces it becomes *Priority Mail*. The same kinds of material that must be sent by FCM *must* be sent by Priority Mail if it exceeds that weight. In addition, you can, of course, send anything mailable via Priority Mail, regardless of the weight, if you believe the extra speed of its delivery is worth the minimum price for packets weighing up to 2 pounds.

But it is not processed exactly like FCM. When you take that tour be sure to ask to see how Priority Mail is separated and processed differently from other mail. It actually receives preferential treatment and that is important to remember, for if you do not mark it conspicuously it may not receive the service for which you have paid. To be sure you do receive expedited service, the Postal Service will provide three sizes of pressure sensitive labels, a large (9 x 12 inch) specially marked flat rate envelope, and a *Priority Mail* carton at no charge. It is a very popular service (with 518 million pieces sent Priority Mail in FY-90) and fills a void between shipping merchandise UPS ground service and expensive overnight service.

It is also very convenient to use as there is a single rate for matter weighing over 11 ounces up to two pounds ($2.90 in 1991) regardless of its destination. Priority Mail packets weighing up to 3, 4, or 5 pounds each take a single rate to all zones, but matter weighing over 5 pounds is rated by eight zones.

Most alert mail managers will develop a general concept of the delivery time of Priority Mail arriving in their mailroom at the same time they are observing the FCM. Priority Mail usually provides two-day delivery between major markets and three-day service nationwide.

Priority Mail Drop Shipment

This service functions similarly to Express Mail drop shipment and expedites movement of any other class of mail between domestic postal facilities. With three-day service standards nationwide, Priority Mail may be quite advantageous for single-piece third-class mail in the 6- to 10-ounce range or for ordinary (last minute) Bulk Business Mail tied to any tight schedule or promotion.

The contents of Priority Mail Drop Shipment must meet the requirements for its class of mail, but the requirements are relatively simple. However, it must be presented to the bulk mail acceptance unit at your postal facility, so ask your local USPS people for assistance. The details are spelled out in the *DMM, Section 136.9.*

Weight and Size Limits

The minimum sizes for FCM apply for *all mail,* but Priority Mail may measure up to 108 inches in combined girth (total of four smallest sides) plus the length (of the longest side). This is the same as Express Mail and fourth-class parcel post.

Marking, Sealing, and Depositing Priority Mail

■*Marking*: Your tour should have convinced you that you must mark anything and everything conspicuously if you expect to get your money's worth. If you send flats be sure to place labels indicating *Priority Mail* on both sides. On sizeable parcels, anything over 8 inches square for example, place the Priority Mail labels so as to be visible from any position.

■*Sealing*: Priority Mail is simply an extension of FCM so it may be sealed and cannot be opened by the Postal Service.

■*Depositing*: The rules on depositing Priority Mail are a little peculiar. Perhaps they are to prevent the stuffing of letter drop boxes with oversize packages. Nevertheless, the *DMM* states, "Priority Mail must be deposited at a post office, branch or station, or handed to a rural route carrier." But it goes on to grant an exception for certain size pieces; "A Priority Mail piece, in a weight category for which the rates do not vary by zone, may be deposited in any street collection box, mail chute, receiving box, cooperative mailing rack or other place where mail is accepted" (*DMM Section 371 & 373.2*). Currently, this covers all Priority Mail weighing up to 5 pounds. But all Priority Mail weighing *over* 5 pounds *must* (according to the *DMM*) be mailed at a post office, station, or branch (or handed to a rural route driver). You are not likely to hear that this is often enforced if the package or envelope is within reason. But it could be a problem and could delay your mail if the limits are abused and the *DMM* restriction is suddenly enforced.

SECOND-CLASS MAIL

This is the most complex class of mail; there are 115 pages of text in the *DMM*, about 15% of the entire book, devoted to the hows, whys, and wherefores of second-class mail. But, fortunately, this class of mail can usually be ignored by the average mail center. It basically covers newspapers and magazines, which are almost always (1) printed in large printing plants, and (2) prepared for mailing by experienced employees working for the printer.

In teaching basic classification be sure to explain why most mailrooms handle so little second-class mail. The transition from First-Class to third-class seems strange, and it annoys people who are trying to learn classification in sequence.

If you are considering mailing a *publication* be sure to talk to your local Postal Service officials. If you think you may qualify as a nonprofit organization, and might qualify to send publications at special second-class non-profit rates, you will also need to discuss your needs with them. But even if you qualify it is highly likely that preparation will take place off of your premises, so you should teach mail clerks to forget about second-class mail.

THIRD-CLASS MAIL

If you go back to the basic description of third-class mail you will see that it is simply matter that is not *required* to be mailed as FCM; that is, circulars, printed matter, or merchandise weighing less than 16 ounces. Third-class breaks down to a rate for *single-piece* third-class mail and a lower but more complex rate for *bulk third-class mail*. The latter rate is applicable to all of the direct mail advertising you receive at home and at the office. It also is known by the more glamorous name of *Bulk Business Mail*.

Third-Class Versus First-Class

Third-class single-piece rates have changed considerably over the past 15 years. It was originally grouped in two-ounce segments costing about 40 percent less than FCM. However, during the rate and classification changes of the 80's it slowly evolved into a totally different structure.

Today, single-piece third-class mail is rated *the same as First-Class Mail* up to 5 ounces. The FCM rate for each ounce is 29¢, 52¢, 75¢, 98¢, and $1.21, up to but not exceeding 5 ounces. The third-class mail rate *is identical* , except that the $1.21 covers from 4 ounces up to 6 ounces. This comparison is very important. *Never* send any envelope weighing less than

5 ounces as *third-class mail*, especially 9 x 12 inch flats. Use green diamond envelopes or mark FIRST-CLASS with a *green* felt marker. Another reason for using FCM instead of single-piece third-class mail is that return postage is charged if the third-class piece is returned for any reason. In contrast, First-Class Mail is forwarded or returned at no charge. So much for the first 5 ounces.

The balance of single-piece third-class mail is rated at 12¢ per each additional 2 ounces and some weights may deserve consideration as First-Class Mail. For example, the 5th and 6th ounces of third-class mail will cost $1.21 while mail not exceeding 6 ounces of FCM is $1.44, a difference of only 23¢. If it is going across the state, the third-class piece may get there in three or four days, but it will take seven to ten days across the U.S., certainly worth an additional 23¢ to get FCM delivery in only three or four days. Such comparisons may be too time consuming for one or two envelopes but imagine the savings if you were based in Connecticut and had 22 branches in California!

Bulk Third-Class Mail

Bulk Business Mail is similar to second-class mail in that it is somewhat complicated to prepare (the presorting is extensive) and to rate. Seasoned mailers who are familiar with the rules and regulations of bulk mail say that the process is not so complicated, but it is difficult to understand without the actual mail with which to physically work.

If your organization decides to get into bulk third-class mail, you might have an outside printer prepare the initial mailing with the understanding that your own people will be taught to do it later.

There are two associations that may be helpful to you if you wish to become more involved with bulk business mail. One is the *Third Class Mail Association*, 1333 F Street, NW, Suite 710, Washington, DC 20004-1108, and the other is the *Graphic Communications Association*, 1730 North Lynn Street, Suite 604, Arlington, VA 22209-2004. In the past they have jointly sponsored working conferences on the fundamentals of third-class mail preparation.

Size Restrictions, Sealing, and Marking

■*Size Restrictions*: Single-piece third-class mail must be rectangular and measure at least 3½ inches high and 5 inches long if it is *less* than ¼ inch thick. It is also governed by the dimensional standards, so it will incur a surcharge if it weighs less than one ounce and exceeds ¼ inch in thickness, 6 1/8 inches in height or 11½ inches in length. Other than that, there are no size restrictions on single-piece third-class mail, it simply cannot weigh over 16 ounces. If it does weigh over 16 ounces it becomes fourth-class mail.

■*Sealing*: All third-class mail is subject to being opened for postal inspection, but should be sealed or secured so that it may be handled by machines.

■*Marking*: Bulk Business Mail must be marked with the class or type of bulk mail being used, as required and explained in the *DMM*. Single-piece third- class *must* be marked THIRD CLASS (*DMM Sec. 629.611*), preferably below the postage and above the address, or it will be treated as First-Class Mail and charged postage at the FCM rate (*DMM Sec. 629.613*).

FOURTH-CLASS MAIL

More commonly known simply as *parcel post*, it is certainly the easiest of all classification, all matter "not mailed or required to be mailed as First-Class Mail, weighing 16 ounces or more, and not entered as second-class mail." In other words, everything that is not First-, second-, or third-class mail! However, there are a few special classifications of fourth-class mail. They can become somewhat complicated, and you should explore that chapter in the *DMM* if you mail bound printed matter. Nor is the rating so simple with *intra* bulk mail center rates and *inter* bulk mail center rates, single piece and bulk bound printed matter, library rates, and several levels of presort and a carrier route rate.

Size Restrictions, Sealing, and Marking

■*Size Restrictions:* Fourth-class mail may weigh up to 70 pounds, and the length and girth combined may not exceed 108 inches. Two or more parcels may be mailed as a single parcel if about the same size and shape and taped together well. *Never* use string on any parcel being shipped any way!

There are about 13 items that are classified as *nonmachinable* and will therefore incur a surcharge. They include items such as extremely heavy boxes, cans of paint, a wooden or metal box, and a large roll or tube. If your organization is planning on shipping such articles via parcel post, be sure to talk with your local USPS people first.

■*Sealing*: Fourth-class mail packages may be securely sealed to withstand the rigors of the transportation system, but they are always subject to being opened for postal inspection.

■*Marking*: No special markings are required on parcel post unless using one of the library, bulk, or presort programs, but the return address *must* be shown.

POSTAGE PAYMENT METHODS

There are a variety of methods for paying postage, and a busy mail center will often find it is using several methods on any given day. While the postage meter is the backbone of business mail, collecting about fifty percent of all revenue for the Postal Service, there are other methods that can and should be used.

For example, if you are a utility and mail out perhaps three quarters of a million statements to customers every month it doesn't make much sense to try to run that mail through a postage meter when you can use a First-Class Mail permit printed on the envelope at the same time that the return address is printed. Or, suppose your management is having an important reception for customers or other business groups and you are sending out high-quality engraved invitations. Most executives would agree that an adhesive postage stamp would add a desirable personal touch to the invitations instead of a red meter impression (which may smear!). So there are different methods for different kinds of mail, and you should be familiar with each of the various means of paying postage.

Printed Stamped Envelopes

Like the postal card, the Postal Service sells several sizes of envelopes that have the postage stamp printed or embossed right onto the envelope. Available either plain or printed with your return address, they are designed for a small medical office or perhaps a retail business which mails about a hundred monthly statements. In general they are inconvenient to order, with few type font selections or variations, inconvenient when rates change, and expensive. In 1991, a thousand #10 window envelopes cost $24 plus $8 for printing (in addition to the postage) whether you purchased a thousand or a carload. If they are messed up in typing, addressing, or inserting, they often end up in the trash (secretly!) instead of being redeemed at the post office. Worse yet, they slow down your mail because they still have to be cancelled, and you also have to lick the flaps to seal the envelopes. It is almost impossible to coordinate their use with a change in postage rates, so you end up licking stamps for several months to meet the new postage rate.

Adhesive Postage Stamps

When you take that tour of your postal facility, ask to see how metered mail bypasses all of the facing and cancelling process and you will really understand all of the benefits of metered mail. When you do, it will be difficult to understand why any but the very smallest business will use anything but a postage meter. And, sometimes the smaller the business the more convenient it is to have a meter. Postage stamps are, of course, good as cash and therefore are always susceptible to theft. They are slow to use in that last rush to get the evening mail out and do not help at all when it comes to sealing envelopes, something every type of postage meter will do.

Admittedly there may be one useful purpose for adhesive stamps in business, aside from an occasional invitation. Each time the rates change, the Postal Service issues a single adhesive postage stamp that is the same denomination as its least expensive Post Office to Addressee Express Mail shipment. If you have any field employees who regularly mail in reports, and those reports come to you via Express Mail, you may find it helpful to provide those field employees with that denomination stamp, particularly if they work out of their homes. However, an Express Mail corporate account may serve you just as well, and you may also prepay self-addressed Express Mail envelopes or packages (up to 70 pounds) with your postage meter.

Precancelled Stamps

Originally designed to eliminate the hand cancelling of bulky pieces of mail or tubes and rolls, precancelled stamps carry the imprint of the post office of origin and two bars that serve to cancel the stamp. They are often used on bulk business mail and on mail sent by nonprofit organizations. Precancelled stamps can only be obtained after making special arrangements with the postmaster and filing *Form 3620, Precancel Permit.*

Meter Stamps and Postage Meters

Perhaps some business people will agree that April 24 should be a holiday, for it was on that date in 1920 that the Post Office Department finally approved the use of a postage meter. Since then, postage meters have saved businesses literally millions of hours of licking and sticking stamps, to say nothing of the convenience of having every denomination of postage stamp right in the office.

Walter H. Wheeler, Jr., who began work as an apprentice and rose to be chairman of the board of Pitney Bowes Inc., was instrumental in getting approval of the postage meter. Mr. Wheeler had an unswerving concept that the business mailer was entitled to use a machine to apply postage as long as the device would provide absolute revenue protection. He spent many years working to obtain approval of the system as it is known today. This system basically gives the mailer all of the privileges with meter stamps that are granted to adhesive stamps. However, there were many regulations and restrictions either imposed or considered as Mr. Wheeler labored to convince Congress and the Post Office Department of the mutual advantages of metered mail. Every year, when the final figures are tabulated, over 50 percent of all postal revenue is collected by postage meters, and the Postal Service sighs with relief that it doesn't have to cancel all of that mail.

A postage meter cannot be sold outright but must be leased from one of the four manufacturers who are approved by the USPS. In this manner the Postal Service is able to exercise full control over their use. The USPS requires a mailer to apply for a license to use a meter, but there is no charge involved. A representative (of the manufacturer) then takes the mailer's check and the meter to the post office having jurisdiction over the location where the mail will be deposited, for its initial setting and sealing. The meter consists of a descending and an ascending register, and the postal clerk sets the descending register to reflect the amount of postage being purchased. The registers change each time the meter prints postage. Some meters have levers that move back and forth to select postage and others use push buttons. Obviously, a postage meter is manufactured so that its accuracy in accounting for postage and overall operation is such that it rarely, if ever, fails.

Some meters will lock as soon as the postage balance (as shown on the descending register) reaches a certain level, and you must then take the meter back to the *same* post office to purchase additional postage. Or, for a fee ($25 in 1991), the Postal Service will send a clerk to your office to reset your meter. Other meters are electronic, and postage may be added to the descending register via a telephone transfer from a trustee account maintained in a bank by the manufacturer.

A small postage meter may be self-contained; others are operated by a larger mailing machine which *can* be purchased from the meter manufacturer. The postage meter sits on top of the mailing machine and is operated, or driven, by the mailing machine. The mailing machine may have a trip release to stamp each envelope, one at a time, as it is inserted into the mailing machine. Others will automatically feed envelopes into the meter, and both types will seal the envelope while it is being stamped. The meter will print postage on gummed or pressure sensitive tape for use on bulky envelopes or packages. Some mailing machines will moisten the gummed tape as it is ejected.

Slugs and Ad Plates

If you are not familiar with a postage meter, some of the terminology will drive you up a wall. To learn more about a postage meter you only need to look at almost any business envelope you receive at home or the office. Reading toward the left, from the right edge of the envelope, you will see the amount of postage imprinted in a box. To the left of the postage is a round "postmark" showing the date and city of mailing. Instead of the city and state, the indicia may show, "Mailed from Zip Code" in the upper half of the circle and the mailer's delivery ZIP Code in the lower portion of the circle. Along the lower edge of the indicia is the meter number.

The postage meter has an opening or slot about 1/8 x 3/4 inches just left of the engraved die which prints the round portion of the meter stamp. This slot allows an engraved *slug* to be inserted with special endorsements such as PRESORTED FIRST CLASS or ZIP+4 PRESORT. The slugs are easily changed to comply with various presort endorsements.

To the left of the slot for the slug is another opening which allows a larger metal engraving to be inserted into the meter head. As the meter revolves it prints a message or an endorsement on every envelope as it prints the postage. Some meters print a message as large as 1 1/8 inches square while others have a print area measuring 2 x 7/8 inches. Since it may be flipped "on" or "off" easily, in addition to using it for advertising, it is convenient for marking envelopes or parcel tapes with classes of mail such as FIRST CLASS or PRIORITY MAIL. But since it was originally designed to advertise on envelopes it is referred to simply as an *ad plate*. It is a very versatile tool in a mailroom.

Depositing Metered Mail

Those conveniences are great, but the real advantage of a postage meter is that mail is already postmarked and dated, so it requires no cancelling. Consequently, it actually moves through the post office of origin faster than stamped mail. To minimize the cancelling of metered mail, the Postal Service *requires* that five or more pieces of metered mail *must* be bundled with all of the addresses facing the same way (see *DMM Section 144.511*). Some people think this is simply a bureaucratic gesture, but it is in fact a method of protecting one of the major benefits of metered mail. It is a very important consideration for those last few letters of the day, which are often the most important ones. Remember your tour, now you can understand why the metered mail bundles are separated from the rest of the mail picked up from collection boxes!

Metered mail *must* be deposited within the postal area served by the post office which sets the meter. However, a *limited* quantity, which is a "handful" according to the *DMM*, may be deposited in a post office other than that shown in the meter stamp as a convenience to the mailer. Metered mail may also be deposited at an *area mail processing center* which performs initial originating distribution for mail deposited at the licensing post office. Such mail must be prepared as specified by the USPS.

Under special authorization, which is carefully spelled out in the *DMM (Section 144.8)* metered mail may be deposited at a *different* postal facility from the one that issued the metered license, and this is called a *drop-shipment*. To use drop-shipment, a written application must be made to the general manager/postmaster of the division whose area includes the licensing post office. Also, there are strict requirements governing the endorsement, which must be printed in the ad plate area. The Postal Service may require special preparation of the mail beyond that which is (usually) required to qualify for the rate paid for the mail.

Refunds of Metered Postage

Should you spoil an envelope or print an incorrect amount of postage on a tape, the entire envelope or entire tape may be submitted to the Postal Service for a 90 percent refund. If the face value of the meter stamps exceeds $250, refunds will be made for the face value of the stamps, less an hourly charge for processing (or calculating) the refund. All of the requirements are listed in *Section 147.252/3* of the *DMM*, but the most important one is that they must be submitted *within a year of their date.*

It is important that your staff be aware of that requirement so you may establish a date, once a year, when all of the meter impressions may be submitted. It would be a good idea to keep a supply of *USPS Form 3533* on hand to facilitate the postage refund. Set aside a cardboard box or a special drawer for spoiled meter stamps. Then make sure all of the mail center employees understand that spoiled meter stamps are redeemable *or else they may hide their mistakes from you and throw the stamps away*. Can't you imagine the embarrassment of a clerk with perhaps three weeks of experience in the mailroom if a stack of envelopes all show $2.90 when the meter should have been set for 29¢? It is impossible to prevent a few mistakes occasionally in a busy mailroom, but with proper training that 90 percent refund will not disappear.

Permit Imprints

Under a system of annual fees and a special permit, a mailer may print the postage directly onto the envelope or card at the same time that the return address or advertising is printed. Known as a *permit imprint*, it is available for First-Class Mail, Priority Mail, third- and fourth-class mail but must consist of a minimum of 200 pieces or 50 pounds. It is particularly suitable for mailing programs involving thousands of pieces of mail. It is widely used for Bulk Business Mail and utilities use it for mailing monthly bills. But there are sortation requirements, so consult your postmaster or account representative if you are considering using permit imprints.

Special Mailing Systems

The Postal Service has developed a series of special mailing systems that tie in with computerized mailing records or other audit trails in order to establish postage costs without going through the laborious weighing and rating of each piece of mail. The programs are somewhat complicated, and are certainly beyond the purview of this book, but they may be of interest to very large mailers. In the past there have been publications covering each type of system and they are: *Manifest Mailing System (Publication 402-B), Centralized Postage Payment System (Publication 406),* and the *Optional Procedure Mailing System (Publication 407).* The details of each are also in the *DMM*.

Always Pay By Check

At the discretion of the postmaster, and with proper identification, your post office will accept checks for the payment of postage or when setting a postage meter. However, it is best to write to the postmaster on your letterhead and advise who will sign the checks, who will present the checks and the location of the post office or station where the transactions are to take place. Obviously, you should never tempt employees by using cash to purchase any kind of postage.

CHAPTER 8

UTILIZING SPECIAL SERVICES

If you eavesdrop on a group of mail managers discussing cost control you are not likely to hear much about the *special services* that the Postal Service offers. Yet you should listen to some of the questions asked of postal officials at Postal Customer Council meetings and other mail management forums. You will learn that even the professionals are not always exactly sure what they are buying when they purchase special services such as registered and certified mail, special handling, or special delivery.

To give you an idea of the potential waste, in FY-90 there were over 45 *million* pieces of registered mail at a cost of $173 million and over 191 *million* pieces of certified mail at a cost of $310 million. Over $6 *million* was spent on special delivery alone. Total revenue for all types of special services totaled *$1.3 billion!* Considering an expense of that magnitude, it will always be worth your efforts to maintain control over all kinds of special services.

If you keep a record of all of the costs of special services for a week during each quarter you will be in a better position to control these expenses. By working closely with the administration people, and the managers who most often order the use of special services, you will be able to explain how they are used unnecessarily. You may be able to significantly reduce costs without reducing essential services.

All of *Chapter 9* of the *Domestic Mail Manual* is devoted to *Special Services* and to help guide you in studying and teaching the specifics of special services the following quick reference list may prove helpful:

Registered Mail	Section 911
Certified Mail	Section 912
Insured Mail	Section 913
C O D Mail	Section 914
Special Delivery	Section 915
Special Handling	Section 916
Merchandise Return	Section 919
Certificates of Mailing	Section 931
Return Receipts	Section 932
Restricted Delivery	Section 933

REGISTERED MAIL (*DMM Sec. 911*)

Registered mail stays under lock and key, or rigid personal control, from the moment it is received at the post office of origin to the time the addressee receives it. It should be used for the protection of valuable documents, jewelry, or other items of real value. However, only First-Class Mail will be accepted as registered mail. Registered mail provides a receipt for the sender at the time of mailing, and a record of delivery is maintained in the office of delivery. It provides indemnity of up to $15 million in the event of loss or damage. In addition, registered mail may be used in conjunction with special delivery and COD services provided the mail also conforms with the requirements of those services.

As a means of further protection for valuables, registered mail may be marked "*Restricted Delivery*." All other such markings (such as "Deliver to Addressee Only") are obsolete. Incidentally, *all* endorsements and labels indicating special services must be placed above the address and to the right of the return address (*DMM Sec 121.44*). After the customer completes *Form 3811* and pays the additional fee for such service, the post office will deliver the envelope or package only to the addressee or a person specifically authorized by the addressee.

Two kinds of *return receipts* are available for registered mail. The return receipt fee (and green return card, *Form 3811)* will provide you with the name of the person to whom the piece is delivered and the date of delivery. For an additional fee the receipt will provide to whom delivered, the date delivered, and the actual delivery address. In the case of delinquent accounts, the new address may be very valuable to further collection efforts, so it is important to understand that registered mail is forwarded when the addressee has filed a *Change of Address Order* (which expires 12 months later). Furthermore, at post offices having letter carrier service, registered mail will be given directory service when the mail cannot be delivered because the address is insufficient or wrong. This service is authorized and explained in the *DMM* and may also be very helpful in collection problems. The details of restricted delivery are contained in the manual.

Since there is a record maintained in the post office of delivery, you may also request the name of the person receiving the registered mail and the date received *after* mailing. This request is made on *Form 3811-A* and requires an additional fee. However, the post office of delivery will not provide the signature of the recipient or address of delivery.

Since mailers requiring receipts must prepare the green return card (*Form 3811*), you should make sure that the mailroom keeps a supply on hand, preprinted with a large return address in bold black letters, to assure a quick return. Or be sure to explore the software and coordinated forms discussed in the section on *Return Receipts*.

The *DMM* covers the preparation for mailing of registered mail. It requires a red label (200-A or 200-B) containing a registration number printed in OCR-A readable font. The USPS will provide large users of registered mail with labels in quantities of 100 or on rolls of 500. The label may also be privately printed with the approval explained in the *DMM*. Several other points should be emphasized. Padded envelopes and spun bonded olefin, such as Tyvek, plastic envelopes, or envelopes with paper coated with a glossy finish, are not accepted as registered mail. You should not place paper or cellulose tape over the intersections of flaps of letter-size envelopes where the registered postmark impressions are made during transit through the postal system. However, packages should be completely sealed with paper tape, and large envelopes (flats) may be sealed with gummed paper tape. But all tape used on registered mail must damage the wrapper if removed, to aid in detecting any tampering. It also must readily absorb a round postmark handstamp. This means that high-gloss self-adhering tape and reinforced filament tape must *not* be used on registered mail.

CERTIFIED MAIL (*DMM Sec. 912*)

Certified mail service provides the sender with a mailing receipt and a record of delivery at the office of addressee, but *no record is kept at the office of mailing*. Only First-Class Mail will be accepted for certified mail.

It is simple to use and relatively inexpensive when compared to registered mail. *Form 3800, Receipt for Certified Mail* is available at your post office, and you should also keep a supply of these forms in your mailroom. Mailers may be authorized to use specially designed and privately printed *Form 3800* if desired. To send certified mail all you need do is complete the form, attach the certified label to the envelope right in the mail center, apply the correct postage, and dispatch certified mail along with your regular mail. If a *postmarked* sender's receipt is desired, you must take the envelope to a post office where the postal clerk will postmark the receipt. *Restricted delivery* and *return receipt* services are also available upon payment of additional fees, and the same (*Form 3811*) card is used as on registered mail.

As in the case with other types of special services, the *Firm Mailing Books, Form 3877*, are permissible whenever the mailer sends three or more pieces of certified mail. At the post office of *delivery*, records are maintained for two years, so return receipts showing to whom the mail was delivered and the date delivered are available *after* mailing with the use of Form 3811-A. (NOTE: See also Walz Postal Solutions for certified mail in *Return Receipt* section).

CERTIFIED VERSUS REGISTERED MAIL

The difference between certified and registered mail is quite substantial.

The 1991 rates reflect a cost of $4.40 minimum for up to $100 valuation for registered mail in comparison to $1 for certified mail. Mail that has no intrinsic value is often sent registered mail when it should have been sent as certified mail. By incorrectly using registered mail a medium size mail center can easily waste $1,000 annually. In addition, because of the very strict controls placed upon registered mail, as postal employees at each point of transfer must account for it, registered mail will usually take two to three days longer to reach its destination. This is another reason why registered mail should be used with caution and only when absolutely necessary to protect valuable merchandise or documents. In addition, registered mail must be taken to a post office for acceptance but certified mail may be mailed anywhere.

INSURED MAIL (*DMM Sec. 913*)

Parcel insurance offered by the Postal Service is useful for the average citizen but it is not usually recommended for business mailers. *Insured mail* provides indemnity coverage for loss, rifling, or damage, but it is available only on third- or fourth-class mail or third- or fourth-class matter mailed as First-Class Mail or Priority Mail, or Federal government mail marked "Postage and Fees Paid." If only for emergencies, your mailroom should be sure to maintain a supply of *Form 3813-P, Receipt for Insured Mail.* This will allow you to prepare your receipt and attach the insured label directly to your mail in preparation for receipt and postmarking by the postal clerk at time of mailing. A *Firm Mailing Book (Form 3877)* may also be used, if larger quantities of packages are to be insured by the post office.

If a package is insured for $50 or less, the post office will stamp the parcel with an elliptical stamp labeled "Insured," but the parcel is not numbered and is delivered as ordinary mail. For parcels valued over $50 you should complete *Receipt for Insured Mail (Form 3813-P)*, preprinted with an OCR number, and attach the pressure sensitive blue label portion to the parcel, above the address and to the right of the return address. (Large mailers may be authorized to privately print *Form 3813-P.*) Delivery requirements of parcels valued over $50 are the same as those for registered mail with a few exceptions at hotels and large apartments. *Insured mail* may be combined with *restricted delivery* and *return receipt*.

OTHER INSURANCE

In addition to Postal Service insurance, there are a number of other ways to insure parcels, and they are all less expensive than that offered by the USPS. The following are a few examples.

■Self-Insurance:　The practice of assuming the risks and replacing damaged or lost merchandise yourself. With low- to medium-priced merchandise and a good packaging program, this may be the least expensive method.

■Free Insurance: Federal Express, Roadway Package System, and United Parcel Service offer free insurance for up to $100 valuation per package. Each carrier charges additional fees for a greater declared value, but they do not publish any restrictions on the limits of insurance on valuable merchandise. The Postal Service offers free insurance on Express Mail shipments valued up to $500 (for loss, damage, or rifling of merchandise), but that is the limit of available insurance. The USPS also covers nonnegotiable documents with $50,000 reconstruction insurance. These may be important factors when evaluating exactly what service to choose.

■Open Form Insurance Policies: These are generally available from the agents of the larger insurance companies and offer loss and damage insurance in addition to protection against pilferage. Usually billed on an annual premium, this insurance is used with an entry book or shipping journal and is less expensive than the USPS.

■Special Parcel Insurance Plans: These plans may be available from several sources, but the largest is probably the Parcel Insurance Plan, 231 S. Bemiston Avenue, St. Louis, MO 63105-1914. This insurance is underwritten by the Fireman's Fund Insurance Company, and the rates are reportedly a fraction of any other parcel insurance. The Parcel Insurance Plan (PIP) claims it will cut your parcel insurance costs by one-third to one-half, while reducing the clerical costs required by most carriers for shipments valued in excess of $100. It also boasts that claims are paid in seven days. A special savings analysis form will allow PIP to customize a proposal for your specific needs.

PIP insures against damage, theft, pilferage, and loss. PIP covers most carriers: UPS, Parcel Post, RPS, Federal Express, First- and second-class mail, international mail, and most air express carriers. Coverage can be extended to include international shipments, both outgoing and incoming. You can call them toll free on 1-800-325-7390.

COLLECT-ON-DELIVERY MAIL (DMM Sec. 914)

Many firms will agree to ship merchandise to a customer and have the carrier collect the money for the merchandise. The Postal Service requires that the merchandise must have been ordered by the addressee, and the amount must not exceed the current limits for *COD mail* established by the USPS. The 1991 rate case established this limit at $600. *COD mail* has certain specific advantages as a marketing tool because customers may order with little or no cash advance. In addition, *COD mail* may be *registered* so as to provide insurance protection, in case of loss or damage, as well as for failure to receive the cost of the article from the addressee. Express Mail, First-, third- and fourth-class mail may all be sent COD, and matter sent as First-Class Mail may also be registered.

Occasional COD parcels may be sent with *Form 3816, COD Mailing and Delivery Receipt.* Mailers with large quantities of *COD mail* may use *Form 3816-AS, COD Card-Firm Mailings,* or privately printed forms and COD tags (as approved by USPS Headquarters). Detailed preparation requirements are extensive, and organizations contemplating large shipments of COD mail should discuss their plans with their postmaster or account representative.

SPECIAL DELIVERY (DMM Sec. 915)

If you want to know the true worth of *special delivery* service you need only look at the statistics. In FY-83 there were 22 *million* pieces of *special delivery* mail, and in FY-90 there were only a little over 1 million! It is highly likely that the other 21 million became disillusioned when the actual delivery service was not very special. If you are not convinced you should read the *DMM* carefully to see the limitations on *special delivery* mail.

Special delivery may be especially wasteful if mailing to medium-size or large mail centers, for rarely does the actual addressee receive the mail any faster than ordinary First-Class Mail. Some organizations may be able to maintain fast special trips for internal distribution. However, with rising operating costs more and more organizations are simply placing such mail in the next internal distribution. With *special delivery* charges for shipments up to two pounds costing $7.65 (in 1991) plus applicable postage, there are several overnight services that are less than $2 more, and you will be *guaranteed* special delivery.

With all of its drawbacks, special delivery can be combined with First-Class Mail, Priority Mail and certified, registered, COD, and insured mail.

SPECIAL HANDLING (DMM Sec. 916)

Third- and fourth-class mail can be dispatched with preferential handling and receive preferential transportation with the payment of a relatively small fee ($1.80 up to 10 pounds and $2.50 over 10 pounds in 1991). Although this *special handling* is not given at the post office of destination, it does expedite the movement of those classes of mail *between* the post office of mailing and the post office of delivery. In some instances fourth-class mail marked for *special handling* to destinations about 200 miles away has received second day delivery. But you must balance third- or fourth-class rates plus the *special handling* fees against Priority Mail (with its nationwide two-day service standards).

If you decide that *special handling* is beneficial to your organization, you should obtain a rubber stamp with letters that are at least ¾ inch high. You will want to train your staff to make sure your parcels are not only well marked but kept separate so that USPS employees can properly expedite the special handling mail and not mix it with ordinary third- or fourth-class mail.

MERCHANDISE RETURN (DMM Sec. 919)

If you are marketing an article it is always desirable to be able to tell potential customers that they may "*return it at no cost.*" This is possible through the Postal Service by authorized permit holders. This return service, with postage being paid by the permit holders, is available for merchandise previously sent as First-Class Mail, Priority Mail, or third- or fourth-class mail.

There is a *Merchandise Return Permit Application (Form 3625)* shown in the *DMM* along with the somewhat extensive requirements. Also explained are all of the special services that may be combined with *merchandise return*.

If this service seems attractive to your organization it will be essential to discuss your needs with a knowledgeable postal employee.

CERTIFICATES OF MAILING (DMM Sec. 931)

With product recall and consumer notification thriving, it may be very important for your mail center to be aware that the new rates for 1991 provide a *certificate of mailing* for only 50 cents. In addition, up to 1,000 pieces may be covered by *one certificate* for only $2.50. This receipt furnishes *only* evidence of mailing. No receipt is obtained when delivered to the addressee, and it provides no insurance against loss or damage.

Form 3817, Certificate of Mailing, is used for individual certificates of mailing, or the *Firm Mailing Book, Form 3877,* may be used. The mailer may also privately print the required forms. Bulk mailings of identical pieces of First- and third-class matter may be issued a Certificate of Bulk Mailings (*Form 3606)* provided postage is not paid by permit imprint.

Familiarity with the provisions of certificates of mailing may be very profitable in satisfying certain legal requirements involving formal mail notification at far less cost than either registered or certified mail. If in doubt this is certainly one area where you should seek the advice of an attorney.

RETURN RECEIPTS (DMM Sec. 932)

While various special services offer *return receipts* it may be helpful to review exactly when they are available. All forms of *return receipts* are requested on *Form 3811* and may only be obtained for mail that is sent COD or Express Mail, is insured for more than $50, or is registered or certified.

If you now send, or you are planning to send, either a large volume occasionally, or just a medium volume of registered or certified mail every day, you should certainly investigate the software (and coordinated forms) offered by Walz Postal Solutions, Inc.,1139 S. Mission Road, Suite C, Fallbrook, CA 92028-3226, telephone 619-728-0565. With forms approved by the Postal Service it runs on IBM-PCs or compatibles (and requires

DOS version 3.0 or above, 640 K, and a hard disk). The pin-fed forms include two copies of a form designed to fit into a #10 window envelope, a numbered Certified Mail Label (*Form 3800*), and a green return card (*Form 3811*). In addition, the return address side of the return receipt card can be preprinted with your address in big 14- or 20-point type. Walz will send samples of the pin-fed forms and a picture of the PC screen produced by the software.

RESTRICTED DELIVERY (DMM Sec. 933)

As an integral part of *Form 3811, Restricted Delivery* is generally self-explanatory. It permits a mailer to direct delivery *only* to the addressee (or the addressee's authorized agent) "*which must be an individual specified by name.*"

It is only available for COD mail, mail insured for more than $50, and for registered or certified mail but may be directed to *two or more persons*, and *all* must sign. For the mailer's protection, unknown persons must provide *proof of identification*.

SPECIAL SERVICES COST CONTROL

There are many areas in the mailroom that require constant cost control so that costs may be analyzed, and one of the more important areas is that of *special services*. You need to be sure that sufficient records are maintained *accurately* so as to determine the number of pieces of mail using each of the services over a designated period, the costs of such services, and perhaps the origin (such as service, sales, billing departments, etc.). If your organization only uses those services occasionally you may wish to simply spot check the usage on a regular basis. However you do it *you must be able to rely on a history of special services if you are to control their costs.*

CHAPTER 9

UNDERSTANDING REPLY MAIL

Reply mail seems to confuse the newcomer to the world of mail management, and a series of changes in postal regulations and reply mail fees haven't helped the more experienced mail manager either. But understanding reply mail actually is not that difficult. It is a series of decisions, a process of elimination. In many instances ordinary economics will dictate what choices you should make.

First of all, you should understand that when speaking of business reply mail decisions you do not need to include the reply cards inserted into magazines, direct mail, and product literature. Those cards are "postage paid" in order to promote replies from prospects for products and services. Literally millions are distributed yet perhaps only two or three percent of the cards will ever be returned to the addressee. No other postage arrangement is practical for that percentage of returns.

The first decision involves what you expect the recipient to do. If you are soliciting only a few facts: "What date would you prefer for an appointment?", "When would it be convenient to discuss this matter?", or "Let me have your date of birth, and I will send you our personalized policy", you need only enclose a return *card*. But if you expect an enclosure of any sort: "Please enclose your check to renew your subscription", "Please send us a copy of your policy for our records", or "We would appreciate your completing the enclosed reference form on our new employee", then you need to enclose a return *envelope*.

The next decision is whether or not *you* wish to pay the return postage. If you are selling something you certainly want to pay the postage and make it quick and easy for prospects to return the card or envelope. If you are soliciting records on employees, on legal matters, or on financial reports, for example, you should have the courtesy to include postage paid envelopes. In those cases you *always* want to provide postage.

On the other hand, there are those groups of recipients who *may* or *may not* require the postage paid on cards or envelopes. For example, suppose you are mailing to all the members of an association. If the dues are substantial, or if it is business oriented, the members are likely to expect the return cards or envelopes to have postage on them. Yet the members of an alumni group might expect to share the postage expense, as would the members of a parents and teachers association. Another example would be a charity that raises funds through the mail. Solicitations going to those who make substantial contributions should certainly include postage paid envelopes. But charities that request smaller contributions often enclose an envelope with the notation that the stamp is appreciated as a further donation.

You would *never* want to prepay postage on return envelopes going to large groups of customers who receive monthly statements such as those from credit card companies, department stores, and utilities. You would not want to prepay that postage because it has become an accepted part of doing business that individuals pay the postage on payments of all kinds. And it would probably double your postage costs.

Thus, as you see, there are times when you *always* want to pay the return postage, times when you *may or may not* pay the return postage, and times when you *never* pay the return postage. Each mail manager must make those decisions based on management's expectations and organizational policy.

TYPES OF REPLY MAIL

The decision to pay or not to pay the return postage is coupled with the decision *how* to pay the postage. There are several types of reply mail.

■*Courtesy Reply Mail* is recommended if you do not wish to pay the return postage but still want to enclose an envelope to assure a quick reply or remittance. This envelope is printed with your return address and includes the ZIP+4 Code and a printed bar code on the bottom 5/8 inch of your envelope. In the upper right corner it carries the recommended notation, "*The Post Office will not deliver mail without postage*", and the recipient is expected to place postage on the envelope before mailing.

■*Metered Reply Mail* is recommended whenever you wish to prepay postage and you have every reason to believe that a large percentage of the cards or envelopes will be returned. You will need to print the required notation above the address (shown in Figure 6) but there are no fees and no extra charges. Simply pre-stamp your cards or envelopes on your mailing machine.

■*Business Reply Mail* is recommended whenever you wish to prepay postage but are confident that only a small percentage of the amount distributed will ever be returned. An annual permit is required from the post office, and the printing on the return card or envelope is dictated by the *Domestic Mail Manual*. That printing will include special marks to speed up processing of business reply mail.

FACING IDENTIFICATION MARKS

There is considerable jargon in mail management and much of it has been adopted from internal mail processing terms used by the USPS. One of those terms is *facing*, which is the process of arranging mail so that all of the addresses *face* in the same direction. That is, with all of the stamps in the upper right corner as you look at the mail and all of the addresses readable. The facing of mail is a very time consuming operation and it was automated as early as 1958. Another term is *raw mail*, which is mail collected from street collection boxes, office lobby boxes, the collection boxes in front of post office stations and branches, and mail dropped in slots in those post offices.

As you may imagine, raw mail arrives in huge quantities contained in large canvas hampers. It is a great mixture, some metered mail bundles, some loose metered mail, a considerable amount of business reply mail and a big percentage of stamped mail.

This mail is dumped onto moving belts where mail handlers try to separate the larger or thicker pieces and First-Class *"flats"* (kraft and white envelopes usually measuring 9 x 12 inches). Then the raw mail continues on moving belts until it is finally stacked up on its edge ready to be *faced*.

At this point (*you really have to go to see it!*) the envelopes can be in one of *four* positions as you look at the stack. The back of the envelope may be toward you with the stamp in the lower position, or the stamp may be in the upper position. The envelope may be facing you with the stamp in the lower position, or the stamp may be in the upper right position. This last position is the way that all of the other envelopes must be shuffled.

Now you should begin to appreciate the problem of facing mail. But the USPS began to use phosphorescent ink in the manufacture of stamps and required the postage meter manufacturers to add a similar ingredient to all postage meter ink. (Such fluorescent ink is referred to as *hot* ink and is a USPS regulation for all mailing machines.) All of those envelopes (millions of pieces every night!) are fed into the *facer-canceller* machine. The machine actually *"sees"* the postage stamps and meter stamp impressions made with hot ink, cancels the stamps, and then sorts the mail with stamps on the front into a separate bin. The mail with stamps facing toward the back are fed into a series of moving belts that flip the mail over so that the machine can "see" the postage stamps and meter stamps, cancel the stamps, and then sort it into another bin.

Right here you should note that the USPS *requires* that five or more pieces of metered mail be bundled so that your mail will miss this entire operation. You should never allow your people to drop loose metered mail in a collection box or lobby box.

There is yet another bin, the reject bin, and a decade ago the facer canceller was filling it up with Federal government "penalty" mail and business reply mail. The facer-canceller "looked" at that mail, saw no phosphorescent stamps or meter impressions, and decided it was unstamped mail. Then mail handlers had to face that mail by hand.

Automation concepts soon brought these problems to a halt, and the *Facing Identification Marks* or *FIM* was born in 1979. The FIM marks do not need any sort of special ink for the facer-canceller to "see" them. The optical systems on the facer-cancellers are fine tuned to identify postage and meter stamps while "reading" several sets of bars in the same general area.

FIM marks are a series of vertical bars printed in the upper right corner of the address side of a business reply card or envelope and within an area that is from 1 3/4 inches to 3 inches from the right edge of the envelope or card.

The FIM mark consists of nine evenly spaced bars (each measuring 5/8 of an inch long and .03125 wide). Different kinds of business reply mail may be designated by the presence or absence of the bars. At the present time there are four combinations in use.

■*FIM A* is for courtesy reply mail with a bar code printed on the bottom of the envelope. The bar code is within the bottom 5/8 inch of the envelope and is known as a *POSTNET* code for Postal Numeric Encoding Technique. The POSTNET (written in all capital letters) Code is a series of tall (1/8 inch high) and short (1/16 inch high) vertical bars that are sprayed on by the USPS optical character readers or by equipment operated by customers who participate in the pre-barcoding discount program. The complete ZIP+4 POSTNET code consists of 50 bars representing the nine digits of the ZIP+4 Code, a correction digit, and a framing bar at each end of the string for a total of 52 bars. You can look at almost any piece of incoming mail (that is not handwritten) to see what the POSTNET code looks like.

■*FIM B* is a different arrangement of bars at the top of the card or envelope. It is used on business reply mail, Federal agency penalty mail, and Congressional mail that is franked. It does *not* have a POSTNET code printed on it.

■*FIM C* is a third arrangement of bars at the top of the card or envelope. It is used on business reply mail, Federal agency penalty mail, and Congressional mail that is franked and it *does* have a POSTNET code printed on it.

■*FIM D* is a fourth arrangement of bars and is assigned to OCR readable mail that does *not* have a POSTNET code. It is usually used on courtesy reply *window* envelopes.

While only those four combinations are currently in use, the nine bars of the FIM marks have the potential of providing many more combinations whenever the need should arise to identify another segment of raw mail.

It may be appropriate here to remind you that whenever there are approximately 500 pieces of metered mail, Congressional mail, or Federal agency mail, it should *always* be sent to a post office in trays provided at no charge by the USPS. Smaller "handfuls" of such mail should always be bundled with rubber bands. Either will keep the mail completely out of the facer-cancelling operation.

COURTESY REPLY MAIL

During the 50's and 60's there were numerous surveys to determine whether the added expense of enclosing an envelope with a monthly statement was beneficial. More and more companies agreed that it did indeed help to accelerate the return of checks from customers, and today no utility, telephone company, or credit card company would think of sending out its monthly statements without an envelope. These envelopes are known as *courtesy envelopes*, and, while they are provided as a convenience to the customer, they do not include postage.

Courtesy envelopes are stamped by individuals paying their bills and dropped into street collection and lobby boxes to become a large part of the raw mail received by the USPS. If your organization only prints its return address on courtesy mail you will experience the normal delays involved in processing any mail with adhesive postage stamps on it. But if you work closely with the Postal Service you can perhaps shave a whole day off of the time it takes to receive your customers' payments.

If you simply add the FIM marks and a POSTNET code to your courtesy envelopes, with free negatives or positives supplied by the USPS, your customers' payments will be received and deposited in your bank earlier. You can go one step further to improve your cash flow and participate in the USPS *Accelerated Reply Mail* (ARM) program, which is described at the end of this chapter.

METERED REPLY MAIL

Once the decision has been made to pay the postage on return cards or envelopes, you must decide whether you want to utilize business reply mail or metered reply mail. A little further along in this text you will learn how to compare the costs of the two types of reply mail, but basically you will want to use metered reply mail *whenever a large (75 to 100) percentage of replies is expected*. Meter stamps may be used to prepay reply postage on

(a) Express Mail; (b) Priority Mail when the rate is the same for all zones; (c) First-Class postcards, letters, and flats up to a maximum of 11 ounces; (d) single-piece special fourth-class; and (e) library rate mail. However, you should review the *DMM (Sec. 144.112a/f)* for full details. There are no fees; you simply run the envelopes through your mailing machine.

However, there are two requirements. You must "turn off" the date and print the meter stamp *without* any date. The date will be established when the card or envelope passes through the facer-canceller machine. And you must *print* "No postage stamp necessary, postage has been paid by" directly above your address as shown in Figure 6.

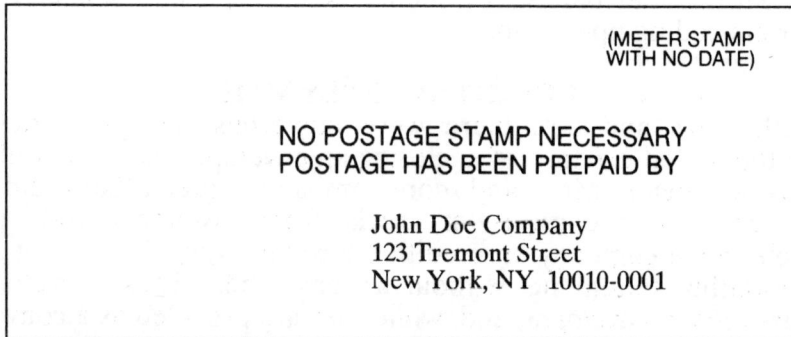

```
                                          (METER STAMP
                                          WITH NO DATE)


              NO POSTAGE STAMP NECESSARY
              POSTAGE HAS BEEN PREPAID BY

                  John Doe Company
                  123 Tremont Street
                  New York, NY  10010-0001
```

Figure 6 Required format for metered reply mail.

The *DMM (Sec 144.112d)* states that "any photographic, mechanical, or electronic process, or any combination of such processes, *other than handwriting, typewriting, or hand-stamping*, may be used to prepare the address side of the reply mail prepaid by meter stamps." This is a security measure which prevents indiscriminate use of your postage meter.

A #9 commercial envelope is the most convenient and useful envelope to provide to the administrative people for it fits inside a #10 envelope, yet will accept several full-size sheets of paper.

BUSINESS REPLY CARDS AND ENVELOPES

Business reply cards and envelopes do not cost you anything *until they are returned.* That is the basic reason for using business reply mail. Whenever you wish to make a wide distribution of cards or envelopes but know very well that only a very small percentage of them will ever be returned, you should use business reply mail.

The format for business reply mail is set forth in the *Domestic Mail Manual (Sec. 917),* and it prescribes the exact location for certain markings and legends that must be printed. Unlike courtesy or metered reply, it *must* have the legend, "NO POSTAGE NECESSARY IF MAILED IN THE UNITED STATES," in a box in the upper right hand corner, large relatively thick bars printed below that notation, and a large rectangular box in the middle of the card or envelope with "BUSINESS REPLY MAIL" printed inside the box. The USPS will provide you with the FIM marks and the POSTNET negatives (or positives) at no charge, and every printer is familiar with the format. However, *before* your printer does the final printing it is suggested that you always have a responsible person at the Postal Service approve the artwork and layout.

The POSTNET code (along with the correct ZIP+4 and FIM C) will qualify you for the *Business Reply Mail Accounting System* which counts your business reply mail and computes the charges, all at a reduced rate.

UNDERSTANDING BUSINESS REPLY MAIL RATES

Business reply mail (BRM) rates may sound slightly confusing at first but not when you understand the whole range of rates. You should understand that business reply mail is like a collect-on-delivery charge. The Postal Service delivers the mail and *then* collects the postage, and that, of course, takes extra accounting which increases the cost. So there are several fees and several levels of participation. If you make an advance deposit to cover your incoming postage and fees, the USPS offers one rate. But if you wish the carrier to collect the fees, or you wish to pay them as you pick up the mail at a post office box, it is considerably higher.

Here are the current (1991) rates, but remember, as explained in previous chapters, the *rate* isn't what is important, *it's what is being compared.*

1. The *annual* BRM permit is $75, *with* or *without* an advance deposit
2. *Without* an advance deposit: 40 cents per piece
3. *With* an advance deposit but *without* a bar code: 9 cents per piece
4. *With* an advance deposit and *with* a bar code: 2 cents per piece

Note: An advance deposit also requires an annual accounting fee of $185.

It doesn't take a CPA to figure out that if you are going to the trouble of printing business reply cards or envelopes at all, you may as well add the bar codes if you can save seven cents on every piece you receive!

Incidentally, the two cent rate is a classic example of participating in a program at one beneficial rate and then having the benefits increase. The original charge for bar coded business reply mail was five cents each, but it was reduced to only two cents when the 1991 rates took effect. This reduction in costs increased the savings (over the previous rate) by 60 percent and it illustrates how the *percentage* of savings in a USPS program often increases with the next rate case.

METERED REPLY VERSUS BUSINESS REPLY

There are hundreds of dollars to be saved when sending out cards and envelopes as either metered reply or business reply mail. Since there are no fees involved in using metered reply mail you must take into consideration the annual fees and extra (two or nine cents) charge per piece when comparing metered reply with business reply mail. If you want to save postage on your returns you must again go through a decision process, "Exactly what percentage of returns do I expect on this mailing?"

For example, if you have 2,000 field sales representatives and send out a mandatory questionnaire or report for them to complete, you can expect about 98 percent of them will return the report. (Some may forget, or lose their envelopes!) Even if your fees have been attributed to another mailing and even with a bar code on the envelopes, you will waste about $40.00 if you use business reply mail. The same thing will happen if you use business reply mail to collect a proxy from stockholders, for you will probably receive a 95 to 98 percent return. So how do you know when to use metered reply mail? The magic figure is around 76 percent (actually 76.78 percent). Here's an example of a 5,000 piece mailing:

$$76.78\% \text{ of } 5,000 \text{ pieces is } 3,839 \text{ pieces}$$
$$3,839 \text{ pieces x } 29 \text{ cent postage \& 2 cent fee} = \$1,190.09$$
$$\text{Plus annual fees of } \$75 \text{ and } \$185 = \underline{\quad 260.00}$$
$$\text{Total for } 3,838 \text{ pieces of business reply} = \$1,450.09$$

$$\text{Total for } 5,000 \text{ pieces metered @ } 29 \text{ cents} = \$1,450.00$$

Therefore, as you can see from the above example, whenever the expected returns will exceed 76 percent of the total mailing it is more economical to use *metered reply*. However, that percentage holds true only when you use envelopes and want to charge off all of the annual fees on that particular mailing. If the fees of $260 have already been paid and attributed to a previous mailing the percentage will vary, and the percentage varies for metered reply versus business reply *cards*.

The break-even point, *the point where metered reply mail becomes more economical*, for envelopes with the fees previously paid is 93.6 percent. The break-even point for cards with all fees attributable to that mailing is 65.7 percent, and with the fees previously paid it is 90.5 percent.

Here is the way to calculate the break-even percentage.

Multiply number of pieces by postage for envelope or card.
Subtract the total fees attributable to this mailing.
Divide that answer by postage rate plus BRM charge per piece.
Divide that answer by the total number of pieces.
The answer is the break-even percentage.

That formula can always be used, regardless of the current rates.

If you wish to be completely economical about reply mail throughout your organization, you should share some of the major concerns discussed in this chapter with any manager who may be responsible for the creation of return envelopes or cards in either sales or advertising literature.

If your organization has been using a considerable amount of metered reply mail over the past 10 years, you should beware of the *"we've always done it that way syndrome."* If the annual BRM permit and accounting fee has already been paid, it only takes a decrease of 6.4 percent in the amount of returns for business reply mail to become more economical than metered reply mail. The only solution in such cases is to maintain a highly accurate count of the number of returns from several mailings.

If you are a non-profit organization that seeks donations through direct mail, you may wish to follow many other such organizations who print a note (often hand-written) in the upper left corner of the business reply envelope. It requests that a stamp be added by the contributor as an added gift. The Postal Service will refund (*only*) the postage (*not the fees*) on BRM returned to your office with postage stamps affixed. Ask your postmaster for details.

ACCELERATED REPLY MAIL

The USPS has a program designed specifically for firms that receive large quantities of First-Class Mail with customers' payments enclosed. The mail is captured at originating postal facilities using automated processing equipment. It can then be picked up at that facility's *caller service* window or can be sent via Express Mail to a postal facility near your office. (Caller service is a premium service provided for a fee to customers using a post office box number who are authorized to pick up their mail at the post office window whenever the post office is open.)

To utilize this relatively new service you need only to coordinate your return envelopes with the Postal Service and pay the caller service fees at each postal facility.

The advantages are obvious. It provides you with your payments much sooner, which in turn makes your funds available for deposit earlier. Your postmaster or account representative can provide you with more information on accelerated reply mail.

CHAPTER 10

SMALL PACKAGE GROUND SERVICES

If you have a small package, one weighing less than 70 pounds, you must either send someone to the post office (and perhaps stand in line) to mail the package as fourth-class parcel post, or pay a weekly service charge of $5.00 (in 1991) to have United Parcel Service (UPS) or Roadway Package System (RPS) pick up the package right in your office.

If you are more than several blocks from a post office or have three or four packages it becomes an easy decision. In addition, if you elect not to have an employee standing around in a post office lobby, you save shipping costs, have free insurance up to $100, undoubtedly speed up the transit time, and perhaps reduce the damage rate. But the most important single factor of those benefits is the rate differential. As long as 15 years ago large mail-order retailers testified before the Postal Rate Commission that "it's strictly the dollars," or "it would cost us several hundred thousand dollars more every year to use parcel post."

But there are additional advantages in using UPS or RPS. As the new kid on the block, RPS may try harder, but both are likely to provide superior service. In addition, while RPS brags about package tracing *en route*, UPS is rapidly developing the same type of service. They have a patented *UPSCODE* backed with a billion dollar budget for computerization and development of the postage-stamp size *"dense code,"* a sort of round bar code with 888 information-carrying cells arranged in a honeycomb pattern.

There are several factors to consider when you must choose between RPS and UPS. Neither carrier is apparently thrilled about delivering to residential addresses. In fact, on February 18, 1991, United Parcel inaugurated a higher fee, a surcharge of 30 cents per parcel, for *residential deliveries* (but not to Canadian addresses). Roadway is even more indifferent to packages addressed to residences as it only solicits business from organizations shipping to *business oriented* ZIP Codes. If RPS does accept a shipment to a home address, it also adds an extra 30¢ fee.

Therefore, if most of your small packages are destined to residential addresses, in all likelihood you will have to choose a carrier other than

RPS. In addition, choosing between UPS and RPS may depend largely on whether or not you already have UPS coming into your mail center for domestic or international air delivery service and the availability of Roadway Package System in your particular part of the country. In any event, it will serve you well to be familiar with both. (RPS and UPS operate with identical rates, and both raised them in February of 1991.)

HAZARDOUS MATERIAL

Just as the Postal Service protects its employees and the general public from the dangers of *hazardous material*, the commercial ground carriers must control what is tendered for shipment via truck.

If you plan on shipping what you suspect may be hazardous material or other regulated materials, you should contact the carrier in advance to determine whether the material will be accepted.

United Parcel Service *will* provide delivery of certain hazardous materials and other regulated materials, but you cannot use *Call Tag* service to pick up hazardous material. UPS will also provide its customers with its own *Guide for Shipping Hazardous Materials* and supplies needed to meet the special packaging, marking, and labeling requirements. (Also see *Chapter 11* regarding hazardous material restrictions on air shipments.)

UNITED PARCEL SERVICE

It was 1907 in Seattle when Jim Casey founded the American Messenger Company. Total assets: six messengers, two bicycles, and a telephone. Now, 84 years later, that humble beginning known the world over by its scurrying brown trucks, has a total work force of 244,000 dedicated employees and 116,000 vehicles. Its founder insisted that the company should be "owned by its managers and managed by its owners." Consequently all UPS stock is held by its more than 18,000 managers (who must sell back their holdings when they retire). The air of mystique surrounding UPS has been referred to as "cross between the Marines and a Quaker meeting."

This of course translates to outstanding service for its customers. Its huge customer base of more than one million shippers who receive automatic daily pickup service are all likely to agree with *Fortune's* regular title of "most admired transportation company."

But it was not all easy. It took UPS 30 years to acquire the rights to serve all 50 states but now it boasts it provides service to *every* address in America. UPS concentrated on over-the-road service until the early 80's, grew tired of coping with commercial airlines schedules and independent operating companies, and in 1987 created its own certified airline. It now owns 133 jets (including seven 747's and 49 DC-8's), operates an additional 240 aircraft under charter, and has 806 daily domestic flight segments out of 399 domestic airports. It also has 402 daily flight segments in and out of

204 international airports.

UPS operates its main U.S. air hub (of one million square feet) in Louisville, KY, and has regional hubs in Philadelphia, Dallas and Ontario, CA. The Louisville hub ranks among the top 10 airports in the world for cargo throughput with the arrival and departure of 77 freighters a day, and half are UPS aircraft. The staff of 1,200 begins the three-hour sort operation about midnight, and only *one error in 10,000* is acceptable.

Ground delivery service works much the same way, with over 100 hubs throughout the U.S. each of which sorts anywhere from 2,000 to 40,000 packages each night. The hubs are organized into a network with a timetable for sorting according to a strict schedule so that the vehicles may move between the hubs within the published delivery standards.

All of those facts about UPS are not included to entertain you but instead to assure you of its commitment to serving its customers very, very well.

Ground Service

It is no surprise that UPS has such an excellent reputation among its customers. It provides every conceivable aid you can imagine to ease your way through the paperwork necessary to prepare shipments via UPS.

United Parcel Service offers a variety of ways to pay delivery charges. They will electronically bill your bank each week, have the bank deduct the amount of the bill from your checking account, and send you bills marked "Paid By Bank." UPS will also invoice a customer each week, with the bill payable within seven days as required by the ICC, or they will participate in one of the many bank freight payment plans where banks consolidate delivery and freight charges for their clients and pay the bills each month. In addition, UPS allows the customer to make a deposit with UPS of an amount equal to four weeks' average billing, accumulate four weeks of bills, and then write one check to cover them, while leaving the deposit intact.

To simplify the record keeping, you may use a *register* that is much like a postage meter. The initial setting is made by United Parcel Service, and thereafter the ascending and descending registers are used to verify the amount "spent" on delivery charges by reading the registers before and after use. It resets automatically, so there is no need to take the register anywhere for refilling. The shipper retains duplicate invoices to provide back-up documentation.

The register is operated by your mailing machine, and a moistened or pressure-sensitive parcel tape is ejected showing the shipper's number, the date, and the charges. All of the postage meter manufacturers can provide UPS registers.

In addition to these methods of recording and paying for UPS shipments, you may choose a computer manifest system. By automatically calculating package weight, zone, and shipping charges, a computer manifest system significantly reduces the amount of time needed to process your packages. The size of your operation, the number of packages you ship, and the degree of automation you need will determine if a parcel register or a computer manifest system is right for you. UPS offers the assistance of its customer service reps to help you decide.

There is an abundance of personal computer software popping up in many different areas of mail management, and preparing UPS shipments is no exception. One such software package, the *Automated Parcel Shipping System (APSS)*, is available from Aristo Computers, Inc., 6700 SW 105th Avenue, Suite 307, Beaverton, OR 97005-5484, telephone 1-800-3ARISTO.

The *APSS* does *everything!* When coupled to a printer it provides manifests, shipping labels, COD tags, and forms for other carriers too. Its menus and prompts glide you along through each step of the preparation process, and as fast as you complete one entry the screen highlights the next data area. Best of all, you can try it before you buy it. Aristo Computers will send you a demonstration diskette (which is quite impressive) for $4 (in 1991) which will allow you to see exactly how the *APSS* works right on your own PC. They also guarantee your satisfaction with a 60-day full refund offer. *APSS* runs on an IBM-PC or compatible computer with 640KB RAM, MS-DOS or PC-DOS, a hard disk, and a printer.

Customer Support

Here are some of the publications and customer aids that UPS will provide to a customer:

■*How to Use UPS*: A 21-page letter-size guide with terrific photos of all types of (completed) forms, labels, and free (Next Day Air) containers, with step-by-step instructions on how to use *all* of the various UPS services.

■*Next-Day Ground Delivery*: A four-page, locally customized, folder, printed on heavy coated stock showing a map of your particular area with *next-day delivery service* identified by ZIP Codes and a second map of the entire country showing *scheduled delivery days*.

■*Weight and Size Limits*: A 11 x 17 inch, heavy-weight folder, suitable as a mailroom poster, illustrating weight and size limits and how to measure cartons correctly.

■*Ground Service Features*: A letter-size sheet, for in-desk reference, listing all of the special services available with ground service.

■*Ground Service Explanations*: Another reference sheet that explains all of the whys and wherefores, the fine print.

■*UPS Delivery Information Services*: A letter-size fold-out brochure containing everything you always wanted to know about tracing and tracking UPS shipments.

In addition, UPS provides a four-color rate chart, in the event you do not have a computing scale, and a compact (5½ x 8½ inches) localized zone chart that calculates the correct zone from your location to any ZIP Code in the U.S. But a word of caution: if you have very many parcels, looking up the zone on one chart and then the rate on another one are both prone to expensive errors. Most of the electronic scales do both for you; all you need do is key in the ZIP Code. Many electronic scales also allow you to "shop" for the lowest rate to any destination.

Features and Special Services

The primary features of UPS ground service include:

■*Pickup:* A driver will stop by *every day*, whether there is a shipment ready or not, for a small ($5.00 in 1991) fixed weekly fee.

■*Delivery*: Whether in a basement or on an upper floor, deliveries are made directly into the premises of the addressee, and a signature is obtained for delivery to all commercial establishments. Three attempts to deliver will be made at no extra charge.

■*Undeliverable Packages*: Refused packages, or any others that cannot be delivered, are returned at no additional cost.

■*Package Tracing*: UPS operates a computer assisted tracing system, and a printed proof of delivery letter, showing the name of the person who accepted the package and the date delivered, is usually mailed the same day that a customer makes an inquiry.

■*Weight and Size Limits*: UPS ground service shipments must not exceed 70 pounds or 130 inches in length and girth combined, and a maximum length of 108 inches. UPS will provide a unique *chain*, similar to the pull chain on a lamp, with markers at 84, 108, and 130 inches. (If the length plus the girth exceed 84 inches, and the package weighs less than 25 pounds, it is considered *oversize* and will be rated as if it did weigh 25 pounds.)

Special services, similar to those offered by the Postal Service, are available from UPS, and they include:

■*Acknowledgement of Delivery:* UPS will provide a signed receipt of delivery when you provide a stamped, self-addressed AOD form at time of shipment. There is a fee of 50¢.

■*Notification of Incorrect Address*: Every effort is made to secure the correct address. Shippers are notified of deliveries made to new addresses and are charged a fee of $3.25.

■*Insurance*: There is no charge for insurance for packages valued up to $100 and additional coverage is available at 30¢ per $100 valuation. (But also see Parcel Insurance Plan in *Chapter 8*.)

■*COD Shipments*: UPS will collect COD charges for a fee of $3.75.

■*Return of Package*: On order of the *original shipper*, prior UPS shipments may be picked up from an addressee and returned to the shipper. This service is known as a *Call Tag*, and the fee is $1.50.

(All of the fees quoted are only for comparison purposes and were in effect in 1991.)

At the beginning of 1991, UPS began offering a new service to its customers that may completely replace the Acknowledgement of Delivery card, which must either have an adhesive postage stamp affixed or be *printed* to comply with metered business reply mail. If you attach a green pressure-sensitive *Delivery Confirmation Request* label containing an OCR readable and barcoded *control number*, UPS can provide confirmation of delivery. Delivery confirmation responses are mailed weekly to your billing address and may even include an image of the recipient's signature for an additional charge. (In early '91, each Delivery Confirmation Response was only 75¢, plus an extra 25¢ for a signature.)

Their headquarters address is United Parcel Service, Greenwich Office Park 5, Greenwich, CT 06831-5150, telephone 203-862-6000. They do not provide an 800 number, but instead you will find their local telephone number listed in the white pages of your directory.

Note: The details of UPS air service are discussed in *Chapters 11 and 12*.

ROADWAY PACKAGE SYSTEM

As is usually the case when an industrial giant has all of the pie, competitors soon start smelling the sweet aroma of profits, and Roadway Services of Akron is no exception. They took one look at UPS domination of the ground shipping business and rolled out the *Roadway Package System, Inc.,* or *RPS*. Now it is reported that RPS has a 5 percent market share and expects a 10 percent slice by the mid-90's.

Stressing that it provides *a better way to ship small packages*, RPS invites a potential customer to simply telephone its 800 number. A customer service representative will then visit you and analyze your shipping patterns to determine the best RPS program to use. Then the rep will order your labels and shipping supplies.

Everything depends on *RPS Barcode Labels.* Each customer is assigned an individual *shipper number*, each package carries a unique number, and both are encoded on every barcode label. Simply affix a barcode label to the left of each package's address label and record the package number in the pick-up record book or on your own manifest. Then that's it. RPS picks up the package, delivers it, and adds the shipping information, including weight and destination ZIP Code, on your itemized invoice. No weighing, no rating, just apply the address label and the barcode label.

The barcode labels are scanned as packages move through the RPS network of terminals and hubs, so each package can be easily traced. In fact, RPS has a special 800 telephone number that allows you to use any push-button phone to punch in your account number, plus your package number, and immediately learn the location of your package.

Roadway reports that in May of 1990, it had expanded coverage to 75 percent of the addresses in the U.S. including Hawaii. They report that their current transit-time guidelines are as follows:

SHIPPING DISTANCE:	DELIVERY TIME:
Up To 450 Miles	Second Day
Up To 900 Miles	Third Day
Up To 1500 Miles	Fourth Day
Over 1500 Miles	Fifth Day

RPS accepts packages weighing up to 100 pounds, the highest package weight allowable in the ground shipping service, and does not publish size restrictions.

RPS Special Services

Like UPS, RPS can provide many of the *special services* offered by the Postal Service and offers exactly the same services as UPS. These include COD service, proof of delivery, address correction, call tags and package insurance. Their fees for those services (in 1991) are identical with those of UPS, including the $5.00 weekly charge for daily pickup. Roadway also offers repeated delivery attempts at no extra charge.

The back of the RPS rate schedule displays a service map indicating the current terminal and service points in the U.S., as well as the Canadian entry points. You can obtain one by writing to Roadway Package Systems, Inc., P.O. Box 108, Pittsburgh, PA 15230-0108, or by calling 1-800-ROADPAK.

CHAPTER 11

DOMESTIC OVERNIGHT DELIVERY SERVICES

If you go back to the volume of Express Mail sent in FY-90, 58,582,000 pieces, and realize that the Postal Service may only have about 10 percent of the overnight market (which may be generous), then the total overnight market exceeds *580 million pieces annually*! This incredible volume has been estimated to be worth about $11 billion in annual sales. Although the growth is slowing somewhat, it has been estimated to equal 8 to 10 percent annually through the 90's. Considering that this market has achieved this enormous volume in approximately 20 years, you must arrive at the conclusion that someone is sending material via overnight carrier that doesn't *absolutely, positively have to be there the next day.*

As in any other case of expenditure for postage and related expenses, a dedicated professional mail manager should agree that overnight shipments need to receive continual close scrutiny. You should establish some sort of appraisal system so that each quarter all of the material being sent via overnight carriers is analyzed to determine if such fast service is actually necessary. If you are doing the proper testing of different methods of mailing and shipping, you should know exactly the time frame for other types of service and be in a position to objectively and economically evaluate the service necessary. If you feel that you do not quite have the authority to question an employee about whether or not overnight service is essential, simply add up all of the costs of such service for a quarter and show the total to your boss or include the total in your monthly brag report. You need not be difficult to get along with; you cannot, of course, impede your organization's legitimate needs. Just make sure that the addressee will actually take action on the material you ship via overnight carrier. A "just to be on the safe side" attitude can be quite an expensive waste.

HAZARDOUS MATERIALS
Earlier chapters discussed some of the precautions necessary when shipping hazardous materials or other regulated materials. Even greater concerns and restrictions develop when you need to ship such material via

air express.

Both domestic and international air transportation shipments are regulated and/or classified by *Title 49, Code of Federal Regulations (CFR), Parts 170-189, The International Air Transport Association* or the *International Civil Aviation Organization.* That section of Title 49, CFR, authorizes the *Department of Transportation* to establish labelling requirements for dangerous and hazardous materials.

United Parcel Service reports that many common items are considered hazardous materials in air transportation. As an example, while this list is by no means comprehensive, UPS may restrict shipments of cigarette lighters and refills, matches, magnets, and small arms ammunition. It may not accept packages containing oil based paints, flammable or corrosive cleaning solvents, or dry ice. And, in addition, it may refuse shipments of aerosol cans or alcohol-based health and personal care products.

Airborne Express however *will* accept certain classes of combustible and flammable liquids for domestic air express but uses a *Hazardous Materials Specialist* in each service center to define exactly what can and cannot be accepted.

Emery states that the shipper must advise whenever a shipment is classified under Title 49 as *Dangerous Goods.* Emery assesses a surcharge for such shipments (weighing less than 100 pounds) between points wholly within the U.S. or wholly within Canada and for shipments originating in either country and destined to the other. A much larger surcharge and rate application applies for international shipments originating in either the U.S. or Canada.

DHL simply states it *will not carry* hazardous materials or combustible articles and lists in its service guide some 33 other substances or products which it considers unacceptable.

The Federal Express guide has two pages of cautions and restraints but appears more lenient toward certain dangerous materials. For example, Federal *will* accept firearms, fireworks, and dry ice under certain circumstances or with prior approval. It has a special *Dangerous Goods Department* to oversee exactly what can and cannot be accepted for domestic *Dangerous Goods Service.*

While some of these cautions begin to get far afield of simple mail management, a decision to ship a new product, or those of a newly acquired subsidiary, or even some corporate gift, can easily run afoul of air transportation regulations.

AIRBORNE EXPRESS

With its own private airport (a former SAC base in Wilmington, OH, certified by the FAA to allow planes to land with ceilings as low as 100 feet) *Airborne Express* is the third largest carrier in the U.S. air express market. In 1989, Airborne delivered over 64 million domestic shipments averaging about 73 percent under two pounds and the balance in the range of 3 to 99 pounds.

The letter-size, 192-page Service Guide that *Airborne Express* provides its customers would be a valuable aid in any mail center. It is large enough to clearly display sample airbills and manifests completely filled out as a guide for new customers. It also includes all of the "fine print" governing Airborne shipments, as well as every U.S. city served and when each may expect delivery.

Special Features

Airborne offers considerable relief for paperwork headaches in the mailroom. If you ship five or more shipments daily, their *Fast Track Express Manifest* allows you to fill in the "shippers" information only once for all five shipments. Airborne may also accept internal documents you are already producing as prepaid airbills.

For high-volume shippers, Airborne will provide the *LIBRA II*, a complete automated shipment processing system, at no cost. Consisting of a personal computer, modem, scale, and printer (with on-site training), it weighs, rates, and labels each shipment in a matter of seconds and prints an invoice.

As an added service, Airborne will provide free personalized airbills imprinted with your organization's name, address, and account number. You need only call 1-800-AIRBILL to order a supply.

Service Options

Airborne Express provides the following domestic service:

- *Letter Express:* Designed for business documents weighing up to 8 ounces, with a special rate for Airborne's (free) Letter Express envelopes, it is usually delivered by 10:30 a.m. the next business day.
- *Airborne Express:* For shipments up to 150 pounds, with delivery the next business morning.
- *Sky Courier:* An independent subsidiary of Airborne Express, Sky Courier provides door-to-door shipment the same day an item is picked up or overnight with delivery by 9 a.m.
- *Hold at Airborne Express:* This service is helpful when your consignee needs the package earlier in the morning than the normal delivery time. Shipments are held for pickup in the nearest Airborne office.

While you can always call for a pickup, Airborne provides over 5,000 secure drop boxes in office building lobbies and other business centers which may have a later pickup time. You may also drop off shipments at any service center listed in the service guide. You can call 1-800-AIRBORNE for the location of your nearest Airborne customer service center, or, in major metropolitan areas, it can be reached through the *Yellow Pages* under *Air Cargo*. Airborne will not accept envelopes or packages addressed to post office boxes. Sky Courier has its own telephone number, 1-800-336-3344.

Special Services

All of the overnight carriers provide substantially the same type of special services. Airborne states that the liability for *Letter Express* shipments cannot exceed $500, and there is an extra charge if it exceeds $100. *Airborne Express* shipments having a greater value than $9.07 per pound will be charged an additional fee. Airborne *will* accept certain classes of *hazardous materials*, but you must seek the help of local Airborne personnel in arranging such shipments. Incorrect addresses or ZIP Codes, post office box addresses, or other errors which make a shipment undeliverable as addressed will incur an extra charge. *Proof of delivery*, a photocopy of the airbill or manifest signed by the consignee, is available for an added fee. Airborne will refund shipping charges when it fails to meet published delivery commitments.

Size Limitations and Packaging

Airborne boldly states that it can ship virtually anything the law allows! Shipments weighing up to 150 pounds receive next-business-day morning delivery as *Airborne Express*, and it will accept practically any size or weight with varying delivery times. Correct weight on an airbill or manifest is very important as there is a fee for correcting the weight on either document.

Airborne provides several free containers. *Letter Express* envelopes are 9¾ x 12 inches and will hold about 40 letter-size sheets of paper. The *Express Pack* envelopes are tear-proof plastic measuring 12 x 15½ inches, and *Express Pack* boxes are reinforced cardboard measuring 3 x 12½ x 17½ inches. Tough triangular tubes with 5¾ inch sides are also available and are 38¼ inches long. Airborne also can provide a leakproof *Lab Pack* envelope measuring 12½ x 15 inches for shipping body fluids that might leak due to internal packaging failure.

Payment Options

Airborne Express primarily works with account numbers and sends invoices that must be paid in 15 days. In the U.S. and Canada, "collect" service (to another Airborne account number) is available, and third party billing is also available in the U.S. Airborne also accepts personal and business checks, but *no credit cards*. Serving more than 45,000 U.S. communities, its headquarters address is Airborne Express, 3101 Western Avenue, Seattle, WA 98126-3349, telephone 206-285-4600.

DHL WORLDWIDE EXPRESS

The world's largest international air express service operator, *DHL*

Worldwide Express, now provides domestic service through its Superhub in Cincinnati. DHL, based in Brussels, began in 1969 and reportedly has 80 percent of some international air express markets. Its fully automatic Superhub in Brussels has the capacity to sort 120,000 shipments in two hours. Serving 70,000 destinations in 187 countries, through 46 distribution hubs worldwide, DHL is rapidly becoming more well known in the U.S. as its trucks fly by on the television screen.

DHL's letter-size, 370-page *Worldwide Express Guide* illustrates completed sample airbills and other documents to help its customers get off to a flying start, and it would be an asset to anyone sending overnight air shipments.

In the U.S. section, the "state" pages show the address and telephone number of every DHL service center in each state, along with a list of cities served and their ZIP Codes. The city listings also provide the scheduled time of delivery in each city.

Special Features

The safety and security of your DHL shipments are ensured by *LaserNet*, a sophisticated electronic tracing system. DHL provides airbills with barcoded numbers on them or barcoded labels for attaching to packages.

To aid its customers in easing paperwork, DHL will provide *USA Multiple Shipment Airbills*, which allow 10 shipments to be dispatched with one manifest.

Service Options

In the domestic market, DHL offers:

- *Same Day Service*: A courier will arrive at your door within an hour, any time, night or day, 365 days a year, to rush your urgent documents to the nearest airport. Upon arrival at the destination airport, most shipments are delivered within 90 minutes.
- *USA Overnight Service*: Documents and packages can be delivered overnight to over 33,000 communities in all 50 states, usually by 10:30 a.m.
- *Express Document*: There is a special lower-cost rate for items of up to 8 ounces, they receives the same service as USA Overnight.
- *Hold For Pickup Service*: This service is available at all of DHL's destination stations in the U.S.
- *DHL WorldMail*: This is a unique service for a non-postal organization. You simply bag or box your international business mail, fill out a standard DHL airbill, and they do the rest. WorldMail then speeds your mail overseas where it's sorted, stamped, and turned over to local postal authorities for delivery to its final destination. Service is available to every country in the world.

For a pickup, rate quote, or estimate of delivery time for Same Day

Service, call 1-800-DHL-ASAP. For other service, telephone 1-800-CALL DHL or check the *Yellow Pages* under *Air Cargo*. You can, of course, drop off shipments at one of the many DHL Service Centers or DHL drop boxes (and receive a discount). Like the other non-postal carriers, DHL will not accept shipments to post office boxes.

Special Services
The maximum liability for loss or damage is $100, but additional insurance is available up to $25,000 for an added fee. There are some 35 products DHL will not accept, including hazardous materials, so new customers should acquaint themselves with the list shown in the service guide. Collect on Delivery service is *not* offered by DHL, but photocopied airbills will provide proof of delivery for an added fee. Saturday, Sunday, and holiday pickup or delivery is available for an added fee.

Size Limitations and Packaging
DHL provides free containers similar to those of all the other carriers. The DHL Express Document envelope is 9½ x 12½ inches, the larger plastic envelope is 12¾ x 16 inches, the DHL box is 3 x 12½ x 16½ inches, and the triangular tube has 6 inch sides and is 38 inches long. DHL also will provide a *Mag Tape Traveler* that is 11¼ inches square and 1¼ inches thick. DHL's polyurethane *WorldMail Bags* are available in two sizes, with the smaller holding about ten pounds of mail.

Payment Options
Primarily using account numbers to invoice its customers, DHL operates a national billing services center, and its telephone number is 713-442-1004. If the recipient has a valid DHL account number, collect billing will be accepted for most countries. DHL offers a drop-off discount when documents or packages are brought to a DHL service facility or drop box. Payment will also be accepted by Visa, MasterCard, or American Express. U.S. operations are managed by DHL Airways, Inc., 333 Twin Dolphin Drive, Redwood City, CA 94065-1401, telephone 415-593-7474.

EMERY WORLDWIDE
Founded by a freight forwarder in 1946, Emery Air Freight Company was primarily serving the international market by 1968, and by 1985 it offered daily trans-Atlantic service with its own planes. Emery entered the domestic overnight package business when it acquired Purolator Courier, and, in April 1989, was acquired itself by Consolidated Freightways. A long haul trucking business with 61 years experience handling freight, Consolidated had 21 years as one of the largest air freight carriers in the U.S.

All of this experience explains why *Emery Worldwide*, now with more than 350 air freight terminals in the U.S. and 90 overseas, can provide same-day, next-day (a.m. and p.m. service) and second-day delivery in both the United States and Canada.

Emery Worldwide operates four international sortation centers and processes more that 40,000 overnight envelopes an hour at its hub in Dayton, OH. The Dayton hub is a 550,000 square foot facility that sorts close to 100,000 shipments every day.

Special Features

Emery uses a computerized tracking and tracing system to monitor all shipments in transit. Their *EMCON* system, said to be the most technologically advanced in the industry, can provide shipment status and time of arrival, as well as quote rates quickly and efficiently. *EMCON* service is available to *Emery Worldwide* customers 24 hours a day, seven days a week, by dialing 1-800-HI EMERY.

Service Options

Emery provides four levels of service in the domestic market:

- *Same Day Service*: Same day pickup and delivery of your most urgent shipments throughout the U.S. and Canada.
- *AM Service*: Scheduled next-business-morning, door to door delivery of your shipments by noon throughout the U.S. and to major destinations in Canada.
- *PM Service*: Scheduled delivery throughout the U.S. and Canada by 5 p.m. the next business day.
- *Second Day Service*: Scheduled delivery throughout the U.S. and Canada by 5 p.m. the second business day.

Special Services

Between points in the 50 states, when the shipper declares the value, Emery assesses an extra charge, with a minimum, when the declared value exceeds 50 cents per pound or $50 (in 1991). A similar charge applies on shipments between points in the U.S. and Canada (or within Canada), but it is calculated differently. As with most air carriers, there are some 25 substances and other items listed in Emery's domestic guide which they will not accept. Both *collect* and *third-party billing* are accepted, and a *Check To Shipper* service is also available. Saturday pickup and/or delivery is available to selected points with prior arrangements. *Proof of delivery* is available at extra cost. Diagnostic specimens are acceptable when certain packaging requirements are met. A special *Signature Security Service* is available for $50 per shipment (in 1991), and it requires the signature of every Emery employee handling the shipment, from pickup to destination.

Size Limitations and Packaging

Emery's domestic guide provides extensive information about the size of shipments. It appears they will accept practically any shipment that will fit on a plane, but there is an extra charge for any piece with a dimension exceeding 85 inches, or any shipment whose length plus girth exceeds 150 inches.

Payment Options

Emery uses account numbers for qualified customers (and penalizes any shipper who fails to show the number on a waybill) and requires payment in 10 days for established accounts.

You can use 1-800-443-6379 to reach Emery's customer service representatives, and the headquarters address is Emery Worldwide, 3350 W. Bayshore Road, Palo Alto, CA 94303-4236, telephone 415-855-9100.

EXPRESS MAIL

Considering the restraints placed on the Postal Service by the Postal Rate Commission--in having the final say about rates and taking ten months to say it--Express Mail has done well to survive in a very competitive arena. Proof of this can be shown in the 58,582,000 pieces of Express Mail that the USPS reported for FY-1990, a very respectable 9.9 percent increase over the previous year. Experienced mail managers have expressed concern about the lack of a telephone number for unscheduled pickups of Express Mail and the lack of the ability to trace shipments. The USPS already has a national 800 number available for pickups and is rapidly working toward the development and implementation of a tracking system.

Special Features

Express Mail has three unique features that are unlike any other overnight carrier. First, it is delivered seven days a week, 365 days a year, *at no additional charge*, including Christmas, Easter, and the Fourth of July. Depending on the physical location of your addressee, and whether it is a business or a residential address, this can be an important benefit.

Second, you may pay for Express Mail with your postage meter, which can be a distinct advantage for the smaller mailroom whenever the question of payment methods arises. In fact, you may even use meter stamps to prepay *reply* postage on Express Mail shipments up to a maximum of 70 pounds, on mail addressed directly to you as the meter license holder. This feature can be quite beneficial in sending weekly sales or service slips to a central location, a simple process which eliminates the need for the sender to become involved in maintaining a postage account or being authorized to charge other carrier shipments to your account.

Third, Express Mail is the only overnight service that can deliver directly to a post office box address.

Service Options

The Postal Service has made several improvements in the service it offers to its overnight customers. In 1988, the rating process was simplified considerably by eliminating the rating by zones, thus it is the same charge whether the envelope or package is destined across the state or across the country. Unless you have an electronic scale, rating by zones is always prone to expensive errors as clerks get into the next higher zone or weight category by mistake.

Another improvement was made in June of 1987, when the USPS established the *Eagle Network* with a fleet of leased aircraft flying in and out of a distribution hub set up in Indianapolis, IN. This arrangement created dedicated air service between all major markets and allowed the USPS to control its own transportation schedules, rather than being subjected to changes and delays triggered by commercial airlines. This has allowed the Postal Service to offer "before noon" service within the major business markets, and it has had a continued 95% success in meeting that service standard.

Express Mail offers the following variety of options:

■*Flat Rate Envelope*: With the implementation of the new '91 rates, the Postal Service introduced a new flat rate envelope which is accepted for Express Mail Same Day Airport, Custom Designed, Post Office To Post Office, or Post Office To Addressee service. You can stuff the envelope full and pay only a flat rate (equal to the rate for *two pounds or less*) regardless of the weight of the envelope. It is made of heavy card stock, measures 9 x 12 inches and will accept at least 100 letter size sheets of 20# paper, or about 7/8 of an inch of material.

    This is not unique, UPS has a similar container and service. But it may be especially helpful for all types of field personnel, or people who travel extensively, who must send relatively heavy and bulky reports in to a central location or home office. It will provide great "no scale required" convenience for such people and could be less expensive than using a "company" envelope and metered reply Express Mail labels, which must be pre-rated and pre-stamped based on anticipated weight.

■*Same Day Airport Service*: To use this service you simply drive, or send a messenger, to the nearest airport and you can dispatch your Express Mail to any of 64 Airport Mail Facilities on the next available flight. The Express Mail clerk will advise you of the anticipated arrival in the destination city but it is your responsibility to notify the addressee when it will be available. All but a few airport mail facilities are open 24 hours a day. *For comparison purposes only*, the rates (in 1991) are $8.35 for up to 8 ounces and $9.70 for up to 2 pounds.

■*Next Day Post Office to Post Office Service:* As the name implies, you must take this Express Mail shipment to a post office and your addressee must pick it up at the destination post office. But for real emergencies, short of going out to the airport, it may be the quickest service for it is ready for a pickup by 10 a.m. or you get your postage returned. The USPS can provide you with a brochure (*Publication 272*) that lists some 6,400 post offices that have *Shipment Claim Locations.* The rates (in 1991) are $9.50 for up to 8 ounces and $11.15 for up to two pounds.

■*Custom Designed Service*: This service is specifically designed to fit your regularly scheduled, or unique, odd-hour, time-sensitive needs. After discussing your requirements with your postmaster or account rep, you will receive a written proposal complete with schedules and costs. You need not always use a pickup to dispatch your Custom Designed Express Mail, there is considerable flexibility, but pickups are the same $4.50 (in 1991) as any on-demand service. The rates (in 1991) are $8.75 for up to 8 ounces and $12.95 for up to two pounds.

■*Next Day Post Office to Addressee Service*: While you or your messenger must take this Express Mail shipment to a post office, it is delivered directly to the addressee's business or residence. Coupled with on-demand service, it provides door-to-door service. The USPS guarantees *morning* delivery in the major business markets or a complete refund of postage, provided you mailed it within the time designated at your post office (usually 5 p.m., but earlier on the West Coast). However, some Divisions, MSC's, and SCF's will accept Express Mail as late as 10 p.m. The rates (in 1991) are $9.95 for up to 8 ounces and $13.95 for up to one pound.

■*Military Service:* Mail order businesses will be pleased to know that two-day service is available to over 200 APO and FPO addresses in Europe, the Orient and Panama. Military personnel and their families may use the same service in returning Express Mail to the U.S. Your post office can provide up-to-date rates.

■*Drop-Ship Service*: If you process several hundred rolls of film or have several hundred invoices or statements for addresses in a state halfway across the U.S., you can put First-Class postage on them, gather them all up and send them via Express Mail. On reaching the city where your customers are located, the USPS will open the special Express Mail sack and distribute your envelopes or packages much quicker than if you had mailed them separately. If you constantly work with customers in distant cities you can utilize this service on a regular basis, or it is a valuable fall-back position when everything seems to go wrong.

■*Reship Service:*   This is the reverse of drop-ship service. If you are expecting orders for merchandise, payments on accounts, or are a film processor, for example, you will want to arrange to have the post office clerks in key cities clean out one or more post office boxes, place everything in a distinct blue and orange Express Mail sack, and dispatch it directly to you. This may not be a unique service but it is doubtful that you can match the cost of $4.50 (in 1991) regardless of how many boxes the clerks check.

The USPS claims that it provides more ways to send Express Mail than all of its competitors combined. Over 26,000 post offices accept Express Mail and there are over 15,000 outdoor and 4,000 office and mall drop boxes dedicated to Express Mail. Any regular mail carrier will accept Express Mail, or you can use the previously mentioned on-demand service by calling 1-800-333-8777. In addition, there are *mobile acceptance vans* and *store front locations* in the larger metropolitan areas that will accept Express Mail. There are more than 15,000 drop boxes, you can give your prepaid Express Mail shipments to any letter carrier, or you can dial 1-800-333-8777 for an on-demand pickup. The pickup charge is only $4.50 (in 1991) regardless of the number of pieces of Express Mail you ship.

Special Services

The Postal Service offers several special services in conjunction with Express Mail. Naturally, you receive free forwarding and free return after five days via Express Mail. But there is also a little known provision in *Section 292.2* of the *DMM* that states, "Directory service *will* be provided for Express Mail shipments which cannot be delivered due to an incorrect or incomplete address." A nice safety net! And other carriers charge extra if the address is wrong! On the other hand, the regulations state that a refund will *not* be given in the event that a wrong ZIP Code delays the shipment.

A *return receipt* can be obtained with Express Mail as with other USPS services. Use the standard Postal Service *Form 3811*, and pay the current fee for that service. *Merchandise insurance* is free, up to $500. *Document reconstruction* insurance is also free, up to $50,000, but limited to 10 times that figure for one occurrence. *Collect-On-Delivery*, or *C.O.D.*, service is available with Express Mail. Typical fees are $4 for collecting from $100 to $200. However, the carrier *will* accept a check which is then sent to you, so you will still run the risk of bad checks in payment for merchandise. Insurance is free on the merchandise you are delivering C.O.D, but limited to $500. Express Mail guarantees on-time delivery every time or your postage back.

Size Limitations and Packaging

Express Mail minimum specifications are simple, shipments should not be smaller than the official labels provided by the USPS, plus space for the postage. Anything smaller should simply be packed in a larger container.

At the other end of the spectrum, an Express Mail container may not measure more than 108 inches in length and girth combined. That is, the smallest four sides added together, which is the girth, plus the length of the longest side. Nor can it exceed 70 pounds in weight.

Other conveniences include several types of free containers available from your local post office. All are especially marked for Express Mail use, an important reminder that emphasizes the fact that the better a package or envelope is marked the less chance it will be misdirected. In addition, the USPS will provide Express Mail labels personalized with your return address, and pin fed, continuous forms for computer addressing are also available.

In addition to the *Flat Rate Envelope*, your local post office can provide a *2-Pound Pak* (12 x 15½ inches) which is made of tear-resistant material and accommodates letters and small packages; an *Overnighter* box (3¼ x 12½ x 15¾ inches) suitable for heavier items, such as computer print-outs, tapes, and merchandise weighing up to five pounds; and a large (4½ x 37 inches) triangular tube for drawings, maps, and blueprints. An *International Express Mail* envelope is also available. The more of these packages you use, the more the USPS will provide, but, of course, you are free to use any sort of package you prefer. However, you *must* use the USPS Express Mail labels.

Payment Options

Obviously, you can use good old-fashioned cash to send Express Mail. Or, if you are not using a postage meter but want to send letters *weighing less than 8 ounces* via Express Mail, the Postal Service can usually provide a single stamp that is the same value as the current rate. Meter stamps can be used to prepay Express Mail and some locations will accept Visa and MasterCard.

By far the easiest method is to utilize the *Corporate Account* and simply write the account number on the label instead of adding postage. Any Express Mail post office will establish a Corporate Account when you deposit an amount equal to your estimated two weeks' Express Mail postage charges or $100, whichever is higher.

Additional information about Express Mail is available in the USPS 28-page *Publication 161, Express Mail Users Guide*, and in smaller folders covering specific types of services.

If you wish to write to the USPS about Express Mail, the address is U.S. Postal Service, Headquarters, 475 L'Enfant Plaza, SW, Washington, DC 20260-6300. In addition to all kinds of USPS listings in the blue "government" pages of your telephone directory, you may request an Express Mail pick-up (for $4.50) from the USPS by calling 1-800-333-8777.

FEDERAL EXPRESS

With over 366 aircraft, including 26 DC-10s and 19 747s, it should be no surprise that *Federal Express* has the largest market share (reportedly over 40 percent) of the domestic air-cargo shipments. Boasting 31,000 vans and over 75,000 employees, *FedEx* serves over 95 percent of the U.S. population and can provide international service to 126 countries.

You will never believe how much information Federal Express will provide in its *Worldwide Service Guide*. Its 252-page book is chock-full of detailed information for shipping to international destinations, in addition to data on its domestic service. It also publishes a list of all of the domestic service centers throughout the U.S. as well those located elsewhere in the world. Federal will also provide potential customers with a 12 x 14 inch *Worldwide Starter Kit* containing a 12-page "quick guide" to their services and rates. The kit will include your Federal customer account card, an initial supply of Federal's free envelopes, both domestic and international airbills, and a business reply card for ordering more supplies.

Special Features

Federal has a *Packaging Lab* that will test and certify your packaging at no charge, and they maintain a special number for answers to specific questions about packaging. Their Special Services desk can be reached via 1-800-238-5355.

As yet another example of electronics invading the mail center, Federal Express provides two computer systems that can help prepare all of the paper work on Federal shipments and also allow you to track your own packages on their worldwide COSMOS tracing system.

A special *Express Manifest* is available from Federal to help reduce paperwork. It allows you to complete airbills for 10 shipments on one manifest and provides barcoded labels for your packages.

Service Options

Federal Express offers a wide variety of services and options but the basic services are:

- *FedEx Priority Overnight Service*: Overnight delivery the following business morning by 10:30 a.m. for documents and small packages.
- *FedEx Standard Overnight Service*: A low-cost alternative when shipped in *FedEx* packaging and weighing less than 5 pounds. Provides overnight delivery the following business day by 3 p.m.
- *Economy Two-Day Service*: A cost-efficient way to send any shipment that doesn't have to be there overnight. Delivery is scheduled on the second business afternoon by 4:30 p.m.
- *Hold for Pickup Service*: Applicable to FedEx Priority Overnight and Standard Overnight, it allows your recipient to pick up a shipment by 9 a.m., Monday to Friday, at most FedEx locations. Also

available for 9 a.m. pickup on the *second* business day for Economy Two-day Service. (Inquire about any restrictions.)

Special Services

Federal offers free *proof of performance* included with your invoice, or you may request a verbal confirmation by phone. Written confirmation is available up to 12 months after delivery. *Collect-On-Delivery* service is available up to $99,999, and you may authorize the acceptance of *only* cashier's checks or money orders, a real security net for the shipper. There is an extra charge for *Address Correction*, if the shipper provides an invalid ZIP Code number, such as that for a post office box, or if some other address correction is necessary. Federal's guide states, "We do not provide insurance coverage," only *liability* for loss, damage, or delay, for the declared value up to $100. There is an additional charge for greater valuation. Saturday pickup or delivery is available at extra cost. As most carriers do (except the USPS), Federal retains the right to open all packages, before and after acceptance. Special handling and shipment of materials defined as *"Dangerous Goods"* by the U.S. Department of Transportation is available but only at designated manned facilities, and at an extra cost. Federal Express offers two *money-back guarantees*. It will refund your transportation charges if your shipment is delivered late (even 60 seconds!) or if it cannot tell you the status of your shipment within 30 minutes of your inquiry.

Size Limitations and Packaging

Federal Express provides the usual containers at no cost to the customer. Their *FedEx Letter* is of heavy card stock, measuring 8½ x 11 inches, and will accept up to 30 pages of correspondence but total weight must not exceed 8 ounces. The water and tear resistant *FedEx Pak*, measures 12 x 15½ inches; the *FedEx Tube* is triangular and measures 6 inches on the sides and is 38 inches long; and the *FedEx Box* is 3 x 12½ x 17½ inches. The smallest package accepted must be at least 2 x 4 x 7 inches.

In the area of packaging, the *Step-By-Step Guide to Proper Packaging* included in the starter kit is of particular help. For domestic delivery, except for *heavyweight shipments*, Federal Express will only accept packages weighing up to 150 pounds, 130 inches in length and girth combined, and with a maximum length of 108 inches.

Payment Options

Relying essentially on account numbers, Federal may offer the widest choice of payment methods. They will invoice the shipper, or invoice the recipient's FedEx account, or invoice a third-party account number. In addition to cash (but not accepted at all service center locations) or a check, they will also accept American Express, Visa, MasterCard, Diners

Club, and the Discover Card. If you choose to use their invoice system, they will sort your invoices by job or department.

In addition to using local numbers (in the Yellow Pages or business section of your telephone book) it is easy to do business with them by telephoning 1-800-238-5355, either for answers to your questions or for a pickup. For added convenience, Federal has service centers, or retail acceptance counters, in major U.S. metropolitan areas and street drop boxes in many other business areas (and each offers a discount on every package dropped off). Their headquarters address is Federal Express, P.O. Box 727, Memphis, TN 38194-0727.

UNITED PARCEL SERVICE

There is considerable background information on United Parcel Service ground service in *Chapter 10* along with full details of the special services available from UPS. They also provide an *Air Service Guide*, which would be invaluable when preparing priority shipments.

Special Features

Very likely the most outstanding special feature about United Parcel Service is that the UPS drivers make so many pickups and deliveries every day. With over one million customers it is no surprise that you see their brown trucks everywhere, and this makes UPS very convenient to use.

Service Options

UPS offers the following expedited services:

- *Next Day Air Letter*: This is another flat-rate, regardless of weight, service for an unlimited number of documents (stuffed!) in a 9½ x 12½, heavy card-stock container provided by UPS at no charge.
- *Next Day Air Service*: Next day air service is available to every address in all 50 states and Puerto Rico. There are 15,000 ZIP Codes that UPS will deliver to by 10:30 a.m. on the next business day, including all metropolitan areas. Over 9,000 other ZIP Codes will receive next-business-day delivery by noon. You may look up any ZIP Code in the *Air Service Guide*, and it will indicate whether that area will receive the earlier delivery or the noon delivery.
- *Second Day Air Service*: Offering substantial savings compared to the cost of overnight service, delivery on the second business day is offered to the entire U.S. and Puerto Rico.

Special Services

The same special services are available for air shipments that are available for ground shipments, except that Call Tag service is not available. UPS *guarantees* on-time delivery of your air shipments or your money back.

Size Limitations and Packaging

The size restrictions for next-day and second-day air service are the same as those for domestic ground service. Packages must not exceed 70 pounds, or 130 inches in length and girth combined, or exceed a length of 108 inches.

Payment Options

There are a variety of payment methods that you may use to ship via UPS and you should refer to *Chapter 10* if you wish to review the variations.

PRIORITY VERSUS PRICE

United Parcel Service has a 36-page booklet entitled, *"Priority Versus Price."* It is 100 percent consumer oriented with a sub-title explaining that it is, *A guide to saving money on package delivery services without sacrificing necessary speed and reliability.*

Rather than an edited version, here is the exact message on the first page:

"Physical distribution has evolved from a reasonably simple straight-forward field into a sophisticated, complex business. New management philosophies regarding manufacturing and inventory control, competitive changes within a deregulated transportation industry, and the growing practice of rate discounting among carriers have confused what was once a relatively consistent area of endeavor.

"The choices and options available can stagger even the most professional buyer of delivery services. Levels of services, once measured in days or weeks, are now expressed in hours. Territory served and services offered vary with carrier and price. This is true of expedited air service as well as ground service.

"While capabilities and costs are in flux, the overall objectives remain the same, get the package delivered safely and dependably, *when* it's needed, *whenever* it's needed, at the *best price* consistent with the circumstances surrounding the shipment, with a minimum of fuss and bother.

"In short, *value* remains the driving factor in the procurement of small package delivery services."

The booklet goes on to offer a *UPS Package Delivery Express Analysis* and states that UPS studies conducted for nearly 100 major companies identified potential savings of from $2,000 to more than $950,000 annually. It also reports that, according to *The Wall Street Journal*, shipping industry analysts estimate that as much as 30 percent of overnight delivery costs are *unnecessary* or a *result of misuse*.

All of these comments reemphasize the need for close examination of your organization's policies of exactly who has the authority to authorize overnight delivery. They also underline the need to carefully audit every invoice for overnight delivery. Duplicate billings, incorrect account numbers, discounts not taken, and other billing errors can all create havoc with your mail center budget.

As a further note of caution, skyrocketing jet fuel prices in the last quarter of 1990 put a strain on operating profits of all of the overnight carriers, as well as the commercial airlines. Fuel prices may or may not return to their previous levels, depending on events that take place in the unstable Persian Gulf area. This pressure on profits (Emery Worldwide uses 500,000 gallons of jet fuel *every day*!) could very well cause an increase in rates for overnight and second-day delivery, in addition to the fuel surcharge that some carriers previously added. These events will place an even greater emphasis on the importance of controlling such envelopes and packages, while closely monitoring your invoices.

AIR EXPRESS DISCOUNTS

Rumors of discounts on overnight air shipments are always flying around. You can read about discounts offered to special trade groups in mail-oriented publications and in national business magazines. But it is an elusive subject. Several prominent carriers do offer a small discount if you drop off shipments at their service centers or deposit shipments in their drop boxes. But if you look through the shipper's guides which the major carriers publish, most ignore the subject. However, Federal Express does acknowledge "volume discounts" and even invites customers to call 1-800-238-5355 for more details.

Discounts do exist. Airborne Express even distributed a press release when it began its *PACE* program. Designed to recognize small-to mid-size companies' need for competitive air express pricing, *PACE* offers next-morning delivery, usually before 10:30 a.m., while saving up to 40 percent. Details are available by calling 1-800-443-5228.

Of all things, even the staid brown trucks have yielded to customer demand. Now UPS provides a break from tradition and offers a discount (they prefer "price incentives") on shipments through its *GroundSaver* service. They have also experimented with some routine incentive pricing programs for certain quantities of *Next Day Air Letters*. As one market analyst recently reported, as UPS brings on more technology-oriented service and increases in productivity in the next two years, it may be in an even better position to keep pressure on its challengers. Whether they will also yield to competitive pressure remains to be seen.

All of this information may be of little real help to you. But this discount gossip should alert you to the need to shop around and explore where you can get the best rates *without sacrificing service*. It seems few rates are cast in concrete!

In seeking discounts, you should provide the carriers with a detailed explanation or analysis of your exact needs along with the anticipated volume. Once you are successful in obtaining a discount, be sure to institute controls so that everyone in your organization is aware of it and takes full advantage of the savings. Then make sure air invoices are carefully audited and that they include any promised discounts.

One last word of caution in a totally different area. Be sure and learn all you can about local and statewide holidays that occur in the major markets to which you ship. If you do much worldwide shipping it would be very beneficial to create a reference file, either on 3 x 5 cards, a Rolodex file, or on the personal computer, indicating all of the holidays in the foreign countries to which you ship. If you ignore them you may end up paying for overnight air service to office buildings that are closed or for shipments into such cities as New Orleans on Mardi Gras!

CHAPTER 12

BASICS OF INTERNATIONAL MAIL

In an ever shrinking world you don't have to be a huge global conglomerate to need to know some basic information about *International Mail*. As proof of that statement, in FY-90, the USPS reported over 165 million pieces of international surface mail and over 632 *million* pieces of international airmail. With revenue of 1.2 *billion* dollars, international mail certainly deserves close scrutiny and cost control.

ELECTRONIC SCALES
How would you like to purchase steak at $12.65 per pound if the butcher weighed it on an inexpensive spring scale and you knew that every *half-ounce* error would cost you 39¢? Not very cost effective is it? Yet many organizations try to "get by" with an inadequate scale, when international airmail is $12.65 per pound, and waste enough international postage to pay for an accurate scale.

Adding insult to injury, a stricter check is maintained on mail addressed to foreign countries than on domestic mail, and if there is insufficient postage *the mail is returned* to the originator from one of the 26 USPS international exchange offices. This process may take several days depending on your location in the U.S.

Actually, the international portion of an electronic scale will usually pay its share of costs three times faster than domestic mail sections because each mistake costs more. Another reason for having an electronic scale to weigh international mail is that it *computes* the total postage in addition to giving the correct weight. In a busy mailroom, mentally calculating postage such as "50 cents for the first half ounce, 45 cents for the next half ounce, and 39 cents for each additional ounce" can rarely be very accurate. It will certainly waste time, and perhaps result in returned mail if the postage is insufficient. Accurate up-to-date electronic scales avoid these hazards.

INTERNATIONAL MAIL MANUAL
The relatively small section on International Mail in this book cannot

begin to keep you completely informed about international mail. But it does offer some basic information on international mail services. Its primary purpose is to alert you to several major areas of concern and point you in the right direction toward greater knowledge and cost control of international mail.

You should consider the *International Mail Manual (IMM)* a necessity for your mail center even if you have only a small volume of international mail. If it helps you avoid just a few international mistakes, it will more than repay its small cost of $14 per year. Like the *DMM* it is available from the Superintendent of Documents, Government Printing Office, Washington, DC 20402-9371, or the *IMM* may be ordered over the telephone by calling 202-783-3238. Fax orders may be sent to 202-275-0019. The Government Printing Office accepts Visa, MasterCard or checks made payable to the Superintendent of Documents. If you purchase other publications on a regular basis, you may keep a GPO Deposit Account to simplify ordering.

The *International Mail Manual* can serve as a basic textbook for the beginner or an essential aid to the professional mail manager.

PUBLICATION 51

For the smaller mailer who mails only an occasional letter to a foreign address, the Postal Service provides a booklet, *International Postage Rates and Fees (Publication 51)*, which is distributed free and can be a great help in any office. This 36-page booklet is revised whenever the rates or regulations change and should be a part of every mailroom library if the *International Mail Manual* isn't necessary.

ADDRESSING INTERNATIONAL MAIL

International addresses should be printed in Roman letters and Arabic numbers. However, an address in a foreign language is permissible provided the names of the city, province, and country are also indicated in English. The last line of the address block area must show *only* the country name, written in full with *no abbreviations* and in *capital* letters. Foreign postal codes should be on the line *above* the country of destination. However, it is acceptable to place the post code on the last line when addressing mail to Canada.

It is a good practice to type *United States* or *U.S.A.* under your full address to indicate the country of origin to foreign postal clerks in the event a piece of mail must be returned.

INTERNATIONAL POST CODES

Some sort of code for rapid mechanized mail sorting has been in use in various countries since 1961. Today, there are mail "post codes" required in most of the larger countries all over the world, and it is absolutely vital for good mail service in the country of destination that you include the codes (if required) in international mail addresses. Whenever an organization has frequent mail, or a large volume of mail, destined to a specific country, it would be well to write to the postal authorities in that country for details of their requirements. In the case of correspondence to specific branches or dealers in foreign countries, they should be asked to verify the proper format of addresses for their offices. That information should then be relayed to all of the administrative people who originate addresses on either typewriters or computers.

CANADIAN POSTAL SYSTEM

The postal service in Canada separated from the government in October 1981 and became the *Canada Post Corporation*. As such it functions similarly to the U.S. Postal Service.

The Canada Post Corporation provides two manuals for its Canadian customers. One is a *Postal Guide* and the other is the *Postal Code Directory*. While the *Postal Guide* would only be helpful for mailers who plan on *depositing mail in Canada*, the *Postal Code Directory* would aid any mailer, anywhere, who sends mail into Canada.

Both are available from the National Philatelic Centre, Canada Post Corporation, Station 1, Antigonish, Nova Scotia, Canada B2G 2R8. You may telephone them at 1-800-569-4362 or use Fax 902-863-6796. The *Postal Guide* is $49.95 Canadian and the *Postal Code Directory* is $10 Canadian. They will accept checks or money orders made payable to Canada Post Corporation and also accept Visa and MasterCard.

Mailers requiring postal code information on computer tape or information regarding Canadian mailing standards should write to Canada Post Corporation, Postal Code Management, Sir Alexander Campbell Building Annex C, Station 321, Ottawa, Ontario, Canada K1A 0B1 or telephone 613-993-1784. But that number is not intended as an information source to obtain the code for single Canadian addresses.

If you need further assistance in developing mail for Canada, you may wish to contact one of the exhibitors at a recent National Postal Forum who is reportedly the "leading supplier of all types of mailing services to U.S. mailers targeting the Canadian market." Their facilities include Canadian address and Postal Code verification. They are Prism International Mailing Services, Inc., 15 Toronto Street, Suite 1010, Toronto, Ontario, Canada M5C 2E3, telephone 416-860-0165.

If you have other questions about sending U.S. mail into Canada you can contact Mr. John Manzolillo, National Sales Manager, World Post Services, U.S. Postal Service, Headquarters, Room 5437, Washington, DC 20260-6339, telephone 202-268-2274.

If you have a claim or inquiry about lost, damaged, or delayed mail sent from the United States into Canada, you should contact International

Claims and Enquiries, U.S. Postal Service, James A. Farley Building, Room 2029-A, New York, NY 10199-9543, telephone 212-330-3800.

CANADIAN GROUND AND AIR SHIPMENTS

■*Airborne Express* claims it is "bringing good neighbors closer" in its service guide and can provide coast-to-coast service to Canada. Any letter, envelope, or package weighing up to 99 pounds (45 kilos) can be sent as an express shipment. The service includes pickup in the U.S., passage through customs, and delivery in Canada. However, an additional brokerage fee may be applied to dutiable shipments when the customs value exceeds $40 Canadian. Special Canadian Customs Invoices (available from Airborne) must accompany shipments valued over $900 Canadian.

Airborne reports that most non-dutiable deliveries are made in Canada the next *business* day, but Saturday delivery is available at an additional cost. In another area, COD and freight collect services are *not* available between the U.S. and Canada.

The addresses and telephone numbers of Airborne's Canadian customer service centers are all listed in its *Service Guide*. Also, a color-coded list of cities indicates whether delivery is scheduled in the morning, by 5 p.m. on the next business day, or (in the case of extended service) on the second or third day. Airborne asks that questions about Canadian shipments be directed to your local customer center as shown in the Service Guide. Airborne prefers that customers call their local customer service centers for information and pickup requests, but you may call 1-800-247-2676 for the local telephone number of the service center in your area.

■*DHL Worldwide Express* lists six letter-size pages of Canadian destinations in its *Express Guide*, along with the addresses of 21 DHL Service Centers. The guide also projects the estimated delivery schedule for each service point.

DHL limits a "document", which requires no commercial invoice, to one pound. Otherwise shipments must be sent as Worldwide Package Express. Other limitations of certain commodities are also reflected in the guide.

Shippers are cautioned that packages weighing over 70 pounds, or measuring over 40 inches in any one dimension, or measuring over 70 inches when the length plus width plus height is combined, may require additional transit time. DHL provides 1-800-CALL-DHL for courier pickup and customer service, or 1-800-DHL-ASAP for same-day service.

■*Emery Worldwide* publishes a large, easy to read service guide which includes both U.S. and Canadian cities served. Emery's Canadian service is identical to the service it offers to and from all U.S. cities. *Same Day Service* provides pickup and delivery of urgent shipments; *AM Service* provides scheduled next-business-morning, door-to-door delivery of your shipments by noon to major destinations in Canada; *PM Service* provides scheduled delivery throughout Canada by 5 p.m.; and *Emery 2nd Day Service* provides delivery in Canada by 5 p.m. of the second business day. The guide lists every city served and the type of service available to each. Emery charges a premium of 30% of the transportation charges on any package having a dimension (length, width, or height) of 85 inches or greater. CTS, or Check To Shipper, service is available to Canada under certain circumstances, and proof of delivery and insurance are available at extra cost. Further information on Canadian shipments can be obtained from 1-800-323-4685, or a pickup may be obtained by calling 1-800-HI-EMERY.

■*Federal Express* publishes its Canadian service destinations in its *Worldwide Service Guide* along with its other foreign listings but it contains over 30 pages of Canadian cities. It also lists over 30 service center locations in Canada.

Federal's weight limit to Canada is 110 pounds per package, with a maximum of 108 inches in length and a maximum of 130 inches in length and girth combined.

Delivery commitments vary based on the day of the week, and customers are asked to call 1-800-238-5355 in the event they require specific schedules or a pickup.

■*Roadway Package System* serves Canadian destinations with its unique barcode labels (See *Chapter 10*). RPS advertises it can provide ground service to all 10 Canadian provinces, covering 98 percent of the Canadian population. The standard rate schedule chart from RPS includes rates to Canada. To learn the transit times to Canadian destinations, telephone 1-800-762-3725.

■*United Parcel Service* publishes a special 28-page, letter-size shipping guide covering Canadian destinations. It shows all of the area of Canada that receives ground *and* air service, as well as the area receiving *only* air service. This booklet does a fine job of showing all of the necessary documents and labels for shipments destined to Canada. Special Canadian zone and rate charts are available from UPS as well.

Acknowledgement of Delivery, Call Tag, and COD services are *not* available for UPS Canadian shipments, or packages exceeding $25,000 in value. The Canadian government prohibits all alcoholic beverages, articles of unusual value, dangerous or hazardous materials, live animals, and pornographic materials from shipments. Special documentation (invoices and U.S. Export Declarations) is required on all shipments *except* for *Next Day Air Letters*. UPS reserves the right to open and inspect any package tendered to it. Undeliverable ground shipments are returned to the shipper at no charge, but shippers must pay for return transportation of undeliverable air shipments. UPS does not have an 800 number but is listed in the white pages of your telephone directory.

■The *U.S. Postal Service* offers several alternatives to Canadian destinations. There is a special rate for *Letters and Letter Packages* which receives First-Class service in the U.S. and airmail service in Canada (and Mexico). The weight limit is 4, pounds except registered items to Canada may weigh up to 66 pounds. There is *Surface Parcel Post* service to Canada with a one-pound minimum and a 66-pound maximum, plus a length and girth combined limit of 84 inches. Or, you may choose *Air Parcel Post* service with the same weight and size requirements. Finally there is *International Express Mail* service to Canada, with a maximum length of 42 inches, a length and girth combined limit of 79 inches, and a weight limit of 66 pounds. (All weight limits and size restrictions are for reference purposes and should be verified with the USPS.)

In addition to comparing the rates for those services with other carriers, you should remember they can be combined with registered service, insurance, return receipt, and restricted delivery.

Verification of the latest costs and other requirements is easy if you have an *International Mail Manual* or you can call your local post office.

INTERNATIONAL EXPERTISE

In any organization where a considerable amount of international mail is dispatched, it is a good idea to have a specialist who is experienced and well trained in international mail. If that person is kept well informed and armed with the proper tools, then the risk of poorly prepared foreign mail will be greatly reduced, as will the opportunity for postage waste. Such a specialist can train newcomers to the mailroom in the generalities of foreign mail and serve as the resident expert for both the administrative staff and other mailroom employees. A thorough familiarization with the *International Mail Manual* and international priority services will prove to be a very good investment.

Administrative employees preparing international mail should also be taught the vital importance of the red, white, and blue borders on airmail envelopes, as they are readily recognized throughout the world.

OTHER INTERNATIONAL SERVICES

If you look in the average metropolitan area *Yellow Pages* under *Air Cargo and Package Express Service*, you are likely to find more than 30 organizations listed, and over half promise worldwide service. Therefore, you might let your fingers do the walking first in your search for couriers who can provide international service.

In addition to that conglomeration of carriers, each one has a wide assortment of services and an equally wide range of destinations. All of these are subject to change, and it would take several volumes simply to categorize all of the different variations offered by each carrier.

However, it may be helpful to look at the chart in Figure 7 which compares some of the basic services you may require from the major international air express carriers.

When you review the chart, you will see that if you have a large amount of international air express shipments you may well need to use more than one carrier to satisfy all of the requirements of different shipments. The chart also emphasizes the need to keep more than one carrier's service guide on hand in your mail center library.

	COD SERVICE	PROOF OF DELIVERY	THIRD PARTY BILLING	COLLECT BILLING	CHARGE FOR INCORRECT ADDRESS	PENALTY FOR OMISSION OF ACCOUNT NO.
AIRBORNE	YES[1]	YES[2]	YES	YES[1]	YES	YES[4]
DHL	NO	YES[2]	NO	YES	NO	NO
EMERY	YES	YES[2]	YES	YES	YES	YES
FEDERAL	NO	YES[3]	YES	YES	YES	NO
UPS	NO	NO	NO	YES	YES	NO

EXTRA SERVICES AND CHARGES ON INTERNATIONAL SHIPMENTS

1-NOT AVAILABLE TO CANADA
2-ADDITIONAL FEE
3-AT NO CHARGE
4-ON SHIPMENTS THAT QUALIFY FOR A DISCOUNT

Figure 7 A comparison of available special services on international shipnments.

One other point about international air express shipments may be helpful. Whenever a shipment is very bulky but relatively light in weight, all of the carriers will calculate freight charges based on the *volume* of the package. Except for UPS, they will all use the same formula. The rate is determined by multiplying the length times the height times the width and dividing the answer by 166 cubic inches. The final answer is then used as the *weight of the article in pounds*. UPS uses a slightly different formula to allow for excess volume. If the package weighs less than 25 pounds, and the length plus the girth exceeds 84 inches, the package is rated as if it weighed 25 pounds.

When you take all of that into consideration, the most helpful course is to provide you with only the bare necessities about international mail and leave the burden on you to pursue additional information from the organization you believe most likely to help you.

Airborne Express

The international portion of the service guide which *Airborne Express* provides its customers would be a real asset to anyone shipping to a multitude of overseas destinations. It lists the name, address, and telephone number of Airborne's customer service centers in over 180 countries, and some listings provide Telex and Fax numbers as well. With six pages of regulations governing international shipments, you should rely on their service guide for more details.

Airborne's basic international service includes:

■*International Letter Express*:   Designed for non-dutiable shipments of documents weighing up to 8 ounces
■*International Express*: For all other shipments, up to 99 pounds per piece, either dutiable or non-dutiable goods

Airborne uses an on-line, real-time computer tracking system, *FOCUS*, for its international shipments, and it will provide its customers with the location of any shipment in transit.

As with all of the international carriers, there are quite a few articles that Airborne will *not* accept for international service. While most are of unusually high value, or of a dangerous nature, you should check before you attempt to ship unusual items via international air express.

You can telephone 1-800-AIRBORNE for the location of your nearest Airborne customer service center or refer to *Chapter 11* for additional information about Airborne.

DHL Worldwide Express

The *Worldwide Express Guide* that DHL supplies its customers has a uniform format for each foreign country and provides a wealth of information including currency, language, travel documents required, and holidays. A product list identifies what may be sent as a document and what requires additional documentation for customs. A listing of major cities served is also shown for larger countries.

DHL's international service includes:

■*International Document Service*: Air express service for non-dutiable documents weighing up to 125 pounds, with a special low rate for up to 15 letter-size pages.
■*Worldwide Package Express*: Air express service to over 180 countries for dutiable exports and imports.
■*FAXLYNK*: DHL's international Fax service can send your documents to over 30,000 international destinations, with guaranteed overnight delivery, for up to 50 pages, by a DHL courier. To use *FAXLYNK*, simply FAX your documents, along with a DHL Electronic Document Airbill, to the DHL center in Cincinnati at 606-282-0054, or call for assistance at 606-283-2232, Ext. 3502.

For the nearest drop-off location, call 1-800-CALL-DHL. *Collect Ship-*

ment billing is available, which allows foreign shippers to bill to your DHL account. DHL can handle shipments over 125 pounds with special arrangements. See *Chapter 11* for additional information about DHL.

Emery Worldwide

Emery provides its international customers with a separate 112-page service guide that lists every foreign destination. The foreign city listings show the number of days required for delivery both *from* and *to* the U.S. for door-to-door delivery. Another group of pages lists the same information for airport-to-airport service.

Emery Worldwide provides:

- *Courier Express Service*: Emery's fastest door-to-door delivery which includes personal "courier" attention and customs clearance with continual "EMCON" computer tracking. Accepts envelopes and documents with no commercial value as well as commercial value express packages and heavy-weight cargo.
- *Air Cargo Service*: Airport-to-airport delivery service for virtually any size or weight, also with "EMCON" tracking. Pickup, delivery, and customs clearance service options may be added.
- *Air Economy Service*: Economical, reliable, airport-to-airport service for packages and heavyweight cargo that "can wait an extra day or two."

Emery customers 1-800-323-4685 for advice on international shipments and can call 1-800-443-6379 for a pickup.

Federal Express

The details of Federal's 252-page *Worldwide Service Guide*, and the *Worldwide Starter Kit* for new customers, are included in *Chapter 11*.

Federal Express provides:

- *International Priority Service*: For delivery of documents and "brown box" packages up to 150 pounds within one to three days.
- *International Distribution Service*: Airport-to-airport service for shipments of nearly any size or weight within one to three days, designed for freight agents and brokers.
- *International Airport-to-Airport Service*: Traditional air freight service for shipments of any weight or size within two to four days, available through freight forwarders.

Federal's handy reference book tells you everything you need to know about every one of its destination countries. Each country is listed in an identical format that provides the weight, dimensional and value limits, billing options, documentation required, "what's okay to ship," commodity restrictions, and a list of approved commodities. It also lists Federal's foreign service center locations and the cities served. A rate *class* shown for each country assists in determining the rate from a chart, which is also included in the book.

Federal Express also has *overnight service*, for documents only, from New York City to Amsterdam, Brussels, Frankfurt, London, and Paris.

In addition to local numbers (in the *Yellow Pages* or business section of your telephone book), you may reach them by calling 1-800-238-5355, for either answers to your questions or for a pickup. For added convenience, Federal has service centers, or retail acceptance counters, in major U.S. metropolitan areas, drive-thru facilities, and street drop boxes in many other business areas.

TNT Limited

Perhaps lesser known than some of the other overnight carriers, with about 75 percent of its 70,000 employees based in Europe, Australia, and South America, *TNT Limited* offers a wide selection of international services.

Its *TNT Mailfast* service, established in the U.S. in 1984, has become the world's largest privately operated postal system, reportedly handling more than 10 million pieces of international mail each week. TNT Ltd. also offers a variety of express courier services as *TNT Skypak* and an urgent door-to-door service as *TNT Sameday*.

For more information you can telephone 1-800-558-5555 for TNT Skypak or write to 990 Stewart Avenue, Garden City, NY 11530-4837. TNT has over 40 branches in the U.S. so you will often find them listed in the *Yellow Pages* under *Air Cargo*.

United Parcel Service

Anyone who has recently watched television knows that UPS goes to every desolate and out of the ordinary destination imaginable, and with 196 countries shown on its international rate chart the ads are no exaggeration.

UPS will provide international shippers with a copy of its *International Air Service Guide,* a 128-page, letter-size directory that contains everything you need to know to ship to any of the destinations.

Of special significance is the size of the guide. It provides ample space for large, easy-to-read photographs of required shipping documents, UPS waybills, and labels to be displayed, with accompanying "how to" text. Also provided is an 11 x 17 inch illustrated chart listing the six steps for preparing an international UPS shipment which would make an excellent (reminder) poster for any mail center. An easy-to-read rate chart, also 11 x 17 inches, provides zones and rates for every UPS destination.

UPS provides:

■*Next Day Air Letter*:   Provides a special low, flat rate for urgent correspondence and documents when shipped in (free) UPS container. No limit to number of pages.

■*Next Day Air Pak*: Designed for flat non-breakable articles and heavier document shipments.   Container provided (free) by UPS with charges based on weight and zone.

■*International Package Service*:   Provides air shipment for merchandise weighing up to 70 pounds but not exceeding 130 inches in length and girth combined. The usual prohibited articles are listed in the UPS guide as well as special commodity restrictions established by each destination country.

Since any international shipment must be cleared by customs inspectors in the destination country, you may be interested in learning more about United Parcel's *UPSnet*, their global data network. UPS claims it gives their customs brokers a head start to sort out potential clearance problems before the packages even arrive. UPS advertises that its international shipments are often well on their way while other delivery companies are still getting their paperwork in order.

UPS also provides barcoded *Air Tracking Labels* and *Export Shipment Control Stickers* to aid in tracing international shipments. They do not provide an 800 number; instead you will find their local telephone number listed in the white pages of your directory. Note: Also see the additional information on UPS in *Chapters 10* and *11*.

U.S. Postal Service

In addition to ordinary international surface mail and airmail, the Postal Service has put together a group of services it calls *Worldpost Service* to provide business mailers with a wide range of transit times to destinations all over the world. A very informative booklet covering *Worldpost* is available from a USPS account representative. There are also 10 reps who have been designated international specialists, located in major metropolitan areas, and your postmaster can provide the telephone number of the nearest specialist.

Worldpost service includes:

■*Express Mail International Service*: One- to three-day Express Mail service to over 100 countries in the world, either through on-demand service or with a custom designed contract agreement. There are limitations established by each country on what can be sent in via the mails, and your post office can advise you about those limitations as well as the documents you may need. A brochure is available showing all of the ins and outs of International Express Mail. Rates may be obtained by calling your nearest post office.

■*International Priority Airmail*: Available to all countries except Canada, with three- to six-day service. Intended for bulk mailers of all categories of international mail, except parcel post items, who sort their mail by country of destination.

■*Airmail & M Bag Service*: Available for four- to seven-day service.

■*International Business Reply Mail*: Provides business reply mail (returning via air) for overseas mailings.

■*Surface Mail*: The least expensive service with 4 to 6 weeks' delivery.

■*International Surface Air Lift*: Economical air service for bulk printed matter.

If you wish to write to the USPS about International Express Mail the address is U.S. Postal Service, Headquarters, 475 L'Enfant Plaza, SW, Washington, DC 20260-6300. There are many different USPS listings in the blue "government" pages of your telephone directory, or, you may request an Express Mail pick-up from the USPS by calling 1-800-333-8777.

INTERNATIONAL MAIL CONSOLIDATORS

As more and more trade barriers are lowered, all kinds of organizations are rapidly becoming involved in international mail. The U.S. Postal Service initiated the *International Surface Air Lift (ISAL)* program and, more recently, the *International Priority Airmail (IPA)* program to better serve international mailers' needs. However, minimum weight requirements and rather complex preparation rules create a substantial deterrent to the small or medium mailer who wants to take advantage of those programs.

The *consolidator* accepts mail in smaller quantities, prepares the mail according to the USPS requirements, and presents the printed material to the airline specified by the Postal Service.

In addition to the sorting and labelling process, the consolidator can also provide complete advice on international postal restrictions. To learn more about the services that a consolidator can provide you should contact one of the following.

Golbal Mail, Ltd.
22455 Davis Drive
Sterling, VA 22170-4446
703-450-8625

Johnson and Hayward, Inc.
516 West 19th Street
New York, NY 10011-2707
1-800-521-0080
In NY 212-675-4250

INTERNATIONAL MAIL CAUTIONS

If your organization sends a considerable amount of mail to foreign countries you will need to be especially alert for all kinds of *international incidents* that tend to delay or embargo mail. If you can identify problem areas early enough, you often can arrange alternate transportation which, while it may be more expensive, will circumvent the problem. The Postal Service is like a *funnel* serving foreign counties. When the pipelines slam shut to one or more countries, the USPS must quickly turn off the funnel by declaring an embargo on mail to the trouble spot. If you send a great deal of mail abroad, it will behoove you to stay very close to someone in the Postal Service, such as an alert account rep, who can warn you of pending embargos. The secret is not to get important documents trapped in that funnel.

CHAPTER 13

UNDERSTANDING MAILROOM PROBLEMS

It has been said that no one is likely to develop a solution if he or she is not really sure how to define the problem, and mail management is certainly no exception. Problems in mail management are often ambiguous, and it is often unclear exactly where the problems may exist or exactly where to look for problems. It's similar to someone recommending that drivers be sure to check their cars before starting out on a long trip. An inexperienced driver might be quick to say, "I certainly don't want to have problems on my trip, but where do I start to look for potential problems?" And, of course, the experienced driver knows he or she needs a checklist.

You also need a checklist in mail management from time to time. By seeking out small problems you can make changes and improvements before those minor details become a real crisis. And in order to recognize where those adjustments should be made, exactly which areas to fine tune, you must follow an organized, methodical process. First, you will need to review *all* of the potential trouble spots where problems usually occur in managing mail. Then you will need to briefly identify which of those areas you believe will need further investigation in your own operation. Next you need to begin to zero in on those specific problems and explore them in depth for better solutions.

In this review process you should be sure to examine management's policies toward the mail operation, how people are treated, all of your mailroom equipment, the service you receive from external delivery services (including the USPS), and any other influences that may affect mail service in your particular organization. Whether you are new to mail management or are interested in improving your operation because of budgetary pressures, you must look to every available source that can help you to identify problem areas. These include studying your own operation, associating with other mail managers and members of the Postal Service, participating in the USPS sponsored *Postal Customer Councils*, and reading newsletters and other periodicals that deal with mail management.

WHAT'S GOING ON?

In every walk of business life people often say, "Oh, I don't have any problems in that area." Sometimes that may be true, but in far too many instances it is a lack of information, not a lack of problems. How do you know you don't have a problem if you don't know what is going on in every phase of mail management in your organization. Seasoned mail managers have said, "We don't spend much time opening mail" or "We don't have many forms that need folding" or "My mailroom staff is well motivated." Then they are astounded to discover they really were not well informed about any of those areas.

It has also been an unfortunate tradition that if you move up one or two levels of management, away from the day to day chores of the mail operation, there is not a great deal of factual information available. It is easy for outsiders with only a casual familiarity with an operation to make statements about its health, but it takes an intimate knowledge of all of the daily mundane tasks in a mailroom to thoroughly understand whether the system is ailing.

If mail management is your only responsibility you are fortunate. But if you have other responsibilities, other administrative functions to manage, then it is that much harder for you to take the time to thoroughly investigate exactly what is happening in your mail operation. The more responsibilities you have the more careful you should be to search for full answers. The larger your operation, the more difficult it is to monitor the details. You almost need a framed reminder in your office, "Do I really know how and why those things happen?"

If you are to receive the maximum benefit from any studies you make toward improving the overall mail operation, then you must be sure you understand exactly what you are trying to accomplish at each of the various work stations. This is important, for you do not want to build in any actions that are actually unnecessary. For example, many organizations must provide some type of tracking system for certain kinds of documents or correspondence. A bank receiving a registered stock certificate must maintain a record of that document as it passes through the mailroom. In another example, when a federal agency receives an inquiry from certain officials, such as members of Congress, special emphasis must be placed on the tracking of the inquiry while an answer is being prepared or in the event that an interim reply is necessary. Yet in the average mailroom, with the exception of perhaps registered mail, very few documents or pieces of correspondence need to be traced through the mail operation. Therefore, most mailrooms do not require any sort of document control, while others could not survive without it.

So it is important that you know exactly what is going on, and even more important is *knowing whether a specific action is really needed in the system*. Each function or problem area should be examined separately to determine exactly what you *are actually doing* and exactly what you *should be doing*.

CAUSES VERSUS EFFECTS

As you work toward understanding how and why things happen, there is another stumbling block thrown in your way and that is determining whether the problem you identify is the *cause* or the *effect.* Here is an example. Last week you had an unusually large mailing to go out, and you ended up with six people on overtime for two or three hours. Several managers outside of the mail operation observed the mail crew working late and were quick to criticize the operation for its unnecessary overtime, "They need more people in that mess down there!" Sound familiar? But *you* know it is not a need for more people on the mail staff. The previous mail manager simply did not believe in preventive maintenance, so your equipment broke down twice, and even service people with beepers take time to show up!

Recently the mail manager in a medium-size mail operation went to a three-day seminar and returned to hear many complaints about how the internal mail was handled in his absence. He was disturbed to find there were several hours of overtime, which was very rare. He immediately presumed that the mail volume had been slowly growing without his realizing it and that the staff could not cope with the new volume. But he was looking at the *effect.* The *cause* was the lack of supervisory personnel while he was away, the group had simply goofed-off in his absence.

Mail management is not a simple science. Many things done in a mail center may indicate a problem in one area when actually there may be several causes and several appropriate solutions. For example, it was a nice three-day weekend, it wasn't as bad coming back to work as you thought. The morning mail was heavy but that is not unusual. Not a bad day at all, until you discover to your horror that you have 5,000 envelopes meter stamped *with Friday's date on them.* As you arrange to have them run back through the mailing machine with zero postage and the correct date printed on the back of the envelope, you begin to think about what caused the problem and how to prevent it.

Chastise the operator may be your first thought. But if you examined the whole situation you could ask yourself more questions. Was the operator properly trained? Are there reminders around to help the operators remember to change the date daily? Do I have fully trained operators assigned to each machine? Do I have trained backup operators to fill in when someone is absent? Do I have a rule that a supervisor must check the first envelope on any mailing of that size? Have I explained to the operator why the Postal Service believes the correct date is so important?

As you can see, in that instance every question could point to the cause of the mistake, and one or more may lead to the solution. The professional mail manager will be sure to seek out all of the probable causes of a troublesome event and apply the necessary solution to each effect.

IMPACT OF EXTERNAL CHANGES

While most of the possible solutions of the problem described above can be traced directly to the manager of that mailroom, there are many problems that are totally beyond the control of the mail manager. It will be helpful to you, to your career, and to your effectiveness with your senior management if you recognize these events as they occur.

Your organization may completely absorb another organization, or you may learn that a totally new department has been created which will depend heavily on mail services. Events such as these will present your staff with a greater volume of mail, and perhaps some unfamiliar classes of mail. You will be faced with a new group of administrative people putting envelopes into your mail system, a new training challenge for you.

Or, right out of the blue, here comes an enormous mailing, a new concept in your organization, and one that cannot be "farmed-out"--a strain on the already overworked staff because of the sheer volume. Or, still worse, not just a monumental one-time mailing, it is a new program coming from upper management and will involve similar quarterly mailings.

And then, just when you thought that you had your staff relatively well trained, the USPS offers another program that is more complicated and your boss says, "I think we ought to get into that program!"

These are external changes that can suddenly develop over which you have no control at all. You cannot avoid coping with such changes but you have to (1) make sure you realize how they impact the other problems in your overall operation and (2) make sure that you itemize those new work loads in every report you submit to management.

Of course, you cannot constantly complain about new volumes that show up at your door. But you can make sure that your boss and the other people in management understand what is going on. For example, in your monthly report, your chance to brag and to build your credentials, you might say, "We were able to send out *our first full First-Class presort mailing* without any overtime, and the *resulting savings* in postage amounted to ...." or "This month our previously approved budget allowed us to purchase and install the much needed console mailing machine. This will eliminate much of the down time we have been experiencing on the smaller machine and will allow us to process *the new quarterly customer questionnaires without any delay or overtime*." That is the sort of publicity you can give to the mail operation. The more you "educate" your management in the intricacies of professional mail management, the more likely you are to change managements' opinion of the mail operation. You will be more likely to get people when you need them, to get equipment when you need it, and to receive the acclamations you deserve.

GENERAL PROBLEM AREAS

If you talk to half a dozen newly appointed mail managers you will find a track record of managing people well, the capability to manage large projects, and individuals who are relatively well organized. Yet new managers often have no experience whatsoever in mail management and can rightfully become extremely confused when observing a busy mail center about four o'clock in the afternoon. If they are honest with themselves they are likely to mutter, "Wow, where in the world do I start to analyze this jungle?" And sometimes even the more experienced mail manager may echo the same thought. Well, there are several ways to get started and to develop your own check list of potential problem areas.

To develop your own personal checklist you need to seek management's opinions and also circulate a survey throughout your organization to your "customers." In quieter moments you will want to hold a staff meeting with your mailroom people to get their input on building a checklist as they are closer to the problems than anyone. Additional items for later inspection may be gleaned from the agendas of the *Postal Customer Councils*, although some have a tendency to lean toward rules and regulations and other USPS know-how, rather than overall mail management. The *National Postal Forums* and other postal oriented-seminars can also provide a list of areas that may need your attention. And finally, postal newsletters and periodicals can always provide a list of current topics in mail management that may well apply to your own operation.

You may have inherited many of the following trouble spots, and the fact that they were there before you were can make them all the more difficult to resolve, but this list may help you identify areas that need your review.

■*Design and Layout*: Many problems in mail management are a direct result of poor design and layout of aisles, work tables, and machines. But few are bolted down to the floor. You can move everything except the steel posts that hold up the ceiling! You can rearrange almost everything, setup new flow patterns, relocate equipment so that related operations are grouped together, and establish new work areas. Then you can test your operation and the new mail flow you have created, and even rearrange it again if necessary.

■*Personnel*: You need to examine the quality of life that your organization offers to the people who work in your mail center. You will want to ask questions such as: are they poorly motivated, are there any incentives to work diligently, are they underpaid, is the mail staff too small and consequently truly overworked, and are they poorly trained or offered no in-depth training. Further questions might revolve around whether or not there are job descriptions, if the supervisors have become tyrants, and does it seem that no one cares.

■*Unrealistic Work Load*: Most basic business systems can sustain a moderate amount of growth without affecting their capacity to serve. A well-designed computer system is purposely created with ample capacity to grow with the organization. The average sales staff can experience an unusual demand for its products or services and still provide satisfactory service to both its customers and the company. And even production lines have been known to far exceed the output for which they were originally designed. But the average mail staff and mail center doesn't seem to be able to absorb a substantial increase in volume without some deterioration of service. Often originally set up with a minimum of staff and space, the mail operation can suffer severely when there is considerable organization growth. The work loads then become quite unrealistic and may cause many different problems.

■*Security*: The very nature of processing incoming and outgoing mail causes up and downs in the daily work load in most mailrooms. But lulls in the work need not turn the mailroom into a visitor center or a place people from other departments throughout the organization can gather to chat and shirk their own work. This is simply not good business and can contribute to several kinds of problems. In addition to the obvious personnel problems, such an environment can increase problems of controlling accountable mail and has been known to contribute to the misuse of postage meters for personal mail.

■*Incentives*: Few business operations can provide a better opportunity for low production and sloppy work than a mail crew who believes they have no incentives to work diligently. If there is a history of few pay increases, little recognition, no bonuses, and they believe "no one cares," the mail center will never function as it is capable of doing.

■*Training*: The run of the mill mail clerk is a lot more perceptive than most people think. They realize that even repetitive jobs like operating large inserting or mailing machines require considerable training. They can quickly perceive whenever management acts as if they are not worth the time and cost to train them adequately. When continual training tapers off until it becomes nonexistent, when there is no development of specialists, or there are no job assignments, it not only affects morale, but it can cause costly mistakes.

COMMON MAIL CENTER PROBLEMS

The areas mentioned in the previous section are usually suspect in *any* mail operation and should certainly become part of your checklist. Later chapters will address some of these trouble spots in more depth and offer suggestions for improvement, while the next sections will provide you with still other problem areas.

■*Management's Attitude*: If you always wanted to start at the top, this is your chance! You should make appointments with senior managers to discuss the mail operation with them in an unhurried atmosphere. You need to understand *their* perception of the importance of the mail in relation to the primary objectives of the organization. You need to know if they consider the mail only a necessary evil (and therefore how hard you will have to work to educate them about its importance), or if they respect the vital value of the mail but believe the entire operation is riddled with headaches and problems.

These conferences will greatly affect your future budgets and your capital investments so be sure to approach senior officers well prepared, particularly if you have recently taken over the responsibility for mail management. It may be a good idea to have a typed outline of areas you wish to discuss or perhaps the actual questions you plan to ask. Depending on the size of your hierarchy, the rapport you build on these "fishing expeditions" can be most valuable to your personal welfare within the organization and to obtaining the tools (people and equipment) you will need to do the job right. Even if you have been managing the mail for the past 10 years, it will build the image of the whole operation with management to research their feelings about the mail service you provide.

This concept of support from management does not mean that you should be allowed to buy every piece of equipment you see. Or to hire a huge staff far greater than your needs. But it does mean that you and your staff are accorded equal status with all of the other departments in your organization. If the advertising, data processing, and sales department are all walking on thick plush carpet, sitting in brand new chairs, before all-new computer terminals, then your staff should not have to put up with a piece of equipment that you outgrew five years ago!

Your biggest challenge may be in trying to teach your management to *listen better*. Time and again, mail managers have discussed the savings that could be realized from either postal programs or new equipment, only to have their recommendations fall on deaf ears. Today's mailing costs should quickly convince management to fully investigate *any* and *every* money-saving proposition or program.

■*Personnel Problems*: There are many kinds of personnel problems that can haunt dedicated mail managers. But many such problems are brought on by the very managers who contend that they don't understand the people on their staff. You need only look around you to see that it is an ever-changing world in the work place. Every organization needs to get across the message that it must be competitive, but many are being charged with pushing the employees too hard.

The days of harassment of any kind should be gone, and those organizations that ignore all of the many rights of workers may even wind up in court explaining their actions. But, such organizations suffer long before any court action occurs. They lose productivity, and they lose dependable people who can grow into dedicated long-term employees. They drive people away and then pay a high price for training in the same job position over and over again.

It's true that a mailroom job is often the entry level position for an employee, and perhaps the lowest paying job in the organization. But learning to manage the employee of the '90s is an important part of effective mail management. The way you must treat people today is *different*, different from ever before. Unless you are employing inner city people who are borderline-destitute, people will simply not tolerate mean, inconsiderate supervision. Nor will they tolerate inferior working conditions with paltry compensation. They simply will walk out. They might stay until they find another job, but then you will only be training someone else's mail clerk.

You and your supervisors need to be considerate of these people. Be sure that your supervisors do not become arrogant and highhanded in their daily dealings with your clerks. Building stress on the job can be expensive in turnover, retraining, and in overall production. And you should never tolerate any sort of discrimination. Set an example yourself and work toward establishing a friendly rapport with the people who handle your mail, for they often have a different lot in life from yours and probably from most of your supervisors. Your supervisors should try to understand the problems these people are experiencing and have some empathy for their way of life, particularly when the mail staff is made up of inner city individuals. There should be some sympathy for their shortcomings if you and your supervisor expect to obtain the workers' full effort on the job. And, your supervisors should be particularly understanding of minority groups who often suffer indignities other more fortunate individuals could not imagine.

The people at fast food restaurants don't smile just because they are told to. They smile because their management has learned (perhaps the hard way) that if you are nice to people they will usually work hard in return. And if you are not, there is another place right down the street.

■*Lack of Sufficient Help*: "Prove it!" That's what they will say when you tell them you need more people to work the mail as it should be worked. Whether you have personally seen a steady increase in customers over the past six years that you have managed the mail, or whether you were more recently assigned to the mail operation, as soon as you say, "I simply must have more help," someone will undoubtedly say, "Prove it!"

Nowhere is it harder to obtain additional workers than in the mailroom. (Perhaps it reflects on management's attitude toward the mail operation.) You can absorb a smaller organization and take over its mailing. You can absorb all kinds of new mailing programs. Or you can experience enormous growth in customers or clients. But it is still a struggle to obtain more people to handle the increases in volume.

But, once you become organized, whenever you need to add one or more employees to handle your mail you need only to reach for your records to substantiate your request. You need to keep a record of every type of activity that takes place in your area. Records in the mail center do more to paint a picture of what is happening than in perhaps any other area. Not only do the records paint a clear picture of what is going on, but those who are uninitiated in mail handling will be astounded at the size of your volume. The lack of sufficient help is a realistic problem although it usually can be overcome through long-term, thorough record keeping.

■*Mailroom Too Crowded*: Even if you are assigned to a fixed boundary that is too small for a mail operation, and there is absolutely no hope of additional space or expansion, you must learn to live with it. If this is the kind of environment you have then you must become all the more diligent about each of the other factors that have an impact on professional mail management. It will put more pressure on you to make sure you have an efficient operation and utilize every scrap of space.

If this is true in your organization then you also must begin a campaign to be sure that management is aware of the problem. Of course, management will lose interest in a constant complainer, but your monthly (brag) report can continue to emphasize that lack of space is a real problem without your becoming a pain in the neck.

The only other recourse is for you to survey the rest of the organization to see if perhaps the mail operation was short-changed the first day you occupied the premises. If everyone else is crowded, you obviously are not going to obtain more space. On the other hand, if the print shop and several other areas look like basketball courts then you need to begin a campaign for equal space. This may take real selling on your part but when you consider the waste and inefficiency that can exist in a crowded mail center you will be doing management a favor.

■*Poor Mailroom Location*: When you first occupied the premises, your predecessors may have located the mailroom in the basement to keep it out of sight. In most cases it is a poor choice. The mail must be lugged down to the mailroom and then lugged back up again. The more out of the way a mailroom is, the more work it is to efficiently distribute the mail. Known as the "basement syndrome," this has long been recognized as a major problem in efficient mail processing.

Yet, if you are operating a relatively large mail center, the basement may be a very practical and efficient location. It all depends on whether you have access to a back dock and where it is located in relation to your mail area. If a truck can bring your mail in on the basement level, as is true in many metropolitan buildings, then you can dispatch your mail through the same dock, and the basement becomes an ideal location. The most logical location for a mail operation is smack in the middle of the organization. But the noise of inserting and mailing equipment may be a deterrent to such a location, as well as the lack of an easy access to an exit for the delivery and dispatch of mail. Therefore, the best location is a compromise between the center of the organization (for the most efficient distribution and pickup of mail), the amount of noise that can be tolerated by nearby offices, and the location of an exit to receive and dispatch mail.

Depending on the size of your organization and its premises, there is one more factor to consider when you have the luxury of selecting a new mail area. That is the location of elevators and the ease with which they may be used. In any multi-story building, the distribution of incoming mail and the collection of outgoing mail can be a real chore. This is particularly true if your organization occupies several floors in the building. Access to a freight elevator is not always available in such buildings, and if passenger elevators must be used there are several restrictions. Often the mail will be ready for distribution early in the morning, about the same time there is a peak in people arriving for work. Then the distribution clerks must waste a great deal of time waiting for an elevator that can accommodate a mail cart along with a large group of people. An intolerant landlord may even complicate this problem further. But some mail managers have been able to obtain a key to control a specific elevator that can be used for a few minutes solely for the distribution of mail to several floors.

Whatever your circumstances, you should know that this is an area that can always stand some improvement. You should investigate such circumstances carefully, seeking ways to expedite your mail and to ease the headaches of your staff. In setting up a new building, utopia would be a relatively large area situated between a back dock or loading ramp and a freight elevator!

■*No Organized Mail Flow*: The lack of an organized flow of mail may be one of the most common problems found in mail centers. All too often you can walk into a mailroom and see the sorting of incoming mail on one side of the room with the mailing machine right next to it and a scale halfway across the room. Whether it is incoming or outgoing, mail will ricochet off of every wall as it is being processed. This system will create confusion for everyone in general and especially for the new employee. A new mail clerk will walk in and wonder what on earth is happening. And it will take twice as long to train someone to understand how the mail is processed in and out of the room.

The most efficient layout is to have the incoming mail flow into the area, go through the necessary steps of sortation, and smoothly flow out to the rest of the organization. The outgoing mail should follow the same sort of route. It should come into the area for consolidation if necessary, be prepared for the post office, and once again smoothly flow out. Such an arrangement is easy to comprehend and consequently easy to teach to new employees. Because it follows a logical sequence of events that are essential to mail processing, there is better productivity, more efficiency, and fewer costly mistakes.

With very few exceptions, all mail processing equipment transports a piece of mail from left to right, and the arrangement of a mailroom should do the same. Regardless of the shape of the room, and how many posts or columns get in the way, a professional mail manager can lay out a reasonably smooth flow of mail if a careful study is made of the various volumes of mail. It can make a world of difference.

■*Poor Lighting*: You will not see "mailroom lighting" on the agenda of any of the mail seminars or forums, but it is just as important as all of the rest of the items usually associated with mail management. Of course, the lack of adequate lighting will not cause any disaster, but it can certainly contribute to low production. The older the building, the more likely you are to be suffering from inadequate light.

You and your staff should be able to evaluate your lighting without any problem. But if you want a more scientific approach (for management!) you can contact a lighting consultant, located via the *Yellow Pages*, to confirm the recommended lighting requirements. In addition, many General Electric Lamp Distributors can provide a lighting cost analysis.

Whether you are only a tenant or your organization owns the building, you should not tolerate substandard lighting, and you will need to insist on the rapid replacement of burned-out fluorescent tubes in either situation.

To aid you further, General Electric has a free 22-page booklet of lighting information for businesses, entitled *Lighting Application Bulletin: Office Lighting,* which any mailroom will find informative and helpful. Any GE district office will mail you the booklet, or you may write to General Electric Company, Nela Park, Cleveland, OH 44112-0001.

■*Inadequate Work Surfaces*: Here's an easy survey for you. Walk into your mail center during an off period, when there is a lull between the incoming and outgoing mail. Look around and see how much work space is available where there isn't some sort of machine located for opening, folding, inserting, weighing, sealing, or stamping mail. If there are not several areas (of two to three square feet) available where you can place a couple of trays of mail, or a box of envelopes, you should investigate rearranging your equipment. Try to provide several areas throughout your mail center that can accommodate someone checking a computer printout, or opening boxes, or any of the other miscellaneous little jobs that turn up in a busy mailroom. It is not unlike a kitchen. Any good cook will tell you that you can have all the food processors and microwaves in the world, but if you do not have adequate counter space your kitchen will not be very useful.

■*Inaccurate Postal Scales*: Walk into any stationery store, and you can buy a fancy looking spring-operated letter scale and even have three or four models to choose from. The current postage rates will be printed on the dial but that's not the only thing it will have. It will have "*NOT LEGAL FOR TRADE*" on it! Do you realize what that means? That means the scale is not accurate enough to be used in trade because *someone will be cheated*. And with every unnecessary ounce of First-Class postage equal to $3.68 per pound, *you* will be the one who will be cheated. Yet you would not believe the number of executives who will outfit their offices with fax machines, the latest copiers, all kinds of modern telephone equipment and balk at the cost of a precision electronic scale.

The longer your mail operation has been established, the more likely you are to have inadequate or inaccurate scales. This deserves your utmost continual observation if you are to enjoy accurate postage rating of your mail. It is a must on anyone's problem area checklist.

MAILROOM EQUIPMENT RECORD

Type of Equipment _____

Manufacturer _____

Model No._____ Serial No._____

Original List Price $_____ Trade-in _____

Date Installed _____

Serviced by _____

Address _____

Telephone_____

over

SERVICE RECORD

DATE: PROBLEM & SERVICE REQUIRED:

over

Figure 8 Form for maintaining machine service records.

■*Worn-out Mailroom Equipment*:   The average piece of mailroom equipment can take a beating and still go on providing good service. Much of it will keep running and doing an adequate job for you long after the financial people have written it off their ledgers. There are two keys that are relatively obvious: is the equipment big enough and fast enough for the volume and kind of mail you have today, and does it operate with a minimum of down time? If it does not break down very often and is adequate for your current needs, it does not matter how old it is.

In the same area, if you take over a new mail operation one of the first things you should do is determine if there is an inventory of all equipment that lists the age of each machine. If there is no such document, you will have to take an inventory and research whatever purchase records that may be available to establish the approximate age of each one. (The staff can usually help with the odds of a breakdown.) These records are essential to your future budget planning, helping you estimate where you may expect the next mechanical crisis. The secret to smoothly running equipment is replace the *oldest* pieces of equipment, one by one, as they begin to give you headaches. You should not try to keep a room full of ancient mechanical wonders year in and year out, because sooner or later you will have to request approval to purchase six or eight major pieces in the same budget year.

■*Inadequate Maintenance*: Any discussion of machines wearing out must be accompanied with a review of the service and cleaning they have received. The expected life of any piece of mailroom equipment is a combination of the service it receives and the use it receives. And the service, or lack thereof, may have a far greater impact than the usage does. So, this is another place where accurate and thorough records are essential to efficient mail management.

All of this information can be set up on a file card system or a personal computer and Figure 8 illustrates a suggested format.

File the cards alphabetically by type of machine for quick and easy reference. With the telephone number of the company who does your service work, the card can provide a complete history of age, the kinds of service required, and the frequency. This is another "must" for anyone's problem checklist.

Problem Checklist

As a checklist and summary, here are the topics discussed as primary potential problem areas:

[ ] Management's attitude	[ ] Personnel problems
[ ] Lack of sufficient help	[ ] Mailroom too crowded
[ ] Poor mailroom location	[ ] No organized mail flow
[ ] Poor lighting	[ ] Inadequate work surfaces
[ ] Inaccurate postal scales	[ ] Worn-out equipment
[ ] Inadequate maintenance	

There are a few other questions that have not been discussed, but they are important enough for your review and possible inclusion on your checklist; they include:

[ ] Is there ample electrical power for all equipment?
[ ] Is space available for mailroom personnel lockers?
[ ] Is the area clean and bright with fresh paint?
[ ] Are double doors available to receive equipment and supplies?
[ ] Is the mailroom separate from printing operations?
[ ] Are noisy operations located in separate room or buffered by special acoustical partitions?

One other word of caution. Frequently there will occur an unpleasant incident or major problem in the business environment, and management often overreacts with some sort of new safeguard. The new safeguard will sometimes remind you of the old saying, "The cure is worse than the disease." In reviewing your mail operation for the first time, or living with it from day to day, try not to overreact to what you perceive to be a real problem. Just because something happens *once* does not mean that it has been happening a great deal in the past or that it will happen in the future. Of course, you should take steps to prevent the recurrence of a major problem, but it may not be necessary to implement enormous preventive measures that will cause disruption elsewhere in the operation. Things are not always as they appear to be, verify the problem well before you take steps to correct it.

MAIL CENTER ANALYSIS		
CURRENT PROBLEM	PROPOSED SOLUTION	JUSTIFICATION
"Visiting" in mailroom causing disruption in processing mail. No security what-so-ever.	Add "dutch" half-door to retard admittance and require sign-in sheet for all.	Small cost of half door will provide business-only atmosphere, more security, and help increase production.
Lack of sufficient help delaying both incoming and outgoing mail.	Contact nearby university to seek students for part-time work.	Compensation for part-time students will be less than current overtime.
Seven-year-old mailing machine causing delays, frequent breakdowns.	Purchase new mailing machine with automatic feed.	Eliminate service delays and costs. Increase production.

Figure 9 Format for scheduled solutions to mail center problems.

ANALYZING YOUR PROBLEMS

Once your problem checklist is written, you will need to establish the priority in which you intend to attack each problem. The most logical step, of course, is to begin work on the problem that is causing the most grief.

Therefore, you need to set up some sort of sheet that will help solve your problems in the order of their importance. And recognizing the impact of budget pressures, you must adjust that list so that you can immediately start work on some of your problems, but be realistic and defer the more costly solutions until later.

Your mailroom analysis might look like the sample sheet in Figure 9.

Once you establish this plan it will serve several purposes. It will be helpful to attach to your monthly report to management to say, "Hey, look at the progress I am trying to make!" At the same time, it will gently alert them that you will be requesting new equipment in the near future. And at the end of the year it will say, "Wow, look what I have accomplished!" If you accurately work up your needs quarter by quarter, and project them to 18 to 24 months or more, this document will almost write your next budget request automatically. A more detailed analysis might well include the planned source of supply or vendor's name and the estimated cost.

Testing Internal Mail Services

Any organization with a large customer base will quickly tell you that if you want to know how well you are serving your customers you should ask the customers. If your organization is large enough to require a mail cart for distributing and picking up mail throughout the building, or has additional branch offices, then you need to ask *your* customers how well you are serving them. They can help you pinpoint unseen problems or reassure you that your efforts are being well received. Figure 10 illustrates a carefully organized questionnaire to survey your service.

The survey will solve another problem, that of being sure what really happens *outside* of the mailroom. It is easy to be lulled into a false sense of security at one time or another by believing that deliveries and pickups are satisfactory for the entire organization. Many mail managers have been known to conscientiously claim that all was well when, in fact, it wasn't. So, in any mailroom survey, study, or appraisal, it is vital to know what really happens, not what someone thinks happens.

KEEPING MAILROOM RECORDS

As in any other business, whether it be financial, marketing, or manufacturing, records in the mailroom are absolutely essential as a barometer of what is occurring. Yet all too often the mail manager is so busy that records are not available to substantiate why the manager is deluged with work. Detailed records will often help identify problem areas and are *always* valuable tools in making reports to management or in the overall volume, practically any size mail center will find each one

MAIL SERVICE SURVEY

MEMORANDUM TO ALL DEPARTMENTS & BRANCHES:

If our internal mail-message system is to be of maximum service to our organization we must be aware of any problems. It is very important to our overall communications that you help us by completing this survey. Please take a moment now to let us have your opinions and then return this form to Central Mail Services. It will be helpful if you would use the "Remarks" section to report any unusual problems. Thank you.

Manager, Mail Services

	Excellent	Good	Fair	Poor	See Remarks
1. What is your overall opinion of our internal mail distribution system?	[ ]	[ ]	[ ]	[ ]	[ ]
2. How would you rate the handling of your incoming mail?	[[	[ ]	[ ]	[ ]	[ ]
3. How would you rate the handling of your outgoing mail?	[ ]	[ ]	[ ]	[ ]	[ ]
4. How would you rate the handling of internal mail messages?	[ ]	[ ]	[ ]	[ ]	[ ]

	Always	Usually	Sometimes	Rarely	
5. Does the first mail generally arrive early enough for your particular department?	[ ]	[ ]	[ ]	[ ]	[ ]
6. Is the last pickup generally late enough for your particular department?	[ ]	[ ]	[ ]	[ ]	[ ]
7. Are the number of daily mail pickups generally satisfactory for your needs?	[ ]	[ ]	[ ]	[ ]	[ ]

	Never	Rarely	Sometimes	Often	
8. Do you have any problems with mail destined to company branches that are located here in town?	[ ]	[ ]	[ ]	[ ]	[ ]
9. Do you have any problems with mail destined to company branches or customers that are located out of town?	[ ]	[ ]	[ ]	[ ]	[ ]

If you would like to know more about any of the special services offered by the Postal Service, we will be glad to telephone you and explain the service. Simply list the service that may be of help to you and indicate your telephone extension.

REMARKS: _____

_____

_____

_____

DATE: _____   Name _____   Ext: _____

Figure 10 Comprehensive mail service survey form.

useful. The larger your operation, the more detailed the following reports should be.

■*Number of Personnel:* This can be very valuable in substantiating the need for additional full- or part-time employees. If you have different grade levels and supervisors, be sure to design a form that reflects each. It would probably be beneficial to complete this report on a monthly basis. A two- or three-year report on one page would be an added asset.

■*Size of Regular Mailings:* A special report should be maintained that describes the type and size of all regular weekly, monthly, quarterly and annual mailings. The figures on the volume of each mailing should probably be updated on a quarterly basis.

■*Volume of Inbound Mail:* This record needs to pinpoint the exact type of mail, i.e., so-called "white-mail" in #10 and #6¾ envelopes, 9 x 12 inch kraft envelopes, and parcels from the Postal Service, RPS, and UPS. This record should be updated monthly.

■*Volume of Outbound Mail:* This record must also identify each type of mail processed. This also needs a monthly update.

■*Volume of Internal Mail:* This may be harder to pinpoint but all of the different sizes and types of mail in this group must be identified as well. Some larger organizations try to count all internal mail one day per quarter, with supervisors spot checking the tallies.

■*Significant Changes:* New department? New mailing to customers? New postal program involved? All of these need to be recorded on a sheet that will track significant changes that affect your total work hours.

■*Volume of Parcels:* While many mail operations receive only a few parcels daily, they do consume time to process properly. Records should be kept if you receive more than four or five parcels a day. If your organization receives a considerable volume of parcels, you may find it helpful to break down the total by carrier.

■*Volume of Overnight Mail:* If you require the overnight service carriers to deliver all *incoming* parcels and envelopes to your mail center you do exert some control over that type of incoming mail. However, having your staff make special delivery trips (which the sender deserves) takes more time so records on all of these pieces of high-priority mail need to be kept accurately. Because of the high cost, *outgoing* overnight mail requires especially close supervision and records of all transactions, broken down by carrier if necessary.

■*Postal Programs Initiated:* The Postal Service is apparently totally committed to work-sharing programs, and, while they eventually pay handsome dividends, they do take some extra time to initiate. The hours of training and supervision necessary to get these programs off on the right foot need to be recorded for several reasons. You need the figures to be included in your reports to management, and you need the figures so that you can be positive the net savings are worthwhile. Also, if a program should take several months to completely install, and you need extra part-time help, these records will assist you in validating the need.

■*Postage Costs per Quarter*: This is one of the great advantages of having a postage charge-back device that is attached directly to your postage meter. It will do the accounting for each department or profit center and give you all kinds of totals. But, you still need to set up a ledger sheet or report form to keep these records over several years rather than relying on hundreds of adding-machine-size pieces of paper. You will also need to capture all of the other costs associated with your mail operation such as UPS, any of the overnight services, and any mailings performed by outside contractors. Knowing these costs is vital when a rate increase looms over the horizon, and you are working on next year's budget.

■*Equipment Breakdowns:* The card file previously suggested will keep track of the individual service problems that you experience, but you need a summary sheet as well if you are to be able to get a picture of your overall operation. Such records can pinpoint undue problems with a specific manufacturer's equipment, identify the need for better training in the case of operator-related service problems, or emphasize the need to replace several machines at once.

■*Training*: Chapter 17 provides suggestions and emphasis on adequate training, but this will serve as a reminder about the importance of keeping adequate records of that training. You should have a complete and detailed record of the exact training each member of your staff has received. If you are to reap the benefits of graduated pay scales, it is imperative that you maintain accurate and comprehensive training records. Otherwise you will be unable to grade the progress of the individual.

For complete convenience, all of your records could be set up in one loose-leaf ring binder with a suitable index. With the convenience of computer terminals and printers available in the average office, it should be a simple task to design forms that can provide you all of the suggested information at a glance. Keep the form layouts on a floppy disk, and then you will be able to amend any form without having to redraw a whole new form. As you develop your record system, remember to stay flexible and to make adjustments to suit your own particular needs; you are not likely to design the ideal form the very first time. Obviously, many of the totals in the reports could be more versatile if entered into a data processing system, but this may be a luxury you cannot always obtain. Mail clerks will always be able to post figures to a record sheet, or a machine service

---

QUARTERLY MAILROOM ANALYSIS

ESTIMATED DAILY <u>INCOMING</u> MAIL VOLUME:

PIECES/TRAYS/SACKS	#10 WHITE ENVELOPES
PIECES/TRAYS/SACKS	#6 3/4 WHITE ENVELOPES
PIECES/TRAYS/SACKS	9"X12" KRAFT ENVELOPES
PIECES/SACKS/TUBS	PARCELS FROM UPS
PIECES/SACKS/TUBS	PARCELS FROM USPS

ESTIMATED DAILY <u>INTERNAL</u> MAIL PIECES:_____

ESTIMATED DAILY <u>OUTGOING</u> MAIL VOLUME:

PIECES/TRAYS/SACKS	#10 WHITE ENVELOPES
PIECES/TRAYS/SACKS	#6 3/4 WHITE ENVELOPES
PIECES/TRAYS/SACKS	9"X12" KRAFT ENVELOPES
PIECES/SACKS/TUBS	PARCELS VIA UPS
PIECES/SACKS/TUBS	PARCELS VIA USPS
PIECES VIA OVERNIGHT SERVICE	

AVERAGE DAILY PIECES OF USPS SPECIAL SERVICES

_____ PCS. CERTIFIED	_____ PCS. CERT. OF MAILING
_____ PCS. C O D MAIL	_____ PCS. INSURED MAIL
_____ PCS. REGISTERED MAIL	_____ PCS. SPECIAL HANDLING

SPECIAL MAILINGS IN PAST 3 MONTHS:
_____
_____

SPECIAL REMARKS:
_____
_____

QUARTERLY POSTAGE: ACTUAL $_____   BUDGETED $ _____   DATE:_____

Figure 11 Design of comprehensive mail analysis report.

record card, but may shy away from any sort of data terminal keyboard.
    One final note on record keeping. Review all of the records you are

keeping, perhaps every six months, to see if you are actually making use of the information you are collecting. More than one business has experienced the futility of collecting data of some sort, only to learn later on that there is no earthly use for the information!

Figure 11 may help you get started toward a quarterly report that will contain most of the information you will want. Depending on the size and scope of your operation, you may want to use it on a monthly basis.

All of that information may seem like overkill but it will record everything that is going on in your operation and save you from that famous lament, *"I sure do wish I had maintained a record of all the times we shipped ...."*

CHAPTER 14

DESIGNING EFFICIENT MAIL FLOW

Some mailroom problems are not exactly hidden, they hit you right between the eyes. Such obstacles usually are close to being immovable, and the professional mail manager facing them must use a considerable amount of nimble footwork to overcome them. For example, if the rapid growth of an organization has resulted in very crowded conditions throughout the entire organization, the mail center manager may as well forget about asking for more space. Instead, he or she should concentrate on improving the logical flow of mail in and out of the mailroom in spite of space restrictions.

The alert manager doesn't let such immovable problems result in losing sight of other questionable areas. If anything, they should serve to emphasize the importance or downright necessity of sound mail operations in all other areas. Instead of an alibi for poor service, so-called immovable obstructions can serve as the very reason to update mailroom equipment and furniture. At the same time, one big problem shouldn't overshadow all of the little ones. However corny it may sound, a river really is made up of little drops of water, and poor mail service and the resulting needless waste are likewise made up of little mistakes and little problems.

A well-organized flow of mail is essential to a smooth operation, for both incoming and outgoing mail, if the total system is to function as it should. The lack of smooth circulation as the *incoming mail* is sorted, opened, and distributed can waste time and money. The lack of a smooth flow of *outgoing mail* through necessary batching, weighing, stamping, and sealing operations can also waste time and money and delay important mail. Improvements in mail flow can be made with very little cost in any mail center, so there is certainly no excuse for mail being passed all over the room when a well-planned flow will improve the entire operation.

DIAGRAMMING YOUR MAIL FLOW

Before you begin to change the present mail flow it would be helpful for you to get a sort of "snapshot" of what is happening now. If you are fortunate enough to have some sort of "property management" office that can provide a photocopy of the blueprints of your area all the better. But an hour or two with a pad of graph paper with quarter-inch squares will provide you with what you need just as well.

Floor tiles are usually 12 inches square, and acoustical ceiling tiles are usually either 12 inches wide and 24 inches long or occasionally 36 inches square. In any event, they can serve as your measuring device, and in a short time you can have a scale drawing of your entire mail layout on graph paper. With a little accurate counting, you will also be able to pinpoint the doors, pillars, and posts, and all the other obstructions with which you have to live.

Next you want to sketch in, with a fair amount of accuracy, the location of all of the furniture, work tables, mailing machines, and other pieces of mailing equipment. Remember to label each one so you will know their function. Then take a light color felt marker, or preferably a highlighter, and indicate the path that incoming mail follows as it moves through each of its operational functions and out to your offices. Then do the same thing with your outgoing mail, from the time it comes in the door until it is packaged for the Postal Service in bundles, trays, or sacks.

Now you have a "snapshot" of your *present* mail operation, and you may very well already have a relatively good flow of mail into and out of your mail center. But, unless you were there when it was first established and you set it up yourself, the odds are it could stand some refinement.

Before you begin to think of making changes, take the time to identify the trouble spots and make small notes in red right on your "snapshot." You might make note of a too-narrow aisle that causes congestion half the time, a worktable that is located in an out-of-the-way location, or a scale that was somehow set up halfway across the room from the mailing machine. This identification of known problem areas will be a great help to you as you begin to redesign your mail center layout with improved mail flow.

MAIL FLOW GUIDELINES

No one is better suited to establish the flow in your mailroom than you are because the whole secret is *to follow the sequence of events* as you process your mail. No two mail operations are exactly the same, and only you know what is best for your particular operation. But, if you follow the sequence of events and have your mail move smoothly from one function to the other you will improve your productivity and eliminate wasted time. At the same time, a smoother flow will be easier to teach to newcomers who also must learn the sequence of events.

The next factor to consider is to make sure that all of your functions move the mail from left to right as it is processed. The reason for this is simple. *Practically all mailing equipment processes mail from left to right.* About the only exception to this rule is a Bell & Howell Phillipsburg large inserter, but most large inserters are operations unto themselves, and they will not disturb your overall mail flow.

Finally, as you have begun to get your flow smoothed out to coincide with the sequence of processing, you only need to *adjust the flow* lines to meet your own organization's volume. While many firms have approximately equal incoming and outgoing operations, many do not. For example, telephone sales or outside sales personnel may create a big volume of items to be shipped out from a mail center that has a relatively small amount of incoming mail. Conversely, print ads or direct mail promotions may develop an enormous amount of incoming sales or inquiries, but the product is shipped from another location. When such events make the incoming volume far less than the outgoing, or when the reverse is true, you must adjust the flow to meet the volume. You may have only 10 percent of your floor space devoted to the incoming or outgoing mail flow, but the other 90 percent should still be set up to preserve the flow and sequence of events for the larger portion of the operation.

As you revise the layout of your mailroom you can often squeeze out a little more space when you begin to arrange the tables and mailing equipment to fit *the sequence of things*. If so, or if you are working with a completely new area or mailroom, the following recommendations may help.

■Don't skimp on the space between two different operations, try to leave an eight foot space wherever possible to minimize noise and distractions.

■Two doors are better than one, if you have the wall space. This allows you to route traffic in one door and out of the other.

■Don't push everything up against the wall. Try some work tables and mailing machines with aisles 30 inches from the wall.

■Try to leave 24-inch "service access" space where possible for mailing, inserting or other machines.

■If two people will sort mail into sorting bins set at a right angle from each other, allow at least 12 inches between the corners of the bins so the people doing the sorting will not get in each other's way.

■Try to preserve six foot aisles for hand trucks and mail carts.

You may not be able to maintain such spaciousness, but these arrangements would be an ideal setup if you had the space.

Last of all, but equally important, you will need to *stay flexible.* It has been said that "everything changes," and this may be truer in the mailroom than anywhere else. Changes *will* come, and you will need to stay flexible to cope with them. New programs, new products, new associates will cause increases in either the inbound operation or the outbound operation, or perhaps both, and you will need to adjust your flow lines accordingly.

IDENTIFYING MAIL PROCESSING FUNCTIONS

To aid you in making sure you include every function that occurs in your particular mailroom, you need to find a quiet place and "think through" exactly what happens to all of your incoming mail and then do the same with your outgoing mail. Suppose you decide that your present setup is lacking a certain desirable function area, for example, a special table for incoming overnight air express. You should be sure to include this new area in your plans to improve your mail flow.

It is equally important to label your "snapshot" with *every* function that now occurs so that a new design does not leave something important out of the scheme of things. Perhaps you have had that sort of thing happen when you were rearranging storage at work or at home. You think you are all set with items A, B, and C when you suddenly realize you didn't allow space for D.

Figure 12 will help you make sure none of the functions are omitted, but in your operation you may have several of those functions consolidated. At any rate, the list covers practically every operation you may encounter.

WHAT'S HAPPENING

As mentioned in *Chapter 13*, it is not just the final result that you must concentrate on if you are to receive the maximum benefit from these mail flow discussions. You must understand and examine each of the various work stations independently to prevent including any unnecessary procedures. You may recall the examples from that chapter describing how banks and Federal agencies must track certain types of mail. But in your own operation, with the exception of perhaps registered mail, you may have very few documents or pieces of correspondence that must be tracked through the mail operation. Therefore, you may not require any sort of document control, it would be totally unnecessary, but others could not survive without it.

So it is important that you know exactly what is going on, and even more important is *knowing whether a specific action is really needed in the system at all.* Each function should be examined separately to determine exactly what you *should* be doing and exactly what you *are currently* doing.

CREATING A NEW BLUEPRINT

By now you should have your present layout well defined, with each function identified and with special problem areas noted in red. Using the checklist in Figure 12, you will be able to identify each of the *desirable* work areas that you need to add. Using the mail flow guidelines, you also know if some of your present functions should be relocated to improve productivity and the overall flow.

Next you need to create another scale drawing of your mailroom in

[ ] Receiving parcels from the Postal Service

[ ] Receiving parcels from UPS or RPS

[ ] Receiving overnight air shipments

[ ] Receiving incoming letter mail and flats

[ ] Dumping incoming mail

[ ] Opening and extracting incoming mail

[ ] Reading and/or locator station

[ ] Tracking/dispatching accountable mail

[ ] Primary sorting of incoming mail

[ ] Secondary sorting of incoming mail

[ ] Receiving internal mail

[ ] Sorting/dispatching internal mail

[ ] Folding/inserting outgoing mail

[ ] Consolidating branch or interoffice mail

[ ] Wrapping parcels

[ ] Weighing parcels and letters

[ ] Applying postage and sealing

[ ] Preparing UPS/RPS shipments and documents

[ ] Holding area for UPS/RPS shipments

[ ] Bag racks or trays for outgoing letter mail

[ ] Outgoing overnight air express mail

Figure 12 Typical mailroom functions.

order that you may arrange each function in a location that will maximize its effectiveness. Depending on how involved the changes are to be, you may want to use a larger piece of graph paper and make your diagram to a larger scale. The larger the scale, the more accurate your layout will be.

You may feel that you can simply pencil in the approximate size of each machine or work table onto your layout and that will suffice. But to be more accurate, and to be able to rearrange the layout several different ways, it is *very* helpful to take the time to make scale cutouts of each piece of furniture and machine in your mail center. These can be cut from colored 3 x 5 cards to facilitate moving them about with ease. This is somewhat time consuming (and your peers may think you have finally gone over the edge). However, saving the scale cutouts in an envelope becomes a real bonanza the next time you want to make a few adjustments.

Once you have your cutouts, you can arrange the furniture and mailing equipment exactly the way you want them on the new larger scale drawing. When you achieve the ideal arrangement, pencil in exactly where each piece will be situated by tracing around the cutouts and identifying each function on the scale drawing. Photocopies of this final arrangement can then be distributed to the people who will help you make the move.

A TIMETABLE FOR CHANGE

Before you take your new mail flow design to management, you will want to establish a detailed plan of action. You should carefully review any "slow" time that occurs in your operation. For example, in some manufacturing organizations the entire plant shuts down for two weeks in the summer. In other organizations, business almost comes to a complete standstill during the last two weeks in December. If those situations are not applicable in your organization, or your need to make the changes is more urgent, try to find a three-day weekend (i.e. a USPS holiday) as the target date.

After you select the date, you will have to develop an action plan that answers all of these questions. Who will participate, your present mailroom employees (are they willing) or commercial movers? If you do use your employees, how will they be compensated, by overtime or compensatory time off, and will your company pick up child-care fees if necessary? (Do *not* allow children to be brought to the mail center in any event!) It is not unusual for a move to involve several 12 hour days. If that is the case, will meals be provided by the organization? What extra equipment will be needed such as dollies and hand-trucks, and will commercial movers need to move the larger equipment? What cleaning supplies will be needed when you move a cabinet away from a wall where it has been for the past seven years! Will you need some custodial people part of the time to aid in cleaning behind the movers? If you are a resident in a building you may need to arrange access to your offices over the weekend as some buildings are completely closed on Sundays and holidays. If your switchboard normally shuts the telephones down, you will have to arrange for phones to remain on in your area for emergency use and as a courtesy to your employees and their families. Depending on the season, you will need to arrange for the air conditioning or the heating system to be operating. If your employees are likely to drive in to help you make the move, but normally take public transportation, you will need to provide prepaid parking spaces. If you are to work into the evening, you will need to arrange some sort of security as your people depart, especially for any women employees. Then you may want to add a few personal touches such as soft drinks and coffee, especially if a cafeteria or nearby convenience store usually provides such things during the workweek (happy people work harder).

Armed with the answers to those questions and your new blueprint, you will have no trouble getting the approval from your management to improve the mail flow in your mail center. But don't neglect the final step, which is to publicize the move very well within the organization. Depending on the scope of the changes that you wish to make, four or five extra hours on Friday evening can mean a big head start on your move. So you may want to encourage a tough "mail early" policy, seek the cooperation of all of the administrative people, and shut down early in the afternoon. Most often the prospect of better mail service pleases management and everyone else in the organization, but you will need to monitor every detail to assure success.

CHAPTER 15

UNDERSTANDING MAILROOM FUNCTIONS

This chapter discusses the three areas of mail processing--incoming, internal, and outgoing--both in detail and in conjunction with an overall system of mail flow. It will provide the professional mail manager with an overview of the entire processing system and will also supply an in-depth knowledge of each of the three functions. In each there are specific trouble spots that can be smoothed out to produce better mail service, often at a lower cost.

INCOMING MAIL

You should, of course, provide a separate area for incoming mail for there are several advantages to such an arrangement. It allows the mail to flow into the mailroom in an orderly fashion, and it provides for the proper step-by-step processing of the incoming mail. It reduces the confusion by providing a specific space for mail that may arrive later in the day, when there is likely to be more activity in other parts of the mailroom.

The usual arrangement for handling incoming mail efficiently consists of *a dumping area*, *a primary sorting area* which will lead to *a reading area* (if necessary), *a secondary sorting area*, and (possibly) an *opening station*. This provides a smooth flow of the mail into, through, and out of the mailroom with a minimum of wasted effort and space. Incoming mail should be analyzed carefully, and if the volume warrants, then "flats" (9 x 12 inch envelopes), "white" mail (#6¾ and #10 business envelopes), incoming advertising leads, accounts receivable, and other types of identifiable mail should be processed separately in order to provide better service in less time.

Receiving Your Mail

How you receive your mail from the Postal Service will, to a large extent, govern how you should plan your processing of incoming mail. The Postal Service processes letter-size mail separately from large flat envelopes that measure 9 x 12 inches and larger. In a post office they are separated early in the processing cycle and kept separate right up until the time they are delivered to you. Therefore, you will usually get your #10 business-size envelope letter mail (the "white" mail) in trays or bundles, with flats kept separate. You should process yours the same way, even perhaps in separate sorting bins because of the different sizes.

You should be sure to take full advantage of the separations that the USPS makes when it delivers the mail to your office. You should make sure someone isn't dumping all the mail together again, for it will usually be "faced" (with all of the addresses facing the same way) when you receive it.

Again, depending on the kind of mail that you receive from the Postal Service, whether it is in a bundle, a tray, or a hamper, there are advantages to using an advance deposit or trust account to prepay *postage due mail* as well as for *business reply mail*. If your postage due amounts to approximately $10 or more every 60 days, you will be allowed to make an advance deposit at the post office (see *DMM, Sec. 146.33, Collection of Postage Due*). The mail will be delivered to you with all postage due charges paid out of the advance deposit. This eliminates one of your clerks from having to run all over the office looking for $8.77 in cash (since postage and meter stamps are not acceptable for postage due mail).

Controlling Incoming Mail

At this point, consider what you might do to control the manner in which you receive your mail. The first area you might explore is the method and time of day that you receive it from the Postal Service. In order to receive your mail earlier you might consider switching to a post office box. Your local post office staff will be able to advise you the earliest time that your mail would be ready for pick up in contrast to having a carrier bring it to your office. If it is not convenient to have an employee pick up your mail at the post office, you are permitted to have it picked up by a messenger. (The *DMM* explains the requirements for allowing someone other than an employee to pick up your mail.)

If you are using a post office box address, one of your employees, or a messenger, may pick up your mail at a *caller window* or at the back platform. The *DMM* explains the details of such arrangements (*Section 965*) and your local post office can provide the current charges.

Then there are several methods for having the Postal Service separate your incoming mail. You might explore the possibility of utilizing more than one post office box, or post office boxes at more than one station or branch post office. For example, a service organization may use a special post office box to cull out all of the previous day's service tickets for posting to customer account cards and for immediate invoicing.

Another method is extremely effective when you are providing return envelopes, especially if the USPS gives you the mail in trays. Envelopes may be printed with different colored borders on one or more sides for rapid identification and separation from the rest of the mail. Also, envelopes may be constructed of light-colored paper to provide a quick visual separation.

Examine your own situation, and ask yourself if your organization is getting its mail in the most expeditious manner possible and what could be done *internally* to improve those conditions. Then sit down with someone from your local post office and discuss your *present* postal service and what service you believe might be more helpful. Only then will you be getting the best possible incoming mail service.

Tracking Incoming Mail

It is very important that you maintain records that will accurately reflect the volume of your incoming mail. As a long-range control device, you must have the history of the mail volume to properly evaluate the personnel, the space, and the equipment needed for incoming mail. The *Quarterly Mailroom Analysis*, shown in *Chapter 13*, will help you maintain those records. The details and frequency of the records should be customized to your particular needs and generally related to the annual growth of your organization.

Many organizations weigh the incoming mail to determine the piece count, and this can be used as an accurate gauge to keep track of your present volume and future needs. At the same time, some organizations will use those figures to obtain piece counts for incentive pay. Even larger quantities of "white" mail containing miscellaneous correspondence can be accurately counted for your purposes. In addition, an even greater degree of accuracy is possible with large quantities of incoming payments contained in uniform envelopes provided by your organization when the statements are sent out.

At least one vendor (Omation Corporation, 253 Polaris Avenue, Mountain View, CA 94043-4514, telephone 415-966-1396) sells equipment that will count a wide variety of envelope sizes, cards, and folded forms. Several models are available, some with printing capability. With through-put speeds of up to 30,000 per hour with only one operator, such equipment may be a great asset in maintaining volume records of incoming mail, as well as in a variety of other tasks.

Organizations that receive a large number of parcels will often spot-check the zone, weight, and rate used on incoming parcels. With the cost of postage or other shipping charges being passed on to you on many invoices, there can be a sizable amount of excess charges included as a result of sloppy weighing, inaccurate rates, and/or inaccurate scales being used by a vendor. Usually, if several tests prove that a company is weighing and rating a few parcels accurately, they will generally be accurate. On the other hand, overcharges caused by a vendor's unskilled mailroom personnel and inaccurate scales are likely to continue indefinitely until major changes are made in *their* mail preparation habits. Most vendors will probably welcome your complaints, for they never know whether the errors are in their favor or if they, too, are often losing money on a shipment.

Priority of Incoming Mail

Depending on the size of your organization, it is usually advantageous to work incoming mail on somewhat of a priority basis whenever all of the mail cannot be distributed on the first internal delivery. Whenever it is possible to quickly deliver a large volume of incoming orders or checks, for example, to a point where they will receive immediate action, it is very desirable to give those items priority service. Such a system might have a dramatic effect on the turnaround time of orders or, in the case of incoming checks, the daily cash flow. Therefore, analyze white mail carefully and look for ways to speed up the delivery of such items as incoming orders, checks, sales leads, advertising inquiries, and financial documents.

After processing the white mail, the flats or kraft mail must be given special attention, and if you are receiving mail from branch offices in flats they should have some readily recognized mark or code on them so that branch communications may be moved quickly into the internal distribution system. A well-marked envelope for interbranch use is essential.

Many daily newspapers are an important part of the business day. Your mailroom staff should recognize that many executives depend on the *Wall Street Journal* or the *Journal of Commerce* for important daily information and those newspapers must move promptly. Whenever all the mail cannot be processed for the first delivery, few executives will tolerate not receiving those two papers. But you will have to evaluate the time needed to process many newspapers against the value of having all of the orders reach the shipping department immediately or all of the checks reaching the accounts receivable department rapidly.

Most magazines received in the mailroom for the employees are sent as free subscriptions to qualified individuals. They are largely devoted to a specific skill or science and carry informative advertising important to the particular field involved. Often, such magazines may appear to be a burden to the mailroom personnel. Some well-meaning mailroom managers have even questioned if they should process so many magazines. But the professional mail manager should recognize that those magazines provide important industry-oriented information to the recipient and are therefore very beneficial to the organization, not just to the addressee. No organization should ever divert such magazines or try to discourage the employees from receiving them, for they provide a valuable source of current data, and every attempt should be made to deliver them throughout the organization.

Parcels received from the Postal Service, UPS, RPS or others should be carefully examined to determine if they could be handled better in the area of shipping and receiving, rather than the mailroom. Depending on the nature of the apparent contents, and their weight, parcels may be handled efficiently along with the other mail if the volume isn't too great. But if large parcels are the rule rather than the exception, it is usually best to provide parcel delivery *after* the white and kraft mail has been distributed. This is another area where accurate records, providing both average weights and the number of pieces, are essential to a complete analysis of the situation and the most efficient method of delivery.

Accountable Mail

Financial institutions have an expression that clearly identifies the importance of certain mail and the necessity for its careful processing. They call financial documents *accountable mail*, and that is a good expression to use in any mailroom to stress the fact that certain mail requires special controlled handling.

Depending on the quantities of registered, certified, and overnight air express mail that your mail center may receive, you will want to establish a series of controls to assure delivery to the addressee without loss and at the same time maintain records that will substantiate the delivery later. If such items are rarely received in your mailroom, then you may wish to send them out by the regular mail clerk and obtain receipts as needed. In another case, you may wish to telephone the addressee and require that the mail stay in the custody of the mailroom supervisor until picked up. In situations where there are considerable quantities of registered, certified, and overnight air express mail, a special messenger can be assigned to the task of delivering the accountable mail, and you may even want the messenger to be bonded. (See Accounting Systems in Chapter 16.)

Keep in mind that the sender pays an extra fee on Express Mail delivered by the Postal Service directly to your organization, and that should not mean dumping it in the door of a mailroom! *Inside* delivery is also a feature of all of the other overnight air express companies, so they should not dump on you either. Actually it is a policy *you* should control. If you have no problem with overnight carriers delivering to specific rooms throughout your building, *then you should require that deliveries are made as addressed.* On the other hand, if you think you can provide some additional security, and want the responsibility for seeing that the overnight envelopes and packages are delivered to individual addressees promptly, *then you should enforce a rule that all overnight deliveries are to come to the mail center.* Whichever way you wish deliveries to arrive, you should teach everyone in your organization to have incoming overnight shipments addressed accordingly, either showing the room number and floor location of the addressee, or the intended recipient's name, care of the mail center and its location.

Establishing Incoming Mail Flow

All of those factors are just some of the many ingredients that make up the incoming mail processing operation. The next step is to begin to establish the actual mail flow.

When you set up the dumping area, which would be more appropriately called a staging area for mail shouldn't be *dumped* anywhere, make sure there is ample room to accommodate the mail on the days when the volume is the heaviest. Think of the dumping section as a kind of primary sorting area. Allow sufficient room to provide easy separation of white mail from all other mail. Allow space to move the flats, magazines, and newspapers directly into their sorting area in an even flow. If you decide to process the white mail separately, with larger bins for flats (as the Postal Service does), make sure that the sorting bins allow for an even flow from the dumping tables to the primary sorting area.

The primary sorting area is also where you begin to discourage *personal mail* from entering your mail stream, whether it be inbound or outgoing. Unless you are completely isolated from all other postal services, personal mail has no place in any organization's operations. Employees should be discouraged from receiving either personal letters, non-business magazines, or parcels at a mailroom that serves an entire organization.

Internal Mail Codes

Special envelopes for special applications can lighten your sorting chores considerably. In addition to the colored edges, the light-colored envelopes, and the extra post office boxes, you may find that your organization can benefit greatly from a *mail code*. Many large organizations use a code to identify the mail's final destination rapidly, just as a ZIP Code is used by the Postal Service. It is likely that the first question you will ask is what percentage of incoming mail will actually include the internal code and help reduce sorting time. Mail managers who have instituted such programs have reported that with a good interoffice publicity program it doesn't take as long as one might think. It is helpful if the code is based on actual, physical circumstances. For example, a large bank in Boston uses a code that designates the building, the floor, and the mail station so that a code of *HO-7-J* is mail stop *J* on the *7th floor* in the *headquarters* building. Simple yet definitive.

After you select the code you wish to institute, start your publicity campaign and remember to stress the benefits for the *recipient*, not the mailroom. Emphasize that the mailroom can provide more accurate and quicker distribution to *everyone*; the fact that it will be easier for your mail center staff isn't important to the users of the mail within the organization. After several notices and posters have been distributed with instructions on using the code, set a date to begin. At the same time, you obviously will need to have a directory published showing the mail codes, and this is usually incorporated into the internal telephone book. With top management's endorsement, you should not have any problems. It will not take as long as you may think. Remember, about 99 percent of First-Class Mail shows a ZIP Code in the address, and it is not even mandatory.

The Postal Service has long offered to provide 10 or more ZIP+4 codes to organizations receiving a certain amount of incoming mail every day. It has emphasized the versatility of ZIP+4 Codes as a means of internally sorting your incoming mail. Some mail managers have expressed doubt about the real assistance such codes would add to sorting. They think it is just as easy and quick to sort to the "sales department," for example, as to memorize which last two digits are assigned to sales. This may be true, so there are pros and cons of promoting the ZIP+4 Code as a sorting tool for incoming mail.

But there is an unknown factor involved! For the technology in the Postal Service to leap from being able to read only the last line on an envelope (when the ZIP+4 program began) to the present capability of reading an area 4 x 10½ inches is somewhat incredible. You will recall that now the USPS is working with an Advanced Bar Code (ABC) which translates the address information into a *delivery bar code.* Experimental offices have been set up so that carriers receive their mail *already in delivery sequence through the extensive use of automated equipment.* The Postal Service has stated that it expects to have over 5,000 delivery unit bar code sorters in operation by 1995 to accomplish this process in many delivery units. Some mail managers have speculated that sooner or later the Postal Service will offer organizations an opportunity to have their *incoming* mail presorted to a series of ZIP+4 codes, and that appears to be a logical course of future events. As soon as all of the kinks are out of the process of sequencing the mail for the carriers, there is likely to be some additional time available on the bar code sorters. With such high-speed equipment, the USPS could sort your incoming letter mail into several groups if you desired, much faster than you could, and charge you a fee to do it. The Postal Service would have added revenue, and a larger return on its investment, but still save you money over costly hand sorting. While highly speculative, it is something worth considering if you are examining all of the alternatives of an internal mail code.

Locator Systems

Hand in hand with the considerations of using an internal mail code go the methods used to locate people within your organization. This situation is much like group attempts to decide on mail classification. No organization can afford to have three or four mail sorters gather in the middle of the floor to try to decide to which room Mary Smith or Joe Brown has recently moved. The degree of sophistication needed will depend on the percentage of turnover and moving in your organization and on the total number of people whom you may serve. Usually, anyone relying on an organization's telephone book as a locator is wasting a great deal of time.

The very least that you can get along with is one of the small card systems where the card has holes cut out at the bottom for attaching to a guide or circular holder. The most well-known is probably *Rolodex*, and they make several sizes that are available wherever stationery supplies are sold.

To create such a system, you simply prepare a card for each person receiving mail within your organization and identify his or her location. (Continuous-form cards for data processing printers are available to fit the rotary files.) Additions, changes, and deletions might be supplied by the personnel department, and could include outside forwarding addresses. Ease in updating is the most important feature of any locator system and is essential to smooth mail sorting without wasted time.

With the widespread use of video display terminals and personal computers, an electronic locator system can be set up without a great deal of difficulty. Even the most humble software usually has a *search* command that allows the PC cursor to locate any item on a list. All you need do is establish a list of names with room or location numbers. Then establish some sort of system to be sure and receive additions (new employees), changes (moves to a different location), and deletions (resignations or retirees), and you will be all set. With five minutes of training, any novice on your staff could locate anyone in the organization. (And you would be able to use the PC on all of the other applications available for the mailroom.) If you have extensive data processing in your organization, your programming people could probably expand your locator system to achieve anything you believe essential. But you will want to keep it simple if you expect everyone in the mailroom to use it.

Opening Mail

If you visited a hundred organizations you would be likely to find that the task of opening the mail is handled a hundred different ways. In a small independent office or a small branch office, a senior secretary may open all envelopes unless they are marked confidential and then distribute the mail to a series of "in" boxes. In an organization with a considerable number of checks being received from customers, the manager of accounting may not want *anyone* opening mail that is returned in courtesy envelopes, except the accounting staff. If large numbers of orders are received daily, the sales manager may feel the same way about incoming orders. In other firms, the mail is quickly and efficiently opened in the mail center, placed right back into the mail trays it arrived in, and then rushed to the accounting or sales departments.

So, while opening mail in the mail center is often a controversial subject, you should remember that one operator can achieve a throughput of about 30,000 envelopes an hour with an automatic mail opener equipped with a power stacker. That saves an enormous amount of time, and it should not be ignored whenever there is a relatively high volume of similar size envelopes arriving frequently. Few organizations may want ordinary cor-respondence opened, but a wise mail manager will be sure to keep man-agement aware of those potential savings. It is equally important to remember that when the mail is opened quickly it allows other workers to begin to process the mail earlier.

Reading Stations

Every organization receives some ambiguously addressed mail that must be opened and read to determine who in the organization should receive it. This reading operation is a "sit-down" operation and may often be set up with staff readers facing each other, using a common section of sorting bins open on both sides and accessible to both readers. Depending on the volume of the mail that must be read, and the mail that must be given directory service, the locator system might logically be a part of the reader's responsibilities. Especially designed desks are available that provide a few sorting bins and room for a video display terminal, or some sort of manual locator system.

Most professional mail supervisors believe that time-stamping the mail is a waste of time and serves only as an alibi for poor handling. In the case of mail that has to be read, however, it may be desirable to use a time stamp. This not only dates the mail, but it also indicates that it was necessary to read the mail, and identifies the station where it was read. The imprint of the time stamp might even incorporate a distribution list showing all of the departments within the organization and serve to direct the mail to its proper department.

Secondary Sorting

Obviously, every organization does not require secondary sorting, for the first sort may direct the mail directly to its final destination. In many situations, however, mail that was originally separated by general product divisions, for example, will need to be broken down to a much finer sort before delivery to the mail stations in the various divisions. The same situation may also occur when sorting for various departments or for sever-al different buildings. Providing sufficient sorting bins to separate this mail accurately and thoroughly is a very important function of the incoming mail operation and should not be neglected because of space or budget restrictions.

Needless to say, if you are managing a truly large operation and are involved in machine presorting or prebarcoding, that equipment can probably help you with the incoming mail. But, because of the high cost, you are unlikely to justify its use solely for incoming mail.

Plastic Bin Labels

If you walk into some mail centers you will be amazed at what passes for bin labels. Often they are handwritten in ink, or even pencil, and sometimes scratched out with a new title scrawled on top of an old dirty card. Instead, you should provide clean, easy-to-read bin labels if you want to receive the maximum return from the people who do your mail sorting. Admittedly, most clerks will memorize a case (of bins) eventually. But they can hardly be expected to sort mail accurately, at the highest possible speed, if the bin labels are small, dirty, nearly illegible pieces of paper. Also, training a new clerk becomes a real chore when the bins are not clearly marked.

Several manufacturers make hand-held embossers that allow you to emboss colored pressure-sensitive 3/8-inch tape with easy to read raised white letters. New clean bin labels will improve both the speed and accuracy of your mail sorting and readily allow substitutes to work the bins when the regular clerk is absent. The tape embossers are available anywhere that stationery supplies are sold.

Analyzing Incoming Mail

You should establish a file for everything that pertains to the incoming mail operation and develop other files for both the internal operation and the outgoing mail. Then if you make an annual survey to look for hidden problems, you will be able to eliminate many of them before they appear. This file should be a reference for anything from records of volume on peak days versus other days to manufacturer's literature on locator systems. It should also include a running log of potential trouble spots or areas that you suspect will need improvement soon. These facts are essential to evaluating your incoming mail operation and will become very valuable in convincing management of the need for such things as additional sorting bins or a larger dumping table.

INTERNAL MAIL

It is difficult to pick the exact spot where the incoming mail process stops and the internal distribution system takes over. But since the delivery of the mail and collection from within the organization are usually thought of as *internal mail processing,* it seems logical to discuss some of the finer points of distribution within the framework of internal mail processing.

Whether you have inherited an internal distribution system or are not satisfied with your present system, the first step toward analyzing the system is to send out some version of the mail service survey shown in *Chapter 13.* The form asks the members of your organization to pinpoint specific problems in the mail distribution operation. In addition to the problem areas that you discover through the survey, you probably will identify other improvements which you can work toward at the same time. As in the case with several other mailroom areas, you should make sure that your distribution routes are checked at least every six months. Make sure that they are serving the volume of mail and customers with the maximum service affordable.

You will want to stay flexible and adjust the routes whenever changes in the location of key offices or the volume of mail demands different distribution patterns. Work toward determining the minimum number of stops that will adequately serve the personnel who are receiving the mail. Keep in mind that *there is considerable prestige connected with a mail stop* and do not become swayed by everyone who states that a stop is essential. Remember you will have to sort to every stop, and that can become expensive if overdone. Make a point to spot-check the volume of mail received at each point or mail stop, but be alert for realistic complaints. You will soon have the best distribution system for your particular organization.

Remember, if you are serving a medium-sized organization, your problems are much like those of a very small city. You have mail to deliver in the town that originates outside the system, and you must deliver mail between points within the town. And, your problems will be in direct proportion to the size of the town.

If yours is a small organization, be careful that you have not grown larger than you realize and actually do need a distribution *system* even though you are relatively small. A pass-it-on approach to mail handling in any but the very smallest organization can be a very poor method of communication. Many organizations have a series of sorting bins and require the various offices to pick up their own mail (like a small town). But, this can become very expensive when you consider all of the time that may be wasted going to and from the mail center. One mail clerk delivering mail may be much less costly than having 16 well-paid secretaries going back and forth all day to pick up the mail.

Utilizing Schedules

After you have investigated all of the possibilities in your distribution system, you should make sure that the entire schedule is well publicized. A well-announced mail program will avoid unfair criticism in mail delays and eliminate the practice of asking route clerks to wait for mail. Obviously, you must base your schedules on when you receive incoming mail and the time necessary to guarantee that your outgoing mail meets Postal Service transportation requirements. Perhaps you need your own mail-oriented newsletter to publicize the pickup and delivery schedules at each mail stop.

Internal Mail Routes

After you have determined the best locations for the mail stops and have established the schedules, you will want to examine a few details of handling mail en route. Depending, of course, on the total number of routes and the number of runs, you should attempt to have as much sorting done en route as possible. For example, suppose you have three runs a day and seven routes. If the messengers can have all of the mail sorted to the other six routes by the time they return to the mailroom, a great deal of time may be saved by simply exchanging the groups of mail. This consumes time en route but it's certainly superior to having seven route clerks return and dump all of the internal mail onto a single table. While working the mail en route requires very little extra time, it will require some extra space on each mail cart.

Another detail to pay attention to involves the mixing of internal mail with outgoing mail. Unless the mail cart is crowded to capacity, it is usually wise to keep all outgoing mail separate and to keep any branch office mail out of the regular mail. Even flats should be kept apart from the white mail for faster handling in the mailroom. And how many times do you have to face mail? Try to teach your route clerks to keep the mail faced *as it is picked up*. It is a simple thing to do and an easy habit to acquire. This will save a great deal of handling time when it finally gets to the mailroom. In most cases, depending on the type of mail, there is no reason why administrative people cannot keep mail faced from the very beginning!

If it is not possible to bring the mail into the mail center with some degree of sortation having already taken place, you may find that the use of sorting bins that are open *on both ends* provides an ideal way to redistribute internal mail. If this is the kind of operation your particular circumstances dictate, you might try having mail sorted into one side of the redistribution table and picked up for delivery on the other side of the sorting table in a *pass-through* fashion. This will keep your route people out of the sorting area, and yet they can pick up their own mail for redistribution on their particular routes. Commercial sorting bins are available that have clear plastic backs held shut with magnets, like any ordinary cabinet door. These allow fast sorting from the open side but easy access at the back for the route clerks.

You may also wish to emulate the Postal Service, particularly when sorting flats. The USPS uses small (venetian blind size) weighted ropes hanging down the middle of the rear of a row of bins that have no back on them. As the flat mail is sorted into the bins the rope keeps the mail from slipping out the back of the bin. Then a distribution clerk can easily and quickly remove the mail from the *rear* of the sorting bin without disturbing the person doing the sorting. If you wish to have such a row of sorting bins constructed, ask your postmaster to show you exactly what one looks like.

Internal Mail Envelopes

Because there is such a wide variety of envelopes available for internal mail handling, there should be one type that is exactly suited to your particular organization regardless of the kinds of material normally transmitted internally. Three or four pieces of paper stapled together with a name scrawled in one corner is no way to send messages and mail through an internal mail system. Both single and stapled sheets are somewhat difficult because single sheets must be separated carefully, and the staples in multiple sheets catch on each other. Nevertheless, they are a necessary evil when notices are frequently sent throughout an organization. You should at least coordinate with the print shop to see that the address labels (which most often are on some sort of computerized list) are always applied in the same place on the memorandums. In all other instances you should forbid loose papers in the internal mail system and require the use of interoffice envelopes.

If you are like most organizations, there will be occasions when *everyone* in the organization is to receive a memorandum, and the departments and executives that might use this type of communication should be aware of your capability to deliver *unaddressed memorandums*. This relieves the originator of having to bother with addressing such notices. However, for this to work smoothly for your route clerks you should provide them with a list showing the number of notices that should be dropped off at each mail stop. The other alternative is to address a single memorandum to department heads and indicate on the address label the number of copies for each office.

The most convenient envelope to both use and process is a 9 x 12 inch or 10 x 13 inch envelope, printed with from 24 to 36 address blocks on its face and a button-and-tie closure. Most have rows of holes punched in the envelope to show whether or not a document is in the envelope. This type is simple for the originator to address (*Mary Brown, Room 6289*, for example), will accept flat unfolded sheets, and is easy to sort and distribute. The buttons and strings do catch on each other occasionally, but this is a small problem compared to the versatility of the envelope and the multiple use it can receive.

Other organizations prefer an envelope similar to the press-and-seal sandwich bags made of clear plastic. These clear vinyl envelopes are usually available in a variety of sizes from your favorite envelope sales representative as are several other types of internal distribution envelopes.

Depending on the nature of your organization and its business activity, your executives may desire some type of confidential envelope for use within the internal mail system. Some organizations utilize a #9 envelope with an opaque design printed on the inside (such as a bank might use) with *"Confidential"* printed conspicuously on the front and back. The #9 envelope will fit whatever type of internal envelope you may be using, and the users of your system will enjoy complete privacy. Obviously, if a customer's confidential artwork or next year's marketing plans pass through the system frequently, larger confidential envelopes would be a good investment. Once again you should call on your envelope specialist to answer your needs.

Analyzing Internal Mail

If your internal mail distribution system has problem areas, you should review the entire operation and see exactly where the trouble spots are located. There are many factors that influence internal mail, and these should be examined systematically if you are to have the best possible internal mail service. (You should also refer to the section on conveyor systems for internal mail distribution in *Chapter 16.*) The following checklist will help you track down potential problem spots:

[ ] How many routes are necessary?
[ ] How many stops are necessary?
[ ] How many daily runs are necessary?
[ ] How much volume per run?
[ ] How early should the first run be scheduled?
[ ] How late should the last run be scheduled?
[ ] Would internal collection boxes help?
[ ] Are mail codes desirable?
[ ] Would pass-through sorting be helpful?
[ ] Would more security be desirable?
[ ] Is mail being sorted en route?
[ ] Are special messengers necessary?

OUTGOING MAIL

In most organizations, much of the daily effort of the employees literally winds up in the mailroom at the end of a busy day. Regardless of how significant or how trivial, each piece of mail is vital, and poor handling can lead to untold aggravation. Each and every piece of mail is important to the welfare of the organization and deserves the very best handling. Delays in handling important documents can cause financial loss or penalties, customer complaints, poor relations with members or customers, and wasted time and money. Therefore, the importance of the outgoing mail system should be emphasized both to management and to those who handle the outgoing mail.

Because of the importance of outgoing mail, all addresses must be accurate and properly formatted. Mail that arrives in the mailroom for dispatch and is improperly addressed--absent ZIP Codes, for instance, should be returned to the originator for correction. If that is not practical, at least the offense should be brought to the attention of a responsible person in the originator's office. The mailroom personnel should never correct or add ZIP Codes because then your people become responsible if the letter is undeliverable-as-addressed.

At the same time, a daily check of the mail will usually reveal any envelopes that are overstuffed and that your experience tells you are not likely to survive the USPS mail processing. Or, you may see window envelopes with the addresses slipping from view or single sheets of paper in 9 x 12 inch envelopes. All of these examples require that you help the originators prepare their mail better. If such poorly prepared mail doesn't make the trip, you can bet you'll hear about it, so you may as well help before the problem arises. This also substantiates why you should have the option of reviewing all types of new envelopes before they are adopted and make sure there are enough different types of envelopes to serve everyone's individual needs.

This, of course, indicates the need to fold material whenever possible. In this way, you can save on postage costs, receive better mail service for white mail than for those envelopes which may look (and travel) like third-class mail, and avoid the oversize surcharge.

Controlling Mail Classification

You will need to establish a series of guidelines within your organization to control classification decisions if you are to receive the correct rates and services desired. It is highly unlikely that you will be able to get all of the administrative people to make the correct decisions. They simply are not trained to do so. But you can help by furnishing them with a small guide, customized to their own needs, that lists your organization's types of mail and the appropriate classes of mail as described in *Chapter 7.*

Next, assume authority for the classification of mail and be responsible for the proper class for each type of mail. If you need something printed, you simply tell the printer what you want. You need not ask what kind of printing plate is to be used or what kind of ink. In a similar vein, administrative or executive personnel who are not well versed in mail services (much less classification) should not dictate which class of mail or special service to use. Instead, try to teach them to request the *kind of delivery* they need, not the service. For example, instead of asking for registered mail, they should simply state that the letter is not valuable but that a receipt for delivery should be obtained. (Of course, you would then use certified mail instead of the more expensive registered mail.) In another example, they may ask for Priority Mail with special delivery to a business address about 900 miles away when what they really want is next-day or second-day delivery.

Obviously, if you are to assume the responsibility for mail classification, then you must study and understand it. In addition to the publications discussed in this book, be sure you get to know an authority at your local postal facility who is dependable for backup information. If you are in charge of a very large operation with a wide variety of mail, you may find it worthwhile to track down the name of a classification expert you can telephone in a real emergency.

Establishing Outgoing Mail Flow

As is the case with incoming mail, outgoing mail must be organized step-by-step so that each function provides the service you need in your particular organization, and the result is a smooth overall system with a good even flow of mail. Whether your mailroom is square, oblong, or L-shaped, you should be able to maintain your operations so that the mail flows in an orderly fashion from one processing station to the next.

There is such a wide variety of outgoing mail in most mailrooms that it is difficult to describe a "typical" situation. If there are three large inserters preparing outgoing First-Class permit mail, then that is a complete system in itself. In that case the flow should be set up so that both the materials being inserted (with an ample staging area) and the sealed envelopes flow into and out of the inserters as smoothly as possible. In other cases, you may have one large inserter handling third-class bulk mail and, at the same time, a medium to heavy load of general mail that will have to be processed in several steps. Then the *sequence of events* should rule. Sorting or batching for branch offices, weighing, metering, and sealing, followed by bundling or placing the mail in trays should all be done in a continuous smooth line, one function after another.

Sorting Outgoing Mail

Outgoing mail should be broken down to two basic areas, classes of mail and branch or interoffice mail. Mail going to customers, suppliers, and others should be sorted by class of mail and then broken down further for any special services that are required. At the same time, the professional mail clerks will use a separate plastic USPS tray for First-Class Mail obviously weighing *less* than one ounce plus another tray (or bin) for other First-Class Mail that will require weighing. In some cases it may be possible for the route clerks to keep one ounce First-Class Mail in a separate group as it is collected from each station.

Incidentally, the recommended method for handling a mixture of weights is to weigh *all of the mail*, sorting it into progressively heavier weight groups, and then run all of each weight group with one setting of the meter. In this manner you will avoid changing the meter every time you stamp a letter. Weighing random weight letters and meter stamping them one at a time is usually much more time consuming.

Sorting bins are required for each kind of mail as it arrives in the mail center during the day. These need to be as versatile as your outgoing mail, with a bin for every type and class of mail. The bins must be large enough to hold all of the mail on the heaviest day so this is an area that may require monitoring from time to time. If you end up with more than one tray of First-Class Mail at the end of the day, you may wish to investigate several wooden (home-made) supports that slant the trays slightly toward the back so that mail stays stacked upright when it is placed in the tray.

This staging area should be the beginning of the flow of the outgoing mail unless some folding and inserting proceeds it. This area of consolidation should be to the left of the scales and the mailing machines so as to provide an even flow from left to right. The mail then passes through the mailing machine and into bundles for mail bags or into trays. Smooth left-to-right processing will help eliminate confusion, will increase production, and will help utilize all of the available mailroom space.

Branch Office Sorting

A completely separate sorting operation is usually necessary for mail destined to branches or other divisions of the organization. It is normally set up as 9 x 12 inch bins, for much of the mail may arrive in the mail center flat, and much of it is classed as First-Class Mail. Some type of reusable envelope, such as a zippered nylon bag, is very desirable at this point. Some organizations that use paper envelopes pre-address them and stack them on the bottom of each bin where they are readily available at the close of the day. In any event, you may want to review *Chapter 6* to be sure you have the best possible container for your particular branch office needs.

In addition to receiving special attention to the container, interoffice mail should also receive extra care in rating and applying postage. Most branch or interoffice mail has a high degree of visibility, and errors here may be unduly emphasized and perhaps blown out of proportion. You must not let careless mistakes in interoffice mail give your entire operation a bad name. On the other hand, if you give such mail the special care that it deserves, the mail system will be held in high esteem throughout the organization.

In another area, your staff should be taught to pay special attention to the address format, for mis-addressed interoffice mail is sure to incur the wrath of the recipient and perhaps others. If you do not utilize a reusable pouch, then explore the small additional cost of having large kraft envelopes (with green diamonds, of course) *printed* with big bold addresses for your branch offices at the same time the return address is printed. But try to avoid rubber stamps for imprinting branch addresses. A poorly stamped envelope with faint letters can easily be misdirected.

Weighing Operation

The next station in the processing flow is the weighing operation, and this is a very important function that can become quite expensive if not properly set up. If all of the mail can be weighed in a few minutes, 5 or 10 at the most, then perhaps a mail scale mounted on a shelf near the mailing machine is a satisfactory arrangement. But if your mail requires a longer period of weighing, it may be to your advantage to allow the operator to sit down and weigh the mail (for greater accuracy!). A table with ample work space on both sides of the scale may sound elementary, but it isn't always provided. As is the case in other mail operations, crowded conditions might save a little floor space, but you will pay a dear price for it if there is insufficient space to properly rate the mail--especially if it occasionally slips to the floor or becomes intermixed, and this is doubly true when weighing international mail.

Internal Postal Accounting

Twenty or thirty years ago you would often see a clipboard hanging near the postage meter with a hand-drawn form with several columns on it. Postage charges were determined by reading the ascending register before and after a batch of mail was processed. As cost centers became more prevalent, a few computerized accounting systems appeared in the 70's. But they were nothing like the sophisticated postage charge-back systems available today from several postage meter manufacturers.

These computer-like modules capture the total pieces and dollars by department, by class of mail, and provide totals for all departments. Some systems can keep records for up to 2,000 departments and for 40 different classes of mail.

Keeping a record of postage costs by departments is smart, but only if someone is actually going to use the data for budget planning purposes. If individual departments are not required to forecast their postage expenses by the quarter or annually, or if nothing happens when a department budget has a large over-run, it is a waste of time to keep such records. This is another area where data is often collected but no one ever actually puts the information to use.

To verify the need for such systems you need to gently ask management "why?" about five times. Otherwise you will be burdened with extra work (collecting the data), and no one will use it.

Applying Postage

Once the mail has been weighed, it is ready for postage. In all likelihood you are using a postage meter. Whether or not you value the many other features of metered mail isn't as important as the need to rapidly seal the mail and bypass the cancelling operation. The relatively low cost of an automatically fed mailing machine shrinks even further in relation to the many years of service it will offer and the ever-increasing cost of mailroom labor. Again, whether it is on a table or some type of stand, make sure there is ample space around the machine to properly handle the mail without it slipping to the floor.

It is very important that you have a *legible* meter stamp on all of your mail and that the date is the date it will reach the post office. The Postal Service considers an illegible meter stamp or an incorrect date to be a serious offense and you should impress this fact upon all of the people who operate your mailing machines. If a few pieces of mail with almost illegible imprints are noticed at your post office, you might get a telephone call. If a lot of mail with almost illegible imprints is noticed, you might get your mail back. And you will definitely get it back if a large number of pieces (like a tray full or more) are noticed with the wrong date in the imprint. You will be asked to meter stamp the mail (with the meter set on zero) on the back of each envelope to show the correct date of mailing, and usually you will have to pick it up!

You can avoid all of those inconveniences in several ways. If you have one or more supervisors, make it their responsibility to monitor the print quality of the mailing machine and to change the date daily. If you have an "early-bird" clerk, the one who likes to beat everyone else to work, assign the monitoring and date changing to that person. In other mail centers, the regular operators are *held responsible* for both the quality of the imprint and the daily date change, but that system is weak whenever the regular operator is ill or on vacation. You can also run afoul of the "today's date" requirements when you have a handful of last minute mail that gets dropped into a collection or office lobby box *after* the last collection. The mail is not picked up until the next day (certainly something you try to avoid), and it has a "stale" date on it.

Postal Service Mail Trays

The best things in life may not be free, but the most useful item in a busy mail center is free. The Postal Service will provide you with heavy duty plastic mail trays suitable for holding about 500 to 600 pieces of letter-size mail, at no charge whatsoever. If you need two trays every Tuesday, they will see that you have them. If you need 200 every Thursday, they'll see that you get those too, and loan you enough large rolling hampers to hold them. And if you are using one of the presort programs, you can obtain fiberboard trays (to preserve the presort) with sleeves. They also hold 500 letters but weigh less when flown to other postal facilities.

Whenever the Postal Service moves a batch of letters within a postal facility, it is always contained in a tray. Mail is cancelled and put in trays, it is taken to the letter sorting machines (LSMs) in trays, and it is removed from the back of the LSMs and put in trays. If it is machinable, it is taken to the OCR machines in trays, and it is taken out of the OCRs after processing and put in trays. And, finally, it is kept in delivery order by the carrier *in a tray*.

You can do the same. You can use trays in the mailroom to accumulate mail after it is inserted, ready to go to the post office. Or, if using a smaller inserter, move the tray right to the mailing machine, meter the envelopes, and stack the mail back into the same tray. Trays help you meet the *requirement* that metered mail be faced. Since metered mail is not cancelled, a tray of mail will go directly to the LSM or, if machinable, to the OCR machines. Incidentally, many postal facilities will pick up a large (3,000 to 5,000 pieces) quantity of mail if you have it ready to go about 3 p.m.

To aid in the handling of USPS trays, several commercial manufacturers provide special carts with casters. Holding anywhere from 5 to 30 trays of mail, these carts are very convenient for processing, storing, or transporting large quantities of letter mail in trays.

When you are on that tour, ask one of the mail handlers how much time it saves when mail is received in trays, versus loose mail or bundles in sacks. They will be quick to tell you that the trayed mail will be dispatched up to *four hours* earlier than non-trayed mail, often meeting earlier truck and plane schedules.

If you simply cannot get trays to your postal facility because of location, lack of transportation, or insufficient volume, you should be sure to *bundle* your mail. Whether you use an occasional mail sack (provided by the USPS) or drop your mail into an office or corner collection box, you should *always* bundle your mail. Metered mail *must* be bundled and faced, but you also need to make separate bundles of the "white" mail and the larger (kraft) flats. Of course, you also will want to bundle separately any third-class flats and First-Class Mail in 9 x 12 inch or larger envelopes. And, it is simple to keep your mail bundled with rubber bands. Bundles are the next best thing to a tray, and they allow the mail handlers to give your metered mail the expedited service it deserves.

Presorting Outgoing Mail

The section on First-Class Mail discounts in *Chapter 7* (along with the *DMM*) should provide you with sufficient information to allow you to choose which level of presorting would be most beneficial to your organization. But there are so many variables in the different programs it is difficult to provide intelligent guidance as to the physical arrangement of space to accomplish the desired presort. In some situations you may need to provide bins to separate the mail as required for the presort. In other cases you may need only to gather up each ZIP group, which may have been sorted by computer software, as it exits from an inserter or mailing machine.

Regardless of the manner in which you accomplish your desired presort, you should be sure to leave adequate space in your mail flow scheme. In most cases that space should be *after* the mailing machine, with the mail passing into trays or being bundled as the presorting is accomplished.

The only suggestion or word of caution for this area is to have some actual experience in your chosen program *before* you allocate any tight space restrictions into your mail flow blueprint. Otherwise, without any actual experience, the sortation and bundling or traying functions may require much more space than originally imagined.

Providing for Parcels

If you have only an occasional parcel to ship, then you only need to provide some of the packaging material discussed earlier and use your regular postage meter for stamping the parcel. However, if your mailroom receives a large number of outgoing parcels, you will find it a worthwhile investment to arrange two lines of mail flow. One will handle the letters and large bulky envelopes, while the other will process only parcels.

In this sort of arrangement you will want to provide a large table for wrapping the parcels without interfering with the other mail. Shipping cartons, packing material, sealing tape dispensers, and address label protective tape should all be conveniently arranged for the people doing the packing and sealing.

After you analyze the types of objects you must pack, you should be confident your package will survive *any* carrier's transportation system. Nevertheless, as a security precaution it is recommended that you have a card or sheet of paper printed with the full name of your organization, your address, and telephone number. Such a card or sheet should be included inside of *every* package you ship in the unlikely event your package is damaged in transit and comes open.

From the packing station, the parcels should flow from left to right to an electronic scale. Most models include every conceivabie rate and allow you to "shop" for the least expensive service.

Preparing Nonpostal Shipments

Much of the design of mail flow and the arrangement of the work tables, machines, and sorting bins depends on the *volume* of each type of mail. This is especially true in arranging the outgoing flow lines. But, if you have more than two or three shipments per day via United Parcel Service, Roadway Package System, or any of the overnight air express carriers, you need a dedicated area for their preparation.

Since all of these types of shipments require some sort of documentation, along with the specific carrier's labels, you should provide either a desk or a table with ample work space. The sit-down operation at a desk may be preferable if you are using a remote video terminal or personal computer to prepare your waybills. But, attaching the waybill labels to cartons and envelopes may require so much moving around, and getting up and down, that a stand-up operation at a table may be better. Such tables are usually 36 inches high, providing a comfortable writing surface so there is no need to bend over a standard 30-inch high desk. But make sure the table corresponds to the height of the clerk.

In addition, this area might contain a typewriter or the printer for a computer, to avoid handwritten waybills, and ample supplies of all types of carrier's waybills and labels, stored in readily accessible boxes or bins. Continuing the flow, there will perhaps be a separate mailing machine with a carrier's register on it instead of a postage meter, or an extra postage meter if you use large quantities of Express Mail. Next to that area there should be bins labeled for each carrier to hold the parcels and overnight envelopes until picked up by the carrier's driver. With such a setup you will find that the drivers will go directly to this area to pickup your outgoing shipments. This will minimize the confusion and disruption in the mailroom as each driver arrives and departs. Also, keep in mind that the closer you keep this final outgoing station to the door that the carrier's drivers use, the less confusion there will be.

That should complete your setup for parcels and overnight shipments. However, while the waybill becomes the shipping label on many overnight and two-day services, you need added protection for an ordinary printed shipping label. An ordinary parcel post or ground service label usually has the shipper's name printed in the upper third and the addressee in the lower two-thirds of the label. This is the type of label that is vulnerable. Dishonest mailroom employees or thieves in transportation systems, working hand in hand with a confederate, have been known to *over-label* parcels just prior to or during shipment. The parcel is then delivered to the confederate at the address shown on the top label and it is almost impossible to trace.

There are two ways to prevent this. One is to apply a pressure-sensitive clear vinyl tape (see *Chapter 6*) over the entire label, which will make an added label quite obvious. The other method is to apply the USPS meter stamp, or a carrier's register tape, *over the top corner of and at a 45 degree angle* to the address label. Then any effort to cover the address label also covers a portion of the meter stamp. Postal Service authorities are aware of the problem of over-labelling, and any parcels observed with labels over the top of meter stamps are immediately brought to the attention of the postal inspectors.

In summary, the outgoing mail flow lines would go first to the packing area and then to the weighing station. Then the flow line would split. One line of flow would go to the documentation or waybill table or desk and end at the bins for each carrier. The other flow line would go either to a separate, tape-only, mailing machine for affixing postage meter stamps to a high volume of USPS shipments or, in the case of a smaller volume, to the central mailing machine for postage.

Cutoff and Dispatch Times

The Postal Service establishes two essential schedules with which you and your staff should be familiar. The first is known as the *cutoff time*. It is when the postal employees are preparing the mail for transit and *cutoff* (or stop) preparing and collecting originating mail for a given departure. This usually occurs 10 or 15 minutes before mail is ready to leave the postal facility. The other schedule is the *dispatch time*, which is the actual scheduled time when the mail is to leave the facility. Many postal facilities will post these times for the information of the public, especially smaller post offices or stations or branches that normally close at the end of the day and perform no actual mail processing.

Your mail should be coordinated with those schedules so that it doesn't arrive at your nearby station or branch post office 10 minutes after the last truck leaves for the nearest processing facility. Your account rep or postmaster will be pleased to provide you with all of the cutoff and dispatch times that might involve your mail. These schedules will then allow you to coordinate your mail preparation with the transportation schedules of the Postal Service. But remember, mailing early always pays dividends. Simply meeting a 2 p.m. dispatch, for example, may enable your mail to be delivered a whole day sooner.

Testing Delivery Schedules

It is important to constantly test all of the transportation systems that you use. You need to ascertain the delivery time required for each destination to which you frequently send mail. Testing should be an integral part of the overall mailroom management process and should be done on a regularly scheduled basis so as to be accurate at all times. When you consider how many transportation changes are made in the various schedules of trains, trucks, and planes, you can understand why testing should be a constant ongoing process.

One simple way to keep up-to-date on First-Class Mail is to examine the postmarks on your incoming mail. You will quickly see exactly how many days it takes mail from each location to reach your mailroom. You and your supervisors should have a general "feel," based on reading actual postmarks, for the average transit time from the principal cities with which your organization corresponds. You may want to check such times once a month and keep a written log of the time. If a continuous problem should develop, the Postal Service would have great respect for your log showing that the transit time had deteriorated badly.

To aid you further in assessing delivery times, several commercial organizations monitor mail for a fee. Those firms are often mentioned in the various mail-oriented newsletters and office publications. One such organization is the U.S. Monitor Service, 86 Maple Avenue, New City, NY 10956-5092, telephone 1-800-767-7967. You might also write to the Direct

Marketing Association, 11 West 42nd Street, New York, NY 10036-8096.

If you have branches out of town you should certainly gather data on transit times and develop a list showing the average time to each branch in both directions. This information can be very valuable in handling inquiries from the entire organization and help reduce unnecessary overnight air express service.

Extraordinary Mailings

In the event of special mailings, which are often done on a one-time or annual basis, such as sending out stockholder's reports, make sure they do not disrupt everything else being handled in the mailroom. When faced with unusually large mailings, some firms contract with the printer to do the complete job, including mailing. If that is not practical, have the originators plan ahead so that the mailroom personnel will know what is coming and will not be hit the same afternoon that there is an unusually heavy volume of other mail. With a little planning there is no reason why a large special mailing has to upset the entire mail system.

PRIVATE EXPRESS STATUTES

In 1710, the *Post Office Act* passed by the British Parliament, which became known as "Queen Anne's Act," strengthened the concepts of a postal *monopoly* for all of her Majesty's dominions, and this included the American colonies. Thus the *Private Express Statutes* were born, and 267 years later, in 1977, a court in New York upheld them as valid and directed an enterprising man and his wife to cease delivering letters in competition with the Postal Service.

The former Post Office Department continually published prohibitions against *"persons engaging in the delivery of letters for compensation."* In 1967, it reminded the public that since the days of the *Articles of Confederation*, the establishment of a *"private express for the conveyance of letters or packets"* was expressly prohibited.

In 1973, the chairman of the Board of Governors of the U.S. Postal Service issued a report on behalf of the board which reaffirmed the necessity to protect the right of the Postal Service to retain a monopoly on the delivery of letters. That report discussed in considerable detail the probability of *"cream skimming competition,"* and gave many logical arguments why the Private Express Statutes should continue to be enforced. In 1974, the Postal Service adopted revised regulations to enforce the Private Express Statutes.

Whether or not you agree with this principle is unimportant. What is important is that you realize the ramifications of the statutes and then decide what manner of compliance might be necessary by your particular mail operation.

What Is a Letter?

Naturally, if the Postal Service has a monopoly on carrying "*letters*," the next question is, "What is the definition of a letter?" The *Domestic Mail Manual* states, "A letter is defined as a message directed to a specific person or address and recorded in or on a tangible object." It goes on to say, "A message consists of any information or intelligence which can be recorded on tangible objects including, but not limited to, paper in sheet or card form, recording disks, and magnetic tapes."

Attempts to completely interpret those words may confuse you, but generally (with a few exceptions), whatever you would normally classify as First-Class Mail would in all probability be called a *letter* for purposes of the Private Express Statutes. Although there are many exceptions and qualifications, the regulations basically narrow down to the fact that letters carried by anyone other than the Postal Service must have postage on them! The principal exceptions cover letters relating to a cargo; letters carried by the senders or the recipients, or *by their regular salaried employees*; and letters carried *to and from a postal facility* where they are to be or have been carried in the U.S. mail. Those are *exceptions*.

In addition to exceptions, there are *suspensions* which are more limited but do allow (under certain conditions) a carrier or mail manager more flexibility. Included in the suspensions are data processing materials, *extremely urgent letters*, and letters carried by universities and colleges for their student and faculty organizations.

Section 112.3 of the *DMM* elaborates on the general coverage of the Private Express Statutes and authoritative advice, including written advisory opinions, may be obtained from the Law Department, U.S. Postal Service, Headquarters, Washington, DC 20260-1100.

MESSENGER AND COURIER SERVICES

Most of the advice in this book deals with sending mail and merchandise out of town, or, if in town, through the USPS, on a non-urgent basis. But special local messengers may be essential from time to time, regardless of the versatility and growing popularity of the fax machine. There will be many times that a fax message will not be suitable for local messages, just as they are not always suitable for long-distance messages. Many fax machines use thermal paper with questionable life expectancy. That may make bond paper delivered by the USPS or a messenger much more desirable for documents that are to be retained as a permanent record. Blueprints, technical drawings and completed government forms are other examples of documents that must bypass a fax machine and be delivered by a messenger.

Depending on the nature of your organization, a *reliable* messenger service can be a valuable asset to any mail center. These messengers will allow you to cope with the demand for same-day service right in your own locality, without running afoul of the Private Express Statutes. In larger cities, businesses that must exchange documents with other organizations almost *have* to rely on a messenger service to enjoy the benefits of same-day service. But, this is another area where testing is essential. It is vital that you know what kind of service you are likely to receive *before* you entrust valuable documents to an unknown messenger. In some cases, you may want to ask for references before you use a new messenger service.

Locating a Messenger Service

This is another time to let your fingers do the walking! The best place to shop for a messenger service is in the *Yellow Pages* of your local telephone directory. Although the headings may vary, they are usually listed either under "*Delivery Services*" or "*Messenger Services*," and there is usually an ample list from which to choose. As you do your selecting you may want to determine if the messengers are bonded.

Courier Services

Also advertised in the *Yellow Pages* are courier services, and these too are often found under the "*Delivery Service*" heading. There is only a fine line between a messenger and a courier, but generally speaking, a messenger is more likely to use a bicycle or motorbike to get around within a single large city. In contrast, a courier may serve several metropolitan areas (or a specific industry such as banking) and use both automobiles and the commercial airlines to deliver your urgent envelope or package.

Regardless of their similarity, there are times you may need both kinds of service, and you should have done some testing, or collected references, long before a crisis erupts.

ADMINISTRATIVE SPACE

You can attend one seminar after another and hear all about the basics of allocating space to each of the various mail center functions. You can read articles about assigning space to each important operation in a mailroom. But you will seldom hear or read about one major mail center function which is vital, and that is the space for the administrative or managerial functions. Yet the larger the mail operation is, the more important this space becomes.

Whatever the title may be, the person who manages the mail center, the one responsible for moving the mail, requires (and deserves) certain fundamental resources. At first glance these resources may seem to be luxuries, but they are not.

The first thing the manager needs is *privacy*. There must be privacy to interview, train, encourage, discipline, and even dismiss employees. Privacy is also needed for telephone conversations, for visiting sales representatives, for maintaining all of the many mailroom records, for studying postal information, and for writing newsletters and reports to management. Even if the staff is small, and part of the time the manager must also perform mail handling tasks, he or she still needs that kind of environment to function with the greatest efficiency.

But that privacy must not be at the expense of a *loss of presence*. That is, however reliable and self-motivated the "workers" may be, the presence of the manager should still be very evident. Therefore, the manager's space *must be* (or certainly should be) enclosed with *glass* partitions which give him or her the opportunity to see the entire mail center at a glance. This arrangement will provide a quiet area in which to perform administrative tasks while allowing the manager to generally oversee the various mailing operations that are taking place. In addition to the concrete advantages of this arrangement, it raises the status of the manager somewhat, in comparison to an old desk shoved into the corner.

It is important too for the mail manager to have access to a full range of office supplies, a file cabinet for maintaining records, and a bookcase for easy access to mail-oriented manuals and loose-leaf binders. These things may seem mundane, but they encourage a systematic method of keeping records and providing the staff with a library of postal and transportation information.

Once the space for manager of the mailroom is established and equipped, you should turn to the need for desks for your supervisors. The ratio of supervisors to general mail clerks is difficult to determine without knowing the scope of the mail operation and the types of mail processed. But a good rule of thumb might be one supervisor for every five or six clerks, or perhaps one for every eight to ten clerks as you approach say a total of 50 employees. Often the deciding factor will be assignment to different functional areas, such as incoming or outgoing mail, or international mail. In any event, the supervisors really need their own desks. That will allow them to keep their own records about their area of expertise, and perhaps a telephone to maintain contact with outside sources of information.

The advantages of supervisors are discussed in detail in *Chapter 17*, but the position of *supervisor* becomes a valuable "carrot" for all of your employees. Therefore, although the desk for the supervisor provides a real benefit to performing his or her job well, it also becomes a status symbol and is an added incentive for the other employees to advance. Admittedly, the space will be difficult to allocate in many mail centers, but that does not diminish its importance.

The final area that needs to be set aside in most mailrooms is one for *personal lockers* for your mail clerks. The advantages are also discussed in *Chapter 17*, for they relate to *morale*. But lockers take up space, so you need to consider them in this section.

You can buy a cabinet of lockers that is only about 15 inches deep and, consequently, will even fit in a hallway if necessary. Some have small 12-inch square lockers, and others contain larger lockers measuring 12 x 36 inches. The lockers are valuable for improving morale, but they provide additional benefits to you for they keep lunches and all kinds of personal gear off of the work tables in the mail center. They help send a strong message that you require the mailroom to be neat and uncluttered.

Once again you can let your fingers do the walking, for the *Yellow Pages* will usually list several sources of lockers. If you are in a smaller city and find no such listings, go to your library and look at the *Yellow Pages* from your nearest large city.

CONTINGENCY PLANS

Whenever an emergency arises that affects the delivery of outbound mail, every mail center should be prepared with well-thought-out contingency plans that provide alternate methods of transporting the mail. Such plans need not be elaborate, but a simple outline of probable actions can be a real lifesaver in the event of storms, fires, strikes, and all the other disasters that can affect mail and parcel delivery. For example, suppose you have branches in Akron, Columbus, and Cleveland, and you mail paychecks to about 100 employees in the three branches. If the checks are normally dispatched to the branch managers on Tuesday for distribution on Friday, you had better have a backup system of transportation when a winter storm dumps 15 inches of snow at your front door Tuesday afternoon and literally stops everything in its tracks. With no plan at all, by the time you begin to make telephone calls looking for an alternate method of shipment, you won't get anything but busy signals. The problem involves getting *what's* needed, *where* it's needed, *when* it's needed, *at the lowest possible cost.* Examine the kinds of mail leaving your organization, determine their urgency, and then establish some sort of contingency plan to help solve problems before they happen. You will be glad you did.

WHAT'S NEW?

Mail processing is one area in which there is *always* something new. Whether it is a new work-sharing program from the Postal Service or new software to make a tedious mailroom job a cinch, there is always something new in mail handling. A professional mail manager should never rest on the merits of the present operation but constantly strive to learn about new methods, new ideas, and new equipment. If a mail manager doesn't stay up-to-date in all of the areas of mail processing discussed here, it is unlikely that his or her organization will have the best possible service at the least cost.

CHAPTER 16

INVESTIGATING MAILROOM EQUIPMENT

It is not the purpose of this chapter to compare one manufacturer's equipment with that of another or to evaluate the features of one product against another. Instead it is an attempt to (1) help you understand the function and benefits of a piece of equipment in the event you are not familiar with it, (2) identify the primary features that would be most important and desirable to a first-time user, (3) identify any problems that are often associated with a specific type of machine, and (4) provide you with all known sources of supply (which a reasonable amount of judicious research has been able to identify) and suggest ways to contact those manufacturers or dealers. It is not, unfortunately, a "buyers' guide" for mailroom equipment. While it is useful to see a chart showing all of the *features* of, say, a folding machine, few individuals or organizations have either the financial support or qualified personnel to conduct a full unbiased study of every piece of mailing equipment on the market. It is hoped that the following material will prepare you to "shop around" for the right piece of equipment to do the type of work you have in your particular mail center. But even after digesting the following you must also strongly depend on three other factors: (1) a demonstration of the equipment, (2) a satisfied user, and (3) the manufacturer's sales representative or dealer who can *accurately* describe the features of each piece of equipment and interpret the advantages of each.

Some office and mail-oriented magazines do publish a "buyers' guide," which can be a convenient comparison of *features*, but they do not usually evaluate one against the other. It would be advantageous for you to establish a reference file that would include those kinds of articles plus the literature from sales reps, forums, trade shows, or conferences. Most often the volume of a specific type of operation slowly grows until you begin to realize that you will need to mechanize or automate the operation sooner or later. Then you have time to shop around at your leisure. At other times a new program proposed by management will force you to obtain new equipment *fast*. Then you will be glad you have that file for referral.

ACCOUNTING SYSTEMS

You may recall the description in *Chapter 15* of a typical postal accounting "system" of 20 or 30 years ago, which consisted of "a clipboard hanging near the postage meter with a hand-drawn form with several columns on it." However, the increase of mail volume in well-established firms and the rise in postage costs have largely eliminated the clipboard. A more modern method was needed, and this need developed about the same time that computer chips became so prevalent. Small computerized accounting systems soon appeared as an ideal "bookkeeper" for mail operations.

There are three primary situations when it is desirable, or essential, to maintain an accounting system in the mail center.

■In a *client* relationship where mailings are prepared and dispatched on behalf of a client who will be billed for postage costs. This is often found in advertising agencies, law firms, and research organizations.

■In a *charge-back* system when large organizations require postage costs to be charged back to various departments or divisions. This is often found in large banks, colleges and universities, and manufacturers who make a variety of different products.

■In support of *profit-centers*, which are usually similar to the charge-back system except that the accumulated costs are more vital to the budgetary restraints of each profit-center. The same type of organization that might require a charge-back of postage costs is just as likely to have its departments or divisions set up as profit-centers.

In addition to those specific tasks, an accounting system can provide a complete analysis of the class of mail, number of pieces, and amounts of postage in the support of ordinary cost control and efficient mail management. Its records will also, of course, accurately forecast future needs and expenditures.

An accounting system is an electronic wizard and is either hard-wired to a postage meter or is an integral part of the meter itself. All models provide a detailed paper print-out showing the details of each transaction. Some models can accept a manual code to track such expenses as local courier service or overnight air express charges. Most models will track up to 1,000 different accounts or departments.

When investigating an accounting system you probably will benefit by first researching the system offered by your *present* postage meter manufacturer. But if you wish to make a comparison with the accounting systems that other meter manufacturers offer you can look in the *Yellow Pages* under *Mailing Machines and Equipment* or write to:

International Mailing Systems, Inc.
19 Forest Parkway
Shelton, CT 06484-6122
203-926-1087

Pitney Bowes
One Elmcroft Road
Stamford, CT 06926-0700
1-800-MR BOWES

Friden Alcatel
30955 Huntwood Avenue
Hayward, CA 94544-7005
1-800-624-7892
In CA 1-800-624-7955

There is another type of accounting system, but instead of tracking postage charges it tracks *accountable mail*. You will recall that is the term used by financial institutions to designate mail that requires *controlled handling*.

If your organization receives a relatively large amount of certified, insured, or registered mail, you can handwrite each number in a book for a permanent record and handwrite some type of form with which to obtain a signature on delivery. These records are necessary but very time consuming. Now there is a better way.

With the *EPG Automated Dispatch System* you simply pass an OCR wand over the USPS label used on certified, insured, or registered mail. The number is read and printed automatically, creating an accurate audit trail for every entry. It not only saves time, it eliminates duplications and transposed numbers.

For more information on this unique system write to Essex Products Group, 30 Industrial Park Road, Centerbrook, CT 06409-0307, or telephone 203-767-7130.

ADDRESSING MACHINES

Electronics in general have had an incredible impact on mail management over the past decade. More new mail-oriented products came on the market during the 80's than were introduced during the entire previous 30 years. The most radical changes may have occurred in the field of addressing. At one time there was a metal Addressograph plate in the House of Representatives for every registered voter in the U.S. Today all of the names and addresses are, of course, computerized, and the Addressograph organization has disappeared.

The demise of metal and plastic address plates even altered the meaning of an "addressing machine." It formerly designated a machine that fed address plates into a print area where the envelope or document was printed. Today, there are at least four types of systems that might be called addressing machines.

Some manufacturers characterize a machine which cuts computer generated addresses, printed four-across on a 17-inch sheet, into individual labels and glues each one to a mailing piece as an "addresser." A more accurate description might be a "labeller."

A second type of "addresser" exists with practically any 9- or 25-pin dot matrix or laser printer. It will print addresses on envelopes one at a time or continuously from a special tray. In a sense these feeders make any personal computer an "addressing machine," but they are more likely operated by secretarial staffs than in a mailroom.

The latest technology creates a third type of "addresser," and that is the ink-jet process for high-volume addressing or personalization of catalogs, bulk business mail, and envelopes. In this process electronically charged ink is sprayed directly onto the document to form the letters and numerals at a speed of over 2,000 characters per second! Ink-jet technology is also the method used to rapidly code mail with the POSTNET barcode.

Other manufacturers now advertise an "addressing machine" that actually is simply a printer for a computer with a highly refined and very versatile envelope feeder. In addition, some models contain independent software that can interpret an address and also print its postal barcode.

When you take all of those processes into consideration, you can see why you need to qualify your intentions whenever you discuss addressing machines. But, since the old address plates have become almost extinct, you should accept this latter system as the addressing machine of the future.

If nothing else, the size of these addressing machines is startling to anyone who has ever seen an old console addresser that was as large as a 60-inch desk and weighed 150 pounds. Tabletop models as small as 24 x 18 inches, and standing only about 15 inches high, are capable of printing about 4,000 near-letter-quality addresses an hour. These machines connect to your PC or other computer system and use your existing software to accept print commands. The manufacturers emphasize that direct printing onto envelopes eliminates the need for expensive labels while improving the appearance of your envelopes.

Two factors have captured the attention of mailers and the manufacturers of software and addressing machines capable of printing POSTNET barcodes. At approximately the same time that the Postal Service announced that the 1990 rate case contained discounts for prebarcoded First- and third-class mail it also reported success in having the University of Arkansas develop a wide area barcode reader. The combination of a discount coupled with wide area reading, an area measuring 4 x 10½ inches, made everyone sit up and take notice.

Earlier efforts to add barcodes usually involved equipment and software for either high-volume mailers or the USPS, often with the software on a mainframe computer. But that technology has changed dramatically. If your addresses include ZIP + 4 Codes, and you can economically update your addresses as you add them to your files, software can simply convert the numeric code and print a USPS acceptable barcode. So, there continues to be an energetic growth in the number of firms which are offering POSTNET bar-coding capability in addressing machines, sorters, and inserting machines.

Even if you do not think you will often qualify for the quantity of mail required to receive the discounts for prebarcoded mail, you can improve the delivery time whenever you prebarcode your mail.

High-speed barcode reading is very technically oriented and many factors influence whether or not the barcode is readable, including density, individual bar dimensions, skew, and overall height and width. Therefore, the USPS has a program that *certifies* systems designed to produce the POSTNET barcode.

In addition, *Postal Bulletin 21781B*, of January 28, 1991, announced that *all* mail submitted for a discount as ZIP+4 or ZIP+4 Barcoded Mail *must* have been addressed by a list that has been coded using the USPS authorized *Coding Accuracy Support System (CASS)*, after September 1, 1991. (See *DMM, Chapter 5.*) Thus whenever you are considering either hardware or software you can understand the necessity for ascertaining (1) that the POSTNET barcodes have been certified by the USPS and (2) that the software is CASS certified.

It appears that it would be to your advantage to insist on seeing a demonstration of these machines *running in harmony with your software* before purchasing any model from any supplier. Another criteria might be to thoroughly explore the availability of local service before the addresser becomes a critical part of your operation.

Your *Yellow Pages* may list local sources under *Addressing Machines and Supplies*, or you can write to:

ACTect
2802 Merrilee Drive
Fairfax, VA 22031-4410
703-641-1200

Bryce Office Systems
115 Hurley Road
Oxford, CT 06483-1011
1-800-627-2792

RENA Systems, Inc.
290 Hansen Access Road
King of Prussia, PA 19406-2429
1-800-426-7905

Scriptomatic Division of Datatech
16 Union Hill Road
W. Conshohocken, PA 19428-2744
215-825-6205

BARCODE PRINTERS

For your clarification, the mailing industry identifies a machine that uses software to spray a complete address on an envelope an *addressing machine*, although the machine does "*print*" a barcode as part of the addressing function. In contrast, a *barcode printer* sprays a barcode on envelopes that *have been previously addressed.*

When you start discussing barcode printers you can end up relatively far afield of mail center management. Most barcode printers are designed for extremely high volumes, are frequently added to another function such as complex, multi-piece inserting, or are integral parts of optical character reader sorters. A number of organizations can provide these large ink jet machines; and they include Kodak (513-259-3100), Domino Amjet, Inc.

(1-800-444-4512, Ext. 235), and Cheshire (1-800-323-1249).

However, there are several unique barcode printers for the small- to medium-sized mailroom. The *Zipnet Printer* can handle any size letter or flat and has a manually operated key pad with which the operator can input a 5-digit ZIP Code or a 9-digit ZIP+4 Code. The Zipnet then applies the corresponding POSTNET code by a disposable ink jet head that, reportedly, will print over 18,000 barcodes. A small liquid crystal display allows the operator to verify the key pad input prior to printing the barcode. A ZIP Code range may be programmed into the printer so that the operator need only key in the last four digits of the ZIP+4 Code. The manually fed Zipnet Printer is said to process from 1,000 to 1,500 pieces of mail an hour. A more automated version feeds the envelopes forward as they are barcoded. For more information, contact Loch Ness, Inc., 3700 Colfax Avenue, S., Minneapolis, MN 55409-1024, or telephone 1-800-323-8623.

Another barcoding system, said to operate at speeds up to 10,000 pieces an hour, stresses the ability to barcode mail in-line with your inserter or mailing machine. The *ZBC-10000* is advertised as an affordable system for small, medium, and large mailers. You can obtain more information from M.A.I.L. code, Inc., P.O. Box 5685, Lafayette, IN 47903-5685.

BARCODE SORTERS

Technology has also been steadily developing at the opposite end of the mail spectrum from the table-top barcode printers. As the Postal Service began to offer discounts for presorting First Class Mail it soon became obvious that large mailers needed equipment capable of high-speed, reliable sorting based on the address printed on an envelope or an enclosure in a window envelope. These large machines, often 20 to 30 feet long, use an *optical character recognition* (OCR) system which "reads" the address and ZIP Code, and sorts the mail into several hundred bins. As the Postal Service announced a discount for 5-digit *prebarcoded* mail, the OCR machine technicians and engineers added the capability of ink-jet technology to spray a barcode onto the envelopes as they were being sorted, achieving an additional discount for the mailer.

A typical barcode sorter may have a through-put speed of 35,000 pieces an hour. Other smaller OCR machines may take up only 35 square feet of floor space, have as few as eight pockets or bins, yet process 12,000 pieces of mail an hour. Thus they require considerable daily volume to be practical. In addition, there is a certain amount of sticker shock; the larger OCR barcode sorters begin at about a quarter of a million dollars! However, many organizations that have sufficient volume to warrant such machines for their outgoing mail often have a similar volume of incoming mail, which can be processed by the OCR barcode readers. When that process is beneficial to the mailer it tends to double the efficiency of the machine.

In spite of the sticker shock, if a mailer has sufficient volume, the projected savings in postage will soon amortize the cost of such equipment, particularly if you lease it. As recommended with any piece of equipment that complex and that expensive, you would certainly want to talk to (and visit with) a number of different satisfied customers before making your decision. Considering the investment, or size of the lease, two or three round-trip airline tickets (to visit a happy user) would make good sense.

Most barcode sorter manufacturers regularly exhibit at postal forums and conferences and frequently advertise in trade publications. These are some of the companies:

Bell & Howell Phillipsburg Company
2202 N. Irving Street
Allentown, PA 18103-9554
215-266-4817

ElectroCom Mail Systems
2200 E. Devon Avenue, Suite 309
Des Plaines, IL 60018-4505
1-800-432-2633

EPS Industries
451 Taft Street, NE
Minneapolis, MN 55413-2831
1-800-627-2377

National Presort, Inc.
1539 Round Table Drive
Dallas, TX 75247-3588
214-634-0678

Postal Technologies, Inc.
7214 East 48th Street
Tulsa, OK 74145-0001
1-800-877-7841

Scan-Code, Inc.
One Riverview Square
East Hartford, CT 06108-4110
203-289-5224

Tritek, Inc.
509 Interchange Blvd.
Newark, DE 19711-3570
302-453-9147

CARTS FOR MAIL

There are almost as many varieties of mail carts as there are different kinds of envelopes. The most common, similar to a grocery cart, is about 42 inches long and 24 inches wide, has an upper and lower basket, and is constructed of chrome-plated tubular frames. They usually have 4- or 5-inch wheels and the front wheels swivel for ease in turning corners.

Other models use tubular frames but have painted sheet-steel sides and ends, larger rear wheels, and accommodate legal-size hanging folders for rapid sorting. A lower shelf, also constructed of painted sheet-steel, has room for additional mail or packages.

One major manufacturer of mailroom furniture (Hamilton Sorter) provides mail carts fabricated out of the same aluminum extrusions and high-density laminated wood used to construct their furniture. Their carts have front wheels that swivel and will accommodate hanging folders.

The largest selection of mail carts is available by mail order from a company that has been selling mail handling equipment since 1959 (W. A. Charnstrom Company). Their 1991 catalog includes *11* pages of mail carts, and they have every conceivable design to meet your specific needs.

In the Washington, DC, area some of the large Federal agencies often use a cart that is almost a rolling sorting bin. Measuring 2 feet wide and 4 feet long, it stands 5 feet tall. There is a 12-inch recessed ledge about 2 feet off of the floor, and the balance of the cart provides 16 square feet of adjustable bins, each 12 inches wide. It is an ideal cart for organizations that have a sizable quantity of flats coming in or going out. The large bins also allow for "in-flight" sorting, a definite advantage. Constructed of light-but-strong magnesium, the lower portion has doors that may be locked for security whenever the distribution clerk is away from the cart. The cart is manufactured by Magline, 503 S. Mercer Street, Pinconning, MI 48650-9310, and in the Washington area it is sold by Paul H. Werres Company, Inc., 12022 Parklawn Drive, Rockville, MD 20852-1860, telephone 301-770-4000.

The world of electronics has even invaded the lowly mail cart! Two manufacturers offer robot-like electronically controlled carts that silently follow an invisible guide-path from one station to the next. Loaded with mail, these carts (which are approximately 2 feet wide and 4 to 5½ feet long, with about 15 square feet of sorting bins) will proceed to each pre-selected station, and stop and beep for attention. After removing the incoming mail, and perhaps some stationery supplies, computer printouts, or magnetic tape, the recipient may add outgoing mail, and the automated cart proceeds to the next station.

The *Mailmobile* was originally developed almost 15 years ago by *Lear Siegler*, a company later bought by *Bell and Howell*. When first introduced it received enthusiastic acceptance from several large organizations, among them the Air Force, Citibank, and Sears. The Mailmobile is available in two sizes from Bell and Howell Mailmobile Company, 411 East Roosevelt Street, Zeeland, MI 49464-1395, telephone 1-800-325-7400. They offer suggested criteria for utilizing one of their automated guided carts and a free mail service survey.

The *Transcar* is a similar automated guided vehicle available from the *TransLogic Corporation*. The TransLogic Transcar differs from the Mailmobile in that it consists of a basic low (9 5/8 inch) vehicle that can be used in many different industrial applications beyond mail distribution. The Transcar will also automatically interface with an elevator without human intervention and operates on rechargeable batter-ies that allow a full day of mail distribution. The Transcar is available from the TransLogic Corporation, 10825 East 47th Street, Denver, CO 80239-2913, telephone 1-800-525-1841.

These computer-controlled carts allow a user to increase internal mail distribution from two or three runs a day to hourly service for time-sensitive documents at no additional labor cost. It is slightly eerie to watch these robot-like vehicles, but users think they are an excellent choice if one can be adapted to your office environment. As one satisfied user said, "It's a great mail clerk; it's never late to work, doesn't take coffee breaks, and never calls in sick."

Other mail carts are available from:

W. A. Charnstrom Company
10901 Hampshire Avenue South
Minneapolis, MN 55438-2393
1-800-328-2962

Friden Alcatel
30955 Huntwood Avenue
Hayward, CA 94544-7005
1-800-624-7892
In CA 1-800-624-7955

Hamilton Sorter Company, Inc.
3158 Production Drive
Fairfield, OH 45014-4228
1-800-543-1605

Kwik-File, Inc.
500 73rd Avenue, NE
Fridley, MN 55432-3266
1-800-328-5711

Raymond Engineering, Inc.
704 Vandalia Street
St. Paul, MN 55114-1303
1-800-365-5770

A. Rifkin Company
P.O. Box 878
Wilkes-Barre, PA 18703-0878
1-800-334-3525
In PA 1-800-358-7300

FOLDING AND INSERTING MACHINES

In order to intelligently discuss folding machines and inserting machines you must realize that they usually fall into one of five different categories:

■Table-top folders designed for small to medium office folding.

■Table-top folders designed for sustained folding, which may be coupled with a table-top inserting machine.

■Large floor-model folders designed to make precision folds as required for production work by the printing industry.

■Table-top inserting machines designed to insert only one, two, or perhaps three pieces into an envelope, which often are physically connected to a folding machine.

■Large multi-station inserters that can insert up to 12 pieces, some of which may have been burst, trimmed, and folded directly from computer output, into one envelope.

While mixed typed mail and general correspondence is usually folded and inserted into envelopes at the point of origin, the computer has funnelled more and more folding and inserting work into the mail center. At the same time that the compensation of mailroom employees has increased, there has developed a relatively strong resentment against doing repetitive work that can be more easily and economically done by a machine. Folding statements, invoices, or letters by hand is a boring task that becomes more tedious as time goes on. Also, when more than one person is doing the folding, it almost always involves chitchat, which wastes expensive time.

But there is an even more important area of concern. Casual hand folding of pieces that are designed to fit into a window envelope often results in folds that prevent the address from showing through the window completely. This often causes delayed and missent mail plus customer irritation. In contrast, a folding machine can fold 1,000 statements in about 10 minutes, and every single one will be precisely folded so that the entire address always appears within the window area. Another related problem occurs when mail is folded correctly to allow the address to show through the window properly, but is so small overall that it can slip around in the envelope. Any mail handler in a post office will confirm that this is a common problem that often delays mail. Yet it is easy to eliminate because the machine can fold the piece of mail so that exactly 1/16 of an inch clearance is left when inserted into the envelope. Then the address will always be in full view and cannot slip away from the window. Thus you can see that a folding machine may even be located *outside* of the mail center and still have a positive effect on the characteristics of your mail.

There is another disadvantage in depending on hand folding. If the folding work stretches into four or five hours it becomes increasingly difficult to properly manage the completion and mailing of the job. The longer you must allocate people to the folding task, the more likely you will need them for other important tasks. It is also difficult to properly manage the task when the people who usually do the folding are absent because of vacation or illness. In contrast, it is easy to have a trained back-up operator for a folding machine, which can complete the entire job in 30 minutes or less.

The folding machine is certainly one of the simplest office or mailroom machines to test. All you need to do is plug it in. Many other machines require a great deal of operator training. But the folder can be brought in for a test, set for your particular form in seconds by the sales representative, and you have almost instant proof of the potential savings. Don't be afraid to try a folding machine for fear it will positively prove itself a bargain. The fact that the folder will definitely save time (and money) in your office does not mean you have to buy or lease it right that minute. (Although one mail manager, when asked if he would like to keep the folder, replied, "I guess I don't have much choice, you don't think I can get it away from my clerks now do you!") Instead, you need to test and evaluate equipment *before* you are ready to buy (or lease) it. You need time to determine exactly what you need and where you are going to get it.

If you do begin to look for a folding machine, you will not have far to look. There must be over a dozen folders advertised in the trade publications. But only a few offer nationwide factory-trained service, and that feature *must not be taken lightly*.

All models are simple to adjust in order to change the folds. But, like most products, the more expensive the folder, the more precise the settings become, and consequently the folds are much more precise. It pays too in the quality of the bearings on the various rollers, as that is the primary area of wear. It is not uncommon for the higher quality folders to stand up well for 10 years of service, a handy rule of thumb when calculating the potential savings versus the cost of a purchase or lease.

Some of the higher quality folders offer such options as perforating, cutting, and scoring, which may be welcome additions to the benefits of the folder. Another feature you should examine is how well the folder controls the folded material as it comes out into the stacker. Maintaining the proper alphabetical order on accounts may be important, just as it may be vital to preserve the ZIP Code order.

There is an interesting phenomenon with most folding machine installations that is akin to the skyrocketing number of copies made on office copiers every day in business. When a folding machine is being tested and the cost-savings figures are being developed, there are usually only two or three jobs that are analyzed as prime applications. Yet, invariably, there develops about twice as many folding applications than anyone thought of originally. This is a fringe benefit to the investment or lease cost and is another reason why the folding machine should never be overlooked when you are trying to cut costs and improve efficiency in a mail center. The primary manufacturers of folding machines are:

Friden Alcatel
30955 Huntwood Avenue
Hayward, CA 94544-7005
1-800-624-7892
In CA 1-800-624-7955

GBR Systems Corporation
4100 Corporate Square, #133
Naples, FL 33942-4704
813-643-0530

Martin Yale Industries, Inc.
500 N. Spaulding Avenue
Chicago, IL 60624-1512
312-826-4444

Pitney Bowes
One Elmcroft Road
Stamford, CT 06926-0700
1-800-MR BOWES

Postalia, Inc.
1423 Centre Circle Drive
Downers Grove, IL 60515-1087
708-629-9100

■*Folding/Inserting Machines:* If you progress beyond the folding machine and begin to consider adding an inserting machine to your shopping list, you will be pleased to see that it will offer all of these benefits:

■Ensures accuracy	■Provides greater security
■Eliminates bottlenecks	■Provides greater flexibility
■Improves morale	■Reduces or eliminates overtime
■Meets mailing schedules	■Eliminates "borrowing" personnel

While the Cheshire Company offers a table top-folder/inserter, the two most well-known manufacturers of combination folding and inserting machines designed for table-top use are Friden Alcatel and Pitney Bowes.

Cheshire's folder/inserter is a compact one-piece unit 30 inches long and 22 inches wide and standing only 21 inches high. It can fold an enclosure before inserting it, or insert material that is already envelope size, and also nest cards or return envelopes. It includes an envelope sealer, a counter, and double and miss detectors.

In contrast to the Cheshire machine, both the Friden Alcatel and the Pitney Bowes machines are completely modular. You select the function that exactly suits your particular needs and more or less construct the machine as you wish. You have considerable choices, for the various modules can imprint, slit, burst, fold, insert, count, seal, and meter stamp in a single pass through the machine. Obviously, an added benefit is the capability to add one or more of those functions later should your requirements change. Since the modules are designed for table-top operation, the controls are easy to understand and operate. They do take a certain amount of mechanical aptitude, but you certainly do not need a certified mechanic to operate one successfully.

If these folder/inserters seem complex, you should not be overly concerned; all of the manufacturers usually *guarantee* the successful performance of their equipment on *specific samples of material*. Your biggest area of concern should be the availability of factory trained service people and the quality of service they provide. As is often recommended on equipment of this nature, a *nearby* and *happy* customer, who can provide an opinion of the quality of service you can expect, should be a strong deciding factor in making your selection.

If you are unable to locate these manufacturers, you can write to:

Cheshire, A Videojet Company	Friden Alcatel
404 Washington Boulevard	30955 Huntwood Avenue
Mundelein, IL 60060-3190	Hayward, CA 94544-7005
1-800-323-1249	1-800-624-7892
In IL 1-312-949-2000	In CA 1-800-624-7955

Pitney Bowes
One Elmcroft Road
Stamford, CT 06926-0700
1-800-MR BOWES

Discussing the pros and cons of multi-station, high-production inserting machines in this book is like the author of a book on first aid offering tips on brain surgery! The large inserters are a specialized field in themselves; they are highly technical both in operation and maintenance; and at an average cruising speed of at least 10,000 insertions per hour, they require a great deal of mail. Just the specifications on all the different models and all the options and different configurations may well fill a book by themselves.

It may be rare that a need for such high speed production is created overnight. Usually some experience exists in operating smaller inserters or there may be a need to replace an existing machine. In either case you are likely to know exactly which features you require. But with so much technology changing constantly it would be advantageous for you to examine every source before making a commitment. Remember, many have POSTNET barcode capability.

Multi-station inserters are available from:

Bell & Howell Phillipsburg Company
2202 N. Irving Street
Allentown, PA 18103-9554
215-266-4817

Böwe Systems
& Machinery Corporation
525 Executive Boulevard
Elmsford, NY 10523-9952
914-347-4414

Computer Output Processors
& Engineering, Inc.
2425 East Medina Road
Tucson, AZ 85706-7097
602-746-3241

Kirk-Rudy, Inc.
2700 Due West Drive
Kennesaw, GA 30144-3532
404-427-4203

Mailcrafters
4621 West 138th Street
Crestwood, IL 60445-1930
708-597-8777

Pitney Bowes
One Elmcroft Road
Stamford, CT 06926-0700
1-800-MR BOWES

Remember, if you amortize a folder/inserter over a 10-year period, you *know* what the cost of labor will be over those years to handle your folding and inserting. On the other hand, 9 or 10 years from now, there is no telling how high the cost of labor will be to prepare your mail.

FURNITURE FOR MAILROOMS

Regardless of the manufacturer, mailroom furniture is invariably modular in design. That is, it is constructed with standardized units or components.

This allows the mailroom designer to custom-tailor each assembly to the particular requirements for the type and volume of mail processed. It also allows a greater amount of flexibility *after* installation if conditions change. Furthermore, all furniture offered by the various manufacturers is similar in design because the basic functions are the same.

This design similarity is not generally true in other types of office equipment, as evidenced by the wide variety of copiers available. However, a table designed for dumping mail is almost identical in shape and size regardless of the manufacturer because the *function* of dumping the mail is the same in every instance.

Because the furniture is very flexible, with legs that may usually be extended from about 26 inches to 36 inches, for example, an inexperienced sales representative or your own employees may inadvertently install or adjust a piece of furniture so that it is not suitable for the task for which it was designed. Or else you may try to use a discarded piece of furniture in a mail center when it really wasn't designed for that use. To help you more fully understand what physical dimensions will *best* serve your mail operations you should review each of the different pieces of furniture usually found in the mailroom.

■*Dumping Tables:* Ordinary tables are often used as dumping tables, but their height is usually too low. Dumping and the accompanying preliminary separating is more easily accomplished in a standing position. Therefore, the proper table height is from 34 to 36 inches. As a mental guide, a standard kitchen table is usually 30 inches high, and the standard kitchen counter is 36 inches high. Trying to cook or do woodwork on a 30-inch-high stove or workbench makes the task more difficult and often results in a backache. So the higher 36-inch surface is more desirable. However, for a person who is only several inches over five feet tall, trying to hold a mail sack upside-down over a 36-inch-high table can become a real chore. Therefore, adjustable legs are very practical if they are available.

The dumping tables are usually available from 24 to 36 inches in depth from front to back, but reaching the back of a 34- or 36-inch table may be very uncomfortable for some workers and may result in a reduction in mail handling. The mail tables are available in a variety of lengths from 30 to 84 inches, but not all sizes are available from the same manufacturer. In every case, a rim or guard is attached along the sides and across the back of the mail dumping table. The rims are commonly 4 to 6 inches high and protect the mail from slipping down between either the wall or another piece of furniture. The table should always be kept clear of everything except the incoming mail. Depending on how you receive your mail from the Postal Service a dumping table should not be classed as a luxury, it can be a valuable addition to your mail processing efficiency. One manufacturer (Hamilton Sorter) can provide rims completely around the perimeter of two dump tables to provide a free standing, square, dump table that is accessible from all four sides.

■*Mail Opener Tables:* Table-top semiautomatic mail openers are basically designed to open letter-size "white" mail from a standing position. They automatically feed envelopes and open them so fast (about 500 per minute) that the operator needs to be standing in order to constantly move the mail toward and away from the opener itself. So the semiautomatic opener is best placed on a table about the same height as the dump tables. In contrast, larger flats, which are usually in kraft envelopes up to 9 x 12 inches, can be efficiently opened on a different type of opener while the operator is *seated.* The manual opener should therefore be used on a standard 30-inch-high table. In either case there must be ample work space on each side for opening the mail without any risk of it slipping to the floor.

■*Inbound Sorting Bins*: Since most sorting bins or cells are available in 12-inch-high sections, the height of the tabletop on the incoming sorting table may be governed by the number of sorting cells required. If you place three sections together to form 36 inches, it may be too tall for some employees if it is sitting on a 34- or 36-inch table. On the other hand, while it is true that the lower the table the more sorting bins you can have, too low a table can cause awkward movements in picking up the mail to be sorted and may result in lower production. Other times it may be desirable to raise the sorting sections or cells *above* the table surface to provide more work space, and the overall height of the sorting bins may be a factor in that case, too.

The inbound sorting table(s) should allow for breakdown of the mail at least to each mail stop and often to even additional separations within each mail stop. Therefore, ample bins must be provided for easy, effortless sorting. It can waste expensive time to cope with inadequate bin sizes while sorting mail. It is also desirable to provide the right size bin to match the kind of mail normally received. You should not be jamming flats into a bin designed for white mail, and it may even be worthwhile to provide an arrangement of bins that provide for separate sorting of white mail and large flats (next to each other) for the same destination in your organization.

If you need to sort to a greater number of bins than can be accommodated on one table, it may be desirable to have one person sort to two tables arranged with the sorting bins facing each other or in an "L" shape in a corner. It is also a practical arrangement to have one clerk sort to as many as 200 bins by forming a "U" with the tables.

■*Reading Stations*: Every medium-sized organization receives what some people call "mystery mail," mail that is ambiguously addressed simply to the organization. Such mail must be opened and read in order to determine who should receive it. This operation should be performed from a seated position at a standard 30-inch-high work table or desk. In addition, bins should be within easy reach so that the reader may sort the mail after its destination is determined. One manufacturer (Hamilton Sorter) offers a unique semi-circular work station with multiple sorting bins which would be ideal for this purpose. Another arrangement, as discussed in the chapter on mail flow, is to have two readers facing each other and sitting at double desks or work stations with sorting bins accessible from either side. Such a work station may also be arranged with *pass-through bins* so that a messenger may constantly pick up the mail for distribution without interfering with the reader. As is the case in most of the mail center stations, it is important that this station stay clear of the clutter often found around a mailroom.

■*Worktables*: An area which is often neglected is the space needed to set down a stack of statements prior to inserting them into envelopes or a place to put printed material prior to folding and inserting it into envelopes. Such functions are important tasks for any mail center, yet all too often there isn't any space available for such daily jobs. You could almost grade a mailroom simply by walking in and looking for free space not assigned to any particular duty *but useful for all of them.*

Most of these tasks can best be performed from a standing position, so such tables or counters should perhaps be higher than the regular 30 inches. Tables are available in a wide variety of sizes, and even a little one in the corner of a small mailroom can be a blessing.

■*Mailing Machine Tables*: The key to the proper height of a machine table, such as one used to hold a mailing machine, should depend on the height of the machine that is to be used on the table. As a rule of thumb, the top of the machine should be about level with the elbows of the operator of the machine. This allows the operator to reach out (with arms parallel to the table) and have the primary controls or loading bins at his or her finger tips. The operator should not have to reach upward for the controls for operating the machine, nor have to reach downward to load or unload a machine. This height is very important to combat job fatigue and for the maximum in mail handling efficiency.

■*Parcel Packing Tables*: The height of a packing table is also governed by what is to be placed on it. If you often ship large boxes, 12 to 15 inches high, you do not want the mail clerk to have to *reach up* to pack and seal the parcel. On the other hand, trying to pack and seal a 4-inch carton on a 30-inch-high table is just as difficult for a taller person. This is another area that should be *customized* for both your material and your personnel. (Note: This table was once known as a "wrapping" table, but you should avoid wrapping *any* package with paper whenever possible. Modern processing equipment may tear the wrapping, losing the address.)

The table for the parcel scale should be lowered so that the *top* of the scale is about level with the packing table, to minimize lifting. If there is a special mailing machine for parcels, the table should be a little higher so that the controls are again at about elbow height of the operator. Most manufacturers understand this need of varying heights.

■*Shipping Station*: One manufacturer (Kwik-File) provides a specially designed table to accommodate the necessary components of a manifest shipping system. There is a durable storage table to provide ample room for supplies; an accessory platform, which supports a PC and up to two printers; a keyboard tray, which retracts when not in use; and an adjustable scale support on one side of the table. Another manufacturer (NATCO) also offers a special table for a manifest system that provides space for each of the above items. Other designs that may fit in well with a manifest shipping system may be found wherever computer furniture is sold.

■*Outbound Sorting Bins*: All of the physical characteristics of the incoming mail sorting bins and tables apply to the outbound bins, but the two operations should always be separate. In most cases, the proper design for adequately accommodating the incoming mail (i.e., the number of bins) will not be the same as that needed for the outbound mail. In addition, the bins and tables should be located to provide proper flow for the outgoing mail, and this rarely fits in with the area most suitable for the incoming mail.

A few years ago there were only one or two organizations that offered mailroom furniture, but with the new awareness of mail center management the list has grown considerably. As mentioned previously, all of the furniture is modular so that you can "build" practically any design or configuration you need. While some manufacturers have local sales and service representatives listed in the *Yellow Pages*, some sell through dealers and others sell by mail through a catalog. All have descriptive literature on their furniture and most literature includes dimensions. The following is list of principal advertisers of mailroom furniture in current publications and exhibits:

W. A. Charnstrom Company
10901 Hampshire Avenue South
Minneapolis, MN 55438-2393
1-800-328-2962

Friden Alcatel
30955 Huntwood Avenue
Hayward, CA 94544-7005
1-800-624-7892
In CA 1-800-624-7955

International Mailing Systems, Inc.
19 Forest Parkway
Shelton, CT 06484-6122
203-926-1087

Delco Associates, Inc.
55 Old Field Point Road
Greenwich, CT 06836-6149
1-800-243-8528

Hamilton Sorter Company, Inc.
3158 Production Drive
Fairfield, OH 45014-4228
1-800-543-1605

Kwik-File, Inc.
500 73rd Avenue, NE
Fridley, MN 55432-3266
1-800-328-5711

NATCO, Inc.   Pitney Bowes
4300 Rhode Island Avenue   One Elmcroft Road
Brentwood, MD 20722-1442   Stamford, CT 06926-0700
1-800-55 NATCO   1-800-MR BOWES

Raymond Engineering, Inc.
704 Vandalia Street
St. Paul, MN 55114-1303
1-800-365-5770

■*Important Purchasing Considerations:* After you have decided that you really will benefit by the addition of the right piece of mailroom furniture, there are several important points to examine in addition to the correct dimensions. The first consideration might be whether to purchase from a supplier that does not have local sales representatives. Your furniture will arrive via truck, probably disassembled, and you must be sure that your staff will be able to put it together. If you are buying from a catalog, make sure that you draw both an accurate sketch of the mailroom and the proposed furniture *to scale*, or you may be in for a rude shock when something doesn't fit. There are probably considerable savings in a do-it-yourself project, but there is no room for poor planning. Remember, too, if you must pay overtime to get your people to set up the equipment it will eat away your savings over a supplier that completes the installation as well.

If you decide to talk to a local sales representative, then you must be sure that your particular problems and concerns are clearly understood by the representative. You might ask these questions. Is the salesperson well versed in mail center operations? How much actual experience has the representative had? Can the company give you a local reference where it has designed and installed another mailroom? If the sales representative doesn't understand your problems, they are not likely to be solved to your complete satisfaction. There is a happy medium in allowing enough space in a mail center for anticipated growth, but you must be sure that the design offered by the vendor is not far beyond the needs of many years of growth.

Any local representative selling mailroom furniture should be able to help you lay out a plan for your mailroom improvements and design how the mail will flow into and through the mail center. Any professional sales representative *should* be happy to provide a scale drawing of the proposed furniture and the new mail flow.

Another prime consideration is the flexibility of the installation. Your overall arrangement should be versatile enough to provide for enlarged areas of work space where they are most likely to be needed. You are probably able to predict the area most likely to grow, and this knowledge should be woven into the overall plan.

Finally, make sure that the measurements are taken *very carefully* before the final order is submitted. If you have a wall that is precisely 15 feet long, it is unlikely that you can put three 60-inch tables against the wall because you must allow for the thickness of the baseboard and perhaps a quarter inch extra here and there. If you plan on several inches of clearance between major assemblies, you will enjoy the ease of a simple, problem-free installation.

LABEL DISPENSERS AND GLUERS

If you have to apply a number of pressure-sensitive labels from time to time but do not have sufficient volume to justify the investment in a machine to apply them, you should certainly investigate the *Dispensa-Matic* labelling machines. Available in several widths, these unique machines employ an electric drive to feed the paper label carrier over the top of and around a small chrome-plated horizontal rod. As the sheet is fed around the rod the labels start to peel off of the carrier, and the electric drive stops just a fraction of an inch before the label is completely free of the carrier or backing sheet. Thus the label is sticking straight out ready for you to pick it up and apply it to an envelope or package. When you do pick up the label a micro switch trips the machine to feed the next label out the same distance and then stops automatically. In the case of four-across computer-printed labels, you pick the right hand label first, and so on until, when you remove the left label, the feeder peels and extends four labels out again.

It is so simple and foolproof that the manufacturer will ship it to you for a 21-one day free trial! They are sold by Dispensa-Matic Label Dispensers, a Division of Commercial Mailing Accessories, Inc., 725 N. 23rd Street, St. Louis, MO 63103-1500; and you can call 1-800-325-7303 to arrange a demonstration.

If you do not use pressure-sensitive labels, but glue your present labels onto boxes and cartons there is a small (7½ inches square) machine that may be just what you have been looking for. It feeds a label through and deposits a precise, accurate "corduroy" pattern of glue on the label or it can be fitted with a wick roller for use as a gummed label moistener. It is also available with a solid glue pattern. Available as either a manual or electric model, it can feed any label up to 5½ inches wide. The manufacturer claims it is easy to fill, easy to empty, and easy to clean. The *LABEL-PRO 5.5 Label Gluers* are available from Glue-Fast Equipment Company, Inc., 727 Commercial Avenue, Carlstadt, NJ 07072-2602. Glue-Fast can also provide machines to apply glue onto labels up to 32 inches wide. They also offer water-based adhesives for all kinds of automatic labelling machines. Their telephone number is 201-939-7100, or outside of New Jersey you may call 1-800-242-7318.

LABELLING MACHINES

A little over a decade ago more and more people were discovering that a computer could quickly print a single strip of address labels. Mounted on a fan-fold carrier with sprocket holes on each side, thousands of address labels came spewing out of computers. Then everyone sat down and laboriously applied them one by one by hand. One manufacturer of pressure sensitive labels sold an ugly machine that looked like ET's cousin, but it cost almost 10 grand!

Fortunately, all that has changed. Featuring sleek designs, a variety of different table-top size machines are available from several manufacturers. They often have electronic controls, and some are capable of applying up to 10,000 labels an hour.

You can usually locate a local source in the *Yellow Pages* under *Addressing Machines and Supplies* or *Labelling Equipment*, or you may wish to write directly to the manufacturers.

Accufast Labellers Automecha Ltd., USA P.O. Box 660 Oxford, NY 13830-0660 1-800-447-990	Postalia, Inc. 1423 Centre Circle Drive Downers Grove, IL 60515-1087 708-629-9100
RENA Systems, Inc. 290 Hansen Access Road King of Prussia, PA 19406-2429 1-800-426-7905	Scriptomatic Division of Datatech 16 Union Hill Road W. Conshohocken, PA 19428-2744 215-825-6205

A totally different process of applying computer-printed labels has been provided by other manufacturers ever since the first set of four-across (known as *4-up*) labels rolled off a computer printer. They are incredible machines to watch! The printed computer sheets are fed into the back of the machine, and as they move forward they are chopped into one-inch strips. The strips in turn are then chopped into individual four inch labels and pressed against a five inch rotating wheel about two inches wide. As it turns (counter-clockwise), holes in the wheel allow air to suck a label onto the wheel, roll it against an adhesive roller, and roll the address label onto the envelope as it passes under the wheel. And all of this occurs at speeds of up to 10,000 pieces an hour.

The process is synonymous with the word *Cheshire*, one of the early developers of such equipment, but there are other firms that make the same type of machine. It is *the way* to affix computer-generated labels when the volume exceeds that which seems economical or practical on single-address strips. In addition, the cost of gluing ordinary computer *paper* onto an envelope as an address is a small fraction of the cost of pressure-sensitive labels.

Two manufacturers of such machines are:

Cheshire, A Videojet Company
404 Washington Boulevard
Mundelein, IL 60060-3190
1-800-323-1249
In IL 1-312-949-2000

Kirk-Rudy, Inc.
2700 Due West Drive
Kennesaw, GA 30144-3532
404-427-4203

MAILING MACHINES

You will recall in *Chapter 7*, in the discussion of postage meters, that in order to maintain complete control over any device that prints postage the Postal Service requires that postage meters be *leased* from any of the four licensed manufacturers. Those four manufacturers are:

Friden Alcatel
30955 Huntwood Avenue
Hayward, CA 94544-7005
1-800-624-7892
In CA 1-800-624-7955

International Mailing Systems, Inc.
Hasler Mailing Machines
19 Forest Parkway
Shelton, CT 06484-6122
203-926-1087

Pitney Bowes
One Elmcroft Road
Stamford, CT 06926-0700
1-800-MR BOWES

Postalia, Inc.
1423 Centre Circle Drive
Downers Grove, IL 60515-1087
708-629-9100

You can usually locate representatives of these companies in the *Yellow Pages* under *Mailing Machines and Equipment*. If they are not in your telephone directory, your library should have a telephone directory for the nearest larger city. Friden Alcatel and Pitney Bowes have factory branches in over 100 cities, and IMS/Hasler distributes its equipment through dealers in major metropolitan areas, while Postalia maintains branches in only selected larger cities.

Most of the manufacturers provide a self-contained postage meter and since the USPS forbids the *sale* of a postage meter, it must be leased to the mailer by the meter manufacturer. Although these smaller meters usually do not provide simultaneous sealing of the envelope, they do provide all of the other benefits of the metered mail system.

When greater speeds are desirable, more denominations needed, and sealing becomes a chore, then a larger meter becomes desirable. But instead of being self-contained with its own small motor, it is activated by a base that is a *mailing machine*. Since the meter is detachable from the mailing machine, the machine may be purchased outright by the mailer or leased through a leasing company. The meter sits on top of the mailing machine and operates as an integral unit which seals and meter stamps envelopes or dispenses gummed tape or pressure-sensitive tape for parcels and unusually thick envelopes.

The rental cost of a postage meter will vary with the manufacturer. Some meters are rented based on the amount of postage used, with a minimum and maximum charge. Other meter rental is based on a flat quarterly charge, regardless of the amount of postage used.

The other factor that influences the cost is how the meter is set. Normally when the meter indicates that your postage is running low you take the postage meter to the nearest post office, along with a check for the amount of postage you wish to buy. Or you can pay an extra fee to the USPS and a clerk will come to your office and set your meter at a cost of $25 (in 1991). But in this age of great convenience another method is becoming more and more popular.

Although originally invented by Pitney Bowes, who pioneered the establishment of accounting procedures to the satisfaction of the Postal Service, Friden Alcatel and IMS/Hasler also have postage meters that may be set electronically through a telephone line. Payments are sent to a trust fund operated by the meter manufacturer who, in turn, sends coded signals over telephone lines to reset your meter to the desired amount. The rental on these electronic meters may be somewhat greater than on the meters you must take to the post office, but in locations where the winters are severe, or where the post office might be a cab ride away, one may be very economical. In the past, every meter had to be taken into a post office at least every six months for setting or for verification that it was functioning correctly. But the '91 rate case changes included a provision for *"examination of"* a meter as well as setting a meter on-site at a customer's place of business (for the above-mentioned $25). So now you may have the luxury of having the meter set electronically over the telephone and having a postal clerk "examine" the meter in your office, *and never set foot in a post office at all.*

Thus, the *cost* of a meter may remain the same whether you are using a mailing machine that automatically feeds envelopes through the meter or whether you require an employee to stand and push envelopes into the mailing machine one by one in a semiautomatic fashion. Naturally the question arises of how long you can allow that clerk to hand-feed envelopes before you are wasting labor. The answer lies in the cost differential between the hand-fed mailing machine and one that will feed envelopes automatically. Many a mailing machine runs well in its tenth year, but to be more conservative, divide the difference by 60 months to see the *monthly* difference, and divide that by four weeks to see the weekly cost to have an automatically fed mailing machine instead of a hand-fed one. The difference is likely to be less than you are paying your clerk an hour to stand there and fuss with envelopes. In addition to having the clerk available for more productive work than feeding envelopes, you gain the advantages of a high-speed feeder for an occasional large mailing, the benefits of higher morale, the ability to grow without placing a strain on your services, and the ability to rapidly send out money-producing documents such as dues, invoices, and statements.

As important as the cost of the investment may be in selecting a mailing machine and a postage meter, there are other factors. One of the most significant considerations might be the anticipated growth of the volume of letters and parcels added to your present volume. It is very common for an organization to be overly cautious in selecting a mailing machine only to find that in three or four years business has grown so much that the present mailing machine is inadequate. Since the trade-in value of *used* office equipment is notoriously low, it becomes extremely expensive to "trade up" within just three or four years. If an organization is somewhat in doubt about its anticipated growth, then it is an excellent time to consider a 36-month lease because it is far more flexible if larger equipment is needed after three years.

Another important consideration to explore as you shop for a mailing machine is the availability and quality of service which you can expect. It is generally accepted that any sales person will sing the virtues of his or her organization, so it is not very profitable to depend on them when trying to evaluate the quality of their service. But there is an easy and inexpensive method. In addition to talking to other mailers that you know ask the sales rep for the names of organizations that have been using their equipment for a year or longer. Remember, every smart sales person has at least two pet customers who would readily say anything for them! What you need is a list of *five or six* present users who will be willing to discuss their service experiences with you. Few frustrations exceed having two or three thousand statements ready to mail at noon when the mailing machine breaks down and there is not a service person to be found.

While some cautions about postage meters and mailing machines were discussed under *Applying Postage* in *Chapter 15*, it would be well to emphasize them again. One concerns incorrect dates and the other concerns meter stamps that are almost too light to read. Either one may bring down the wrath of the Postal Service (perhaps justifiably so).

There are several systems that assure the daily changing of the meter date, and one should be adapted that will *guarantee* that the date is changed every day. For example, you may want someone to change the date every day as soon as you open. In another case, one enterprising mail manager uses a large wall calendar near his desk and requires that a tape with the new date be applied every morning. You may not need something so drastic, but incorrect dates do trouble the USPS and will often slow down your mail (for over cancelling).

If the meter stamps are illegible, your mail may even be returned to you. This problem should be an easy thing to eliminate, for the inking of most machines is a simple process of turning on an automatic inking system every so often or replacing a disposable cartridge. The *legibility* of the meter stamp is almost as important as the date. If the date of mailing, or the city and state, on the meter stamp is too light to read it is often over-cancelled, with the usual possible delay.

A third area to which you should pay particular attention is the *sealing system* in your mailing machine. You would be surprised to see how much mail the Postal Service receives that is metered but unsealed. Sealers are easily clogged with paper lint and minerals in the water so that without adequate maintenance they soon stop sealing properly. You should not neglect this, for unsealed mail can be damaged on mail processing equipment, and it really upsets customers to receive mail that is unsealed. (See the section that follows on *Sealing Solutions*.)

You can improve those three areas considerably if they are made the specific responsibility of one individual and included in the job description as an assigned task. Remember, the mailing machine is almost your last opportunity to improve your mail service through proper mail preparation.

MANIFEST SHIPPING SYSTEMS

The computer chip has changed many other methods of handling and processing mail but it has created an entire new user-friendly environment in the area of shipping. It wasn't very long ago that a shipping clerk would have to place a package on a scale, look up the zone on a paper chart and go back to the scale to determine the postage or UPS charge. Then the label had to be typed. If a manifest showing all of the details of the shipment was desired, it had to be hand typed a line at a time. Any summary sheets or analysis of shipments had to be laboriously created by hand, each one prone to omitted items and transposed numbers. If you wished to use the least expensive carrier you had to leaf through three or four tariffs. But the computer chip has done away with all of that tedious work, plus adding many other benefits such as absolute accuracy and communicating with other data systems.

As manufacturers began to put computer chips to work in electronic scales and inexpensive printers smaller than a typewriter, a system evolved that takes all of the drudgery out of shipping any size parcel. Simply set a package on the electronic scale platform, push a button to select a carrier, and enter the destination ZIP Code. The system instantly shops for the best rate (or carrier), prints a postage meter tape or a UPS or RPS shipper ID label, creates a COD form, automatically assigns handling charges for invoicing, creates a carrier's manifest, and prints a label for the package. Later you can automatically print valuable management information through detailed reports of carriers and services used, by department, cost center, or product line. And the list goes on and on.

That's the good news! The bad news is that there are at least 22, yes, *twenty-two*, manufacturers that offer some type of manifest shipping system. With so many different systems available, it will not be easy for you to select the best one for your particular needs. However, if you develop a wish-list for all of the features you need now and those you may want to add later, it will be a start. Also, create a shopping list of all of the reports (weekly, monthly, quarterly, etc.) you need to create, and the communication links you will need to other computer systems. Armed with those lists, you should be prepared to discuss your need with some of the sales reps and view demonstrations and installations of proposed systems. As your selection narrows down to one or two manufacturers, features like ease of operation, methods of changing rates, and quality of local service may be as important as overall cost.

If your system wish-list includes the desirability of an interface with a postage meter, you would be wise to explore what kind of systems each of the meter manufacturers have to offer. Other systems may or may not have that capability.

To help you further, you should be alert for shopping guides and other articles published in some of the publications listed in *Chapter 18*. In order to include every known source of manifest shipping systems, only the telephone numbers are listed:

ADD+ON Software, Mission Viejo, CA	714-582-1555
Advanced Microwave, Sacramento, CA	916-635-1878
Aristo Computers, Beverton, OR	1-800-3ARISTO
ASAM International, Pleasant Hill, CA	415-686-4105
Datacard Corporation,Minnetonka, MN	1-800-826-0490
Detecto Scale, Roslyn, NY	1-800-641-2008
Digi Postal, Lenexa, KS	1-800-SAY-DIGI
FASCOR, Cincinnati, OH	513-421-1777
Friden Alcatel, Hayward, CA	1-800-624-7892
Full/Tech, San Diego, CA	619-297-0454
Harvey Software, Fort Myers, FL	1-800-231-0296
IMS/Hasler, Shelton, CT	1-800-243-6275
Malvern Scale, Malvern, PA	215-296-9642
MH Systems, San Francisco, CA	415-929-0522
Micro General, Santa Ana, CA	714-667-0577
MOS Scale, Cosa Mesa, CA	714-754-7841
Pitney Bowes, Stamford, CT	1-800-MR BOWES
Postalia, Downers Grove, IL	708-629-9100
Rock, F.C., & Assoc., Santa Rosa, CA	707-523-3102
TanData Corporation, Tulsa, OK	1-800-TANDATA
Tech Conveyor, Phillipsburg, NJ	201-454-1515
Weight-Tronix, Fairmont, MN	707-527-5555

OPENERS FOR MAIL

Several kinds of mail openers are available, and their different applications shouldn't be confused with each other. The traditional table-top opener is available for two specific applications. The first is the hand-fed rotary opener, which is used to open large, thick envelopes up to 12 inches long. The other opener accepts a large handful of mail and feeds it into the machine automatically. The automatic openers either feed the envelopes into two circular cutters parallel to the edge of the envelope or feed the envelopes past a thicker cutter turning perpendicular to the top edge. Both machines only trim off a fraction of an inch from the top edge of the envelope. Both types have the capability of opening about 500 letters per minute, depending on the length of the envelope.

In some medium-sized organizations, considerable time can be saved by opening much of the mail right in the mailroom. If there are fears that some mail may be lost while being distributed in a very large organization, then several mail openers might be strategically located wherever the bulk of the mail is destined. The enormous speed of the automatically fed machines make them able to justify themselves rapidly, so several locations are still economical.

When large quantities of mail are received in identical envelopes, they might easily be slit open by high-speed equipment in the mailroom, left in their envelopes and distributed to the proper departments in the same trays received from the USPS. For example, if you constantly receive envelopes from customers containing the top of their statement and a check, this type of mail is ideal for high-speed opening. In any case, whatever you are doing now might be analyzed to see exactly what is happening and what areas may be improved. This is another function that may change rapidly and needs an annual checkup and analysis.

At the other end of the spectrum are machines that accept a stack of mail two to three *feet* long. These machines cut the mail open on three sides and grasp the two sides of the envelope to expose the contents to a series of extraction stations. While they are certainly a part of the incoming mail function, they may actually belong in the area of accounts receivable and should probably be located there in many installations. However, it should be the responsibility of the manager of mail services to keep management up-to-date in the use of such equipment as it is a spin-off of the mailroom operation.

When investigating which machine may best suit your needs, do not overlook the Omation Corporation. They specialize in mail openers, machines that batch count, and machines that verify that your envelopes are empty. The other manufacturers of mail openers are also listed below:

Bell & Howell Phillipsburg Company
2202 N. Irving Street
Allentown, PA 18103-9554
215-266-4817

Friden Alcatel
30955 Huntwood Avenue
Hayward, CA 94544-7005
1-800-624-7892
In CA 1-800-624-7955

International Mailing Systems, Inc.
19 Forest Parkway
Shelton, CT 06484-6122
203-926-1087

Omation Corporation
253 Polaris Avenue
Mountain View, CA 94043-4514
415-0966-1396

Pitney Bowes
One Elmcroft Road
Stamford, CT 06926-0700
1-800-MR BOWES

Postalia, Inc.
1423 Centre Circle Drive
Downers Grove, IL 60515-1087
708-629-9100

POSTAGE METERS AND REGISTERS

If you inherited your present postage meter from your predecessor, or have limited experience with one, you may be surprised to learn that each of the four manufacturers can provide several different models, each with different characteristics. However, only certain models or series of meters will fit on specific mailing machines. In some cases, if you require a feature of a different meter you may need to replace your mailing machine in order to use that particular meter.

Three manufacturers can provide electronic postage meters. Friden Alcatel markets a *Postage on Call* meter; IMS/Hasler rents the *TMS Tele Meter Setting* system; and Pitney Bowes features its *Postage by Phone* meters. Each of those meters is reset through telephone lines, and providing the ultimate in mailer convenience.

In addition to those series of postage meters, each manufacturer has other models with different features. So, there are several factors to take into consideration when selecting a meter. One is the *maximum amount of postage* that can be purchased. Twenty odd years ago you could only purchase $9,999 in postage for most meters, and a meter attached to a multistation inserter might need resetting two or three times a week. Now you can obtain a meter that can be set for up to $99,900 in postage, enabling you to mass produce more metered mail. Therefore, one factor to examine on a meter is the amount of postage it will accept at one time.

Another factor is the highest amount of postage the meter will *print*. In the 60's and 70's, Pitney Bowes had thousands of meters in use that would not print a stamp larger than 20 cents and more that would only print a maximum of one dollar. But times change, and now, in step with rising postage costs and overnight services, you can obtain a meter that can print up to $99.99 in a single stamp. Many mailers find that meters which can print up to $9.99 are quite adequate, but if you plan on sending very many heavy envelopes via Priority or Express Mail you may find it advantageous to use a meter that will print up to $99.99. Remember, anytime you ask a clerk to put *two or three postage meter stamps* on an envelope or package in order to pay the correct postage, you are undoubtedly going to have mistakes that will waste some postage.

Still another consideration is whether the meter is capable of printing postage in *decimal fractions* of a cent. Most meters print postage and account for postage (in the ascending and descending registers) in *whole* cents. But many of the discounts offered by the Postal Service (which frequently change) are in *tenths of a cent*. (There are several ways to pay additional postage when your meter will not print the correct, exact postage but they are somewhat cumbersome and should be avoided whenever possible.) For example, with the '91 rate changes the postage for nonpresorted ZIP+4 mail became 27 and *6/10ths* of a cent, presorted First-Class Mail became 24 and *8/10ths* of a cent and 3-digit ZIP+4 barcoded First-Class Mail became 23 and *9/10ths* of a cent, for one ounce or less.

Other meters have interface connections for electronic scales and accounting systems so that they may exchange data with the meter, but many do not. Some will set the postage amount based on what the scale "instructs" it.

Therefore, in selecting a postage meter (which often determines which model of mailing machine you may use) you must "shop" just as you select any other piece of mail center equipment. You must determine exactly what your needs are, both now and a "guesstimate" for the future, and match those needs with the postage meter features. In considering a postage meter ask yourself if you need:

[ ] an electronic meter?
[ ] to buy more than $9,999 in postage?
[ ] to print stamps larger than $9.99?
[ ] to print postage in tenths of a cent?
[ ] a scale that will "set" the meter?
[ ] a meter to interface with a scale or accounting system?

■*Parcel Registers* look exactly like postage meters but are used to pay shipping charges for United Parcel Service. For easy identification in using the correct unit in a busy mailroom the registers are painted UPS brown! They have been in use for almost 30 years and help to eliminate some of the paperwork associated with preparing a UPS shipment. At one time registers were available for several carriers in addition to UPS.

However, the proliferation of software for PC's and small, inexpensive, 9-pin dot-matrix printers make preparing UPS shipments a snap. They allow UPS-approved labels to be automatically generated, along with a multitude of other forms, plus a simultaneous UPS-acceptable shipping manifest to be printed at the end of the day. These complete systems save so much time and effort that they may well contribute to the demise of the parcel register.

If you are already using a parcel register and are contemplating buying or leasing a new mailing machine, make sure the manufacturer can provide a parcel register to fit the new machine.

RACKS FOR MAIL BAGS

You get the best mail service if you use mail trays and the USPS encourages you to use trays. But certain types of mailings, such as bulk business mail, require bundling, and then you will usually use mail sacks or bags. If that is the case, you will want to use *racks* for holding the bag(s) open. You would think that any kind of hook can be used to hang up a mail sack, but just wait until you get 50 or 60 pounds of mail in one and try to lift it off the hook. Then you will realize that commercial mail bag racks have specially designed hooks that allow you to drop the bag on the floor without lifting it up off of the hooks.

If your types of mail warrant bags instead of the preferred trays, you should be sure your system includes mail bag racks in sufficient quantity to hold your mail on *peak days* as well as others. Racks to hold from one to four bags are commonly available, with and without casters (from Charnstrom Company). If you have several mailing machines, you may find it advantageous to provide mail bag racks near each one rather than having clerks walk halfway across the room to a common set of bags.

W. A. Charnstrom Company
10901 Hampshire Avenue South
Minneapolis, MN 55438-2393
1-800-328-2962

Friden Alcatel
30955 Huntwood Avenue
Hayward, CA 94544-7005
1-800-624-7892
In CA 1-800-624-7955

Frederick Manufacturing
20 South Wisner Street
Frederick, MD 21701-5652
301-662-6811

A. Rifkin Company
P.O. Box 878
Wilkes-Barre, PA 18703-0878
1-800-458-7300
In PA 1-800-358-7300

SCALES

One of the earlier chapters stated that perhaps the computer chip has had a greater impact on addressing equipment than on any other piece of mailroom equipment, but that may be wrong. Perhaps the greatest impact by far has been on *scales*.

New postal rates set by Congress on July 1, 1845, were based on weight rather than the number of sheets, for the first time. Shortly after, small, fragile-looking counter-balanced scales appeared and really didn't change much for a hundred years. But right after WWII, in 1945, Pitney Bowes assigned a sales manager to promote the sales of letter openers, other mailing equipment, and *postal scales.*

All of the moving parts of Pitney Bowes scales were made of stainless steel, and the scales featured a pendulum and weight system with large easy-to-read charts that provided almost 100 percent accuracy. At the same time, the Triner Company was developing a series of precision scales that became the mainstay of the former Post Office Department.

But stationery stores featured spring scales at a fraction of the cost of Pitney Bowes scales. In spite of cautions printed on the face of the spring scales, *"Not Legal For Trade,"* mailers were often "penny wise and pound foolish" as they installed these error-prone devices in their offices.

Then, in August of 1958, one ounce of First-Class Mail increased to *FOUR CENTS!* Businessmen were appalled and began to search for ways to reduce postage costs. By then the P-B precision scales were up to about $135, and a salesman could be ejected from an office as soon as he quoted the price! (But many of those scales were in service 20 years later.)

All that changed with the microprocessor computer chip. Read Only Memory (ROM) chips could be "programmed" by the manufacturers with thousands of bits of rate information which a mailer could access to determine the costs of mailing and shipping. Instead of a serviceperson having to come to your office to replace the scale chart, the manufacturer sends you the *PROM* containing the new rates, and you simply plug it into the scale. But that is just the beginning of many, many advantages found in electronic scales.

There are, of course, many different sizes of electronic scales with different weight capacities. With an average "footprint" of about 10 x 12 inches, a capacity of up to 70 pounds, and weighing less than 10 pounds, an electronic scale will:

- ■Convert ZIP Codes to the correct shipping zone
- ■Provide up to two dozen major rate categories
- ■Add the cost of many USPS, UPS, or RPS special services
- ■Display prompts for operator to add more information
- ■Allow operator to "shop around" for least expensive rate
- ■Provide rates for key air express carriers
- ■Interface with (one or more) postage meters
- ■Interface with a data collection or on-line system
- ■Interface with one or more printers for labels and manifests
- ■Accept barcode data from an OCR wand

And, it accomplishes all of that with up to 1/128th of an ounce accuracy.

Speaking of accuracy, it would be well for you to recall *Chapter 13*, which discussed buying a fancy-looking, spring-operated letter scale and even having three or four models to choose from. The scale will have the current postage rates, but that's not the only thing it will have. *"NOT LEGAL FOR TRADE"* will be printed right on the face of the scale! And you remember what that means? It means that the scale is not accurate enough to be used in trade because *someone will be cheated.* And you should remember the slogan of the harried mail clerk, "Put some extra postage on it and it'll never come back!"

Again, repeating *Chapter 13*, the longer your mail operation has been established the more likely you are to have inadequate or inaccurate scales. But there is a simple test, borrow an electronic scale on trial. The completely accurate way to test your present scales is to weigh, seal, and stamp all of your mail just as you have always done, then *reweigh* your outgoing mail on an electronic scale. Repeat that several times, and you will quickly see how your savings will multiply. The reason of course is that a modern electronic letter scale can provide you with accuracy to within 1/128 of an ounce while most spring scales will be lucky to determine weights within 1/8th of an ounce. This area deserves your utmost continual observation if you are to enjoy accurate postage rating of your mail.

Electronic scales are available from:

Aristo Computers, Inc.
6700 SW 105th Avenue, Suite 307
Beaverton, OR 97005-5484
1-800-3ARISTO

Detecto Scale Company
1044 Northern Boulevard
Roslyn, NY 11576-1507
1-800-641-2008

Digi Postal Corporation
11135 West 79th Street
Lenexa, KS 66215-5239
1-800-SAY-DIGI

Friden Alcatel
30955 Huntwood Avenue
Hayward, CA 94544-7005
1-800-624-7892
In CA 1-800-624-7955

International Mailing Systems, Inc.
Hasler Mailing Machines
19 Forest Parkway
Shelton, CT 06484-6122
203-926-1087

Micro General
1740 E. Wilshire Avenue
Santa Ana, CA 92705-4615
714-667-0557

Pitney Bowes
One Elmcroft Road
Stamford, CT 06926-0700
1-800-MR BOWES

Postalia, Inc.
1423 Centre Circle Drive
Downers Grove, IL 60515-1087
708-629-910

Remember, a good rule of thumb is to take the price of the electronic scale and divide it by a (very) conservative life-span of five years or sixty, months. Then divide that figure by four weeks and see what your losses must equal to break even. Since most cheap scales weigh heavy, you will waste a minimum of 23 cents postage (after 2/3/91) every time your scale is wrong, and who knows how much by the year 2000. Then again, if it is a five-pound scale, and it weighs heavy on a typical air express shipment weighing three pounds to the third zone you will waste about *$5.75!*

SEALING SOLUTIONS

You may have peeped into an automobile radiator after it has been in use for two or three years, or seen the condition of a faucet when the washer was being replaced. If so, you will remember the scale and mineral deposits that begin to corrode the inside of a car radiator and many kinds of plumbing fixtures. Then you will quickly understand why your mailing machine stops sealing your envelopes.

Mailing machine manufacturers try to minimize this problem by constructing the sealers out of plastic, brass, and copper. But if the water contains sufficient minerals, it will clog up anything and everything. This has always plagued mailing machines, but now there is a solution.

There are (at least) three organizations that offer *sealing solution* especially designed to activate the glue on an envelope instantly. While assuring that your mail will remain confidential and secure, it will also eliminate the possibility of mineral deposits.

Mail Solutions, Inc. provides their *Quick Seal* in plastic gallon jugs shipped to you by the case. Pitney Bowes provides *EZ Seal* in half gallon containers, and also provides pre-packaged, disposable bottles that can replace your present water containers on over a dozen different mailing machines. Postmatic provides plastic gallon jugs of *concentrate*, each of which will make 16 gallons of *Seal-Tight*.

For more information on solutions to sealing problems you should write to:

Mail Solutions, Inc.
1904 Calumet Street
Clearwater, FL 34625-1107
813-447-4191

Pitney Bowes
40 Lindeman Drive
Trumbull, CT 06611-4785
1-800-243-7824

Postmatic, Inc.
780 86th Avenue, NW
Minneapolis, MN 55433
612-784-6046

SOFTWARE FOR MAIL CENTERS

Chapter 18 provides guidelines on staying up-to-date and one of the most important suggestions may be the creation of a series of product files. Set up by generic name rather than by manufacturer, the files then become a valuable library of sales literature and magazine articles. You might also include memos or notes you write after having seen a product at a colleague's office or at an exhibit. Depending on the size of your operation and the types of mail you process, you may want to set up files for most of the products in this chapter. In any event, you will certainly need one for "*Software*."

Software programs, encompassing all of the various mail-related computer programs, are involved in so many areas of mail management that they grow in importance every day. This may well be the primary area you should be alert to in every mail-oriented publication, exhibit, or conference. The reason for such vigilance is that when you do find a software program appropriate for your particular needs it usually isn't only a time or labor saver, it's *spectacular!*

For example, the software that *automatically* prints a UPS shipper label, package label, and a manifest, or *automatically* corrects an incorrect or missing ZIP Code as you simply enter an address into your files, is truly spectacular. The complete accuracy, the speed, the versatility, and the labor savings of these programs provide a quick return on your investment. Many professional mail managers believe this is just the beginning of more and more computer programs that will help reduce some of the tedious, time-consuming tasks in a mail center.

The following admittedly may be only a small percentage of all the software programs available, but it will help get you started.

Software Provides:	Vendors Name and Address:
Address file standardization and correction	Postalsoft, Inc. 4439 Mormon Coulee Road LaCrosse, WI 54601-8220 1-800-831-6245
Address file standardization ZIP Codes & ZIP+4 Codes	Polk 400 Pike Street Cincinnati, OH 45202-4280 513-381-3885
Certified and registered mail	Walz Postal Solutions 1139 South Mission Road, Suite C Fallbrook, CA 92028-3226 619-728-0565
List enhancement	Peoplesmith Software P.O. Box 384 North Scituate, MA 02060-0384
List management & all postal programs	Arc Tangent, Inc. 121 Gray Avenue Santa Barbara, CA 93101-1831 805-965-7277
List management	Business Computer Center, Inc. 813 Bedford Lane Libertyville, IL 60048-3001 1-800-397-9069
List management	Group 1 Software, Inc. 6404 Ivy Lane Greenbelt, MD 20770-1400 301-982-2000

<u>Software Provides:</u>	<u>Vendors Name and Address:</u>
List Management (CD-ROM ZIP+4 retrieval)	U.S. Postal Service National Address Information Center 6060 Primacy Parkway, Suite 101 Memphis, TN 38188-0001
Mail Flow Planning System	U.S. Postal Service Any Division or MSC Marketing Department
Postal discount programs	Richard Fleischer & Associates, Inc. 135 Village Road Roslyn Heights, NY 11577-1522 516-621-2826
Postal discount programs ZIP Codes & ZIP+4 Codes	First Data Resources 7302 Pacific Street Omaha, NE 68114-5400 1-800-338-6073
Postal discount programs ZIP Codes & ZIP+4 Codes	LPC, A Pitney Bowes Company 1200 Roosevelt Road Glen Ellyn, IL 60137-6098 1-800-MAILERS
Postal discount programs ZIP Codes & ZIP+4 Codes	Software Marketing Associates, Inc. 415 Silas Deane Highway Wethersfield, CT 06109-2119 203-721-8929
POSTNET Printing System PC compatible bar codes	Harvey Software, Inc. P.O. Box 06596 Fort Myers, FL 33906-6596 1-800-231-0296
Sack labels	Whittier Mailing Products 12435 Mar Vista Street Whittier, CA 90602-1196 213-698-7795
Shipping management for all carriers (Demo diskette free)	Shaw Software Company, Inc. 8930 Tintagel San Antonio, TX 78250-2043 512-681-8572
Shipping manifest systems for all carriers (Demo diskette $4)	Aristo Computers, Inc. 6700 SW 105th Avenue, Suite 307 Beaverton, OR 97005-5484 1-800-3ARISTO

Software Provides:	Vendors Name and Address:
Shipping systems Receiving systems	TanData Corporation 1400 South Boston Tulsa, OK 74119-3612 1-800-TANDATA
ZIP Code Directory & other ZIP products	DCC Data Service 1200 18th Street, NW, Suite 704 Washington, DC 20036-2506 1-800-431-2577
ZIP Code Directory & other ZIP products	Melissa Data Company 32118-8A Paseo Adelanto San Juan Capistrano, CA 92675-3606 1-800-443-8834

SORTING AND CONVEYOR SYSTEMS

How would you like to cope with 30 departments *each* receiving two or three bushels of mail every day, and about 50 percent of it consisting of relatively thick flats? If you tried ordinary sorting bins, your clerks would spend half their time just emptying the bins. But there is an easy solution. The Novak Company custom designs a unique mail sorting conveyor system which can make that volume of mail a snap.

The waist-high sorting section consists of 30 parallel one-inch slots, 15 in the horizontal surface and 15 in a vertical surface just an arm's length away. These one-inch slots lead to a series of rapidly moving belts that carry the mail through aluminum channels to large plastic tubs or "tote" boxes. This arrangement gives the clerk access to 30 different plastic tubs while standing in one spot.

To accompany the unique sorting bin area, Novak can provide a round dumping area, with the usual protective sides to prevent spilling mail, and a conical center that turns effortlessly. This arrangement allows unsorted mail to be brought within easy reach of the sorting clerk.

The mail tubs in turn are suitable for transporting the sorted mail to its final destination on any of several available conveyor systems that can serve multistory office buildings.

For example, if you need to distribute mail or urgent documents to more than one level in an office you can always use a mail cart and push it through the halls to an elevator. But if you must distribute mail to more than perhaps three or four floors in a building, the push cart and elevator solution may be less attractive.

There are three other methods for delivering mail (and other supplies) to multistory buildings.

■*Computerized Pneumatic Tube System:* The size of the plastic cylinders used in a computerized tube system are twice as large as those commonly seen in a drive-in bank station, and they will hold approximately 15 pounds of material. They are excellent as a distribution system for a fax center, for handling cash, or for the rapid distribution of urgent documents that are received during the day. Perhaps the simplicity of operation is another strong point of the computerized tube systems, for anyone can operate the sending and receiving stations. The TransLogic Corporation can provide more information on computerized tube systems.

■*Electric Track Vehicle System:* Operating under the direction of a central controller, the electric track vehicle (ETV) system features self-propelled vehicles (which can contain the tote boxes from a multi-channel sorter) that move along a network of modular aluminum track and switches. The individual vehicles can transport up to 50 pounds at speeds of up to 200 feet per minute with simple push-button controls at each station.

These systems are similar to a subway system, with totes full of mail being dispatched from station to station on a series of tracks, all computer controlled. It is very versatile, carrying computer tapes and printouts, office supplies, and internal mail back and forth throughout the organization. But one happy user said that one of the most valuable benefits may be the elimination of unwieldy mail-cart traffic in corridors and on elevators. Two manufacturers of ETV systems are TeleEngineering and the TransLogic Corporation.

■*Selective Vertical Conveyor System:* A modern-day version of the classic dumb waiter, the selective vertical conveyor, is anything but dumb. Aided and abetted by moving belts that move fiberglass totes into and away from dispatching platforms,the selective vertical conveyor is ideal for the establishment of decentralized mail distribution centers in multistory buildings. With easy-to-operate controls and a computerized monitoring system, it requires only a single vertical shaft. The TransLogic Corporation also manufactures selective vertical conveyor systems.

For obvious reasons, decisions regarding these systems are not to be taken lightly. It may be difficult to install one in an existing building. But whenever you are involved in establishing a mail system in a new building, you should certainly contact these manufacturers so that you may visit several of their installations.

A slightly different type of conveyor is available from Tech Conveyor. They provide a parcel shipping system that is a self-contained conveyor and computer shipping station processing up to 45 parcels per minute. They report that many options are available in addition to the baseline system, including manifesting and cost-center charge backs.

For more information on large sorters and conveyors, you can write to:

The Novak Company, Inc.   Tech Conveyor
55 Old Field Point Road   575 Elder Avenue
Greenwich, CT 06836-6149   Phillipsburg, NJ 08865-1544
1-800-243-8528   201-454-1515

TeleEngineering
P.O. Box 670
Newfoundland, NJ 07435-0670
201-208-0010

TransLogic Corporation
10825 East 47th Avenue
Denver, CO 80239-2913
1-800-525-1841

STAMP AFFIXERS

It has been a long-standing controversy, for at least 40 years, whether a meter stamp or a USPS postage stamp will "pull" better in direct mail advertising. There have been many debates about which type of envelope will produce the greatest number of leads.

Should you or your management consider entering this rivalry, you will want to know that devices containing rolls of 500 or 3,000 stamps can be attached to certain models of mailing machines, and they can apply stamps to envelopes as each one is sealed. Since these devices are driven by the same mechanism that drives a meter, they revolve at the same speed, usually 175 letters a minute on the larger automatic machines. The Postal Service usually provides large rolls of stamps for all levels of bulk and nonprofit mail, in addition to postage for First-Class Mail, so these machines provide you with great flexibility and seal your envelopes at the same time.

You can obtain further information about affixing postage stamps from:

Bowen Industries
7741 Alabama Avenue, Suite 1
Canoga Park, CA 91304-4904
818-340-4000

Mailing Machine Service, Inc.
1425 Chicago Avenue South
Minneapolis, MN 55404-1384
612-333-4291

Postmatic, Inc.
780 86th Avenue, NW
Minneapolis, MN 55433-5970
612-784-6046

STRAPPING AND TYING MACHINES

A decade ago, every time the Postal Service met with major bulk third-class mailers the discussion soon got around to bundles breaking open in the mail and the extra cost for the USPS to re-sort the mail. The bundles were tied on machines that needed careful service and attention if the knots were to survive mail processing en route to the destinations. But, once again, there has been a change. The Postal Service now urges all third-class mailers to use rubber bands to prepare letter-size bulk business mail bundles and encourages them further by providing free rubber bands. Rubber bands hold bundles securely and yet are flexible enough to prevent breaking intransit. However, there is no machine available for placing rubber bands around a four inch bundle of mail, so it becomes a slower operation than the old tying machines. In addition, the bands often break (a major contention of people who prepare bulk business mail) causing a real danger to eyes and a discomfort to hands when they snap.

In spite of the breaking problem associated with rubber bands, in the average mail center there is usually little need for a tying machine for general mail. Tying machines may still be used on bundles of larger flats but often even that operation has been replaced by *bundling machines* that use ¼ inch wide polypropylene strapping. Instead of an intimidating tying machine, table-top models carefully designed for general office use are available.

The bundling machines are great for reinforcing the sealing of boxes and cartons, for securely fastening two packages together for shipping to the same address, and for bundling incoming mail together for delivery to a distant point such as another building or floor.

The company that invented tying machines 75 years ago was B. H. Bunn Company, and their address is 2730 Drane Field Road, Lakeland, FL 33811-1395, telephone 813-647-1555. They also manufacture banding and bundling machines.

Another supplier of bundling machines is Felins, 8304 West Parkland Court, Milwaukee, WI 53223-9873, telephone 1-800-THE-LOOP.

Production size strappers and fully automated strapping machines are available from:

EAM Industries
675 Jaycee Drive
West Hazelton, PA 18201-1155
717-459-3426

Wilton Corporation
300 South Hicks Road
Palatine, IL 60067-6900
1-800-323-6026

TAPE DISPENSERS

The section on *gummed sealing tape* in *Chapter 6* discusses the virtues of using "programmable" tape dispensers. They reduce tape consumption by dispensing the correct length, no more, no less. The other advantage is that some models heat the water in which the sealing brushes rest, and the warm water activates the glue more thoroughly. This in turn provides you with a faster, more secure seal. No one should attempt to use paper tape to seal cartons without a dispenser unless he or she expects to waste considerable time in cutting tape by hand and working with messy moisteners that may or may not fully activate the glue.

The tape dispenser market appears to be totally dominated by one organization, Better Packages, a division of International Mailing Systems, 19 Forest Parkway, Shelton, CT 06484-0903, telephone 203-926-1087. They provide a variety of models, and if you are contemplating buying either your first tape dispenser, or simply replacing an old model, you should write or call for a brochure showing the different models and features of each. Carefully consider the advantages of being able to print on the tape simultaneously as it is ejected, push button control of the length of the tape, and the plus of having a foot pedal for continuous production.

OTHER MAIL EQUIPMENT

■*Bag Tag Printer:* A complete system is available, consisting of a small computer, printer, and software, under the trade name of *BagTagger.* When you need a tag for a bag of mail, instead of trying to locate it in a cabinet, you simply enter the correct destination ZIP Code and mail class, and the printer prints the correct bag tag. It not only formats the tag exactly as required by USPS regulations for each class of mail, it includes a barcode on the tag. The system is updated quarterly to remain current with the latest USPS revisions. For additional information, contact Whittier Mailing Products, 12435 Mar Vista Street, Whittier, CA 90602-1196, telephone 213-698-7795.

■*Bag Tag Racks*: Whether you stock 100 or 1,000 bag tags, a rack is available to hold each ZIP Code for easy selection. A free guide to bag tag storage is available from Viking Metal Cabinet Company, Inc., 5321 W. 65th Street, Chicago, IL 60638-5692, telephone 708-594-1111. The guide describes how best to use their all-steel racks.

■*Canvas Mail Pouches*: If you have branch offices nearby and use a courier or employee to deliver mail to the branches, or have several buildings that you deliver mail to in all kinds of weather, you may find that canvas mail pouches are very worthwhile. They are available in a variety of sizes and are also available with a hasp for a lock for added security. Both of the following will send you a catalog featuring their products, which include canvas mail pouches:

W.A. Charnstrom Company
10901 Hampshire Avenue, South
Minneapolis, MN 55438-2393
1-800-328-2962
In MN 612-944-8555

A. Rifkin Company
P.O. Box 878
Wilkes Barre, PA 18703-0878
1-800-458-7300
In PA 1-800-358-7300

■*Drop Boxes:* Unless there is no USPS collection box for miles and miles, you should not accept stamped employee mail into an organization's outgoing business mail. You must keep it separate from metered mail, so it often becomes just another unnecessary bundling separation. If you do want to provide personal mail service to employees, you will find that some type of collection box will keep it all together. Some boxes even hold bags so the personal stamped mail drops directly into a sack. Various sizes are available from W.A. Charnstrom Company.

■*Mail Boxes*: Many mail operations in addition to colleges and universities could benefit from individual mail boxes. Among other things, they allow you to provide off-premise delivery with absolute security and the versatility of having recipients pick up mail from individual boxes. You may even aid the sorting by requiring addresses to contain the box numbers. Boxes are available that load from the front, or the traditional box as used by a post office, which loads from the rear and is emptied by individual doors at the front.   The Charnstrom Company sells several kinds of these boxes, as does Salsbury Mailboxes, 1010 East 62nd Street, Los Angeles, CA 90001-1598, telephone 213-232-6181

■*Rubber Floor Mats*: Many jobs in the mailroom must be done standing up, but that doesn't mean that the mail handlers must stand all day on a hard concrete or asphalt tile floor. Rubber matting, from 3/8 to 1/2 inches thick, placed in front of inserting machines, mailing machines, and sorting bins can be a big factor in increasing productivity. The mats can boost morale, help fight fatigue, and improve efficiency at very little cost. They are available in ready-cut mats or in continuous rolls, measuring up to 36 inches wide, and will be a welcome addition to your mailroom. You can purchase rubber matting, cut to size, from companies listed in the *Yellow Pages* under *Rubber Products.*

■*Stitcher for Shipping Bags*: Similar to a small sewing machine, a stitcher is available which, according to the manufacturer, can close padded envelopes "in less than 2 seconds" with a chain stitch similar to the one you may have seen on fertilizer or bird seed bags. This may be a welcome change from metal staples, which can catch on other mail and, more important, cut mail handlers' hands. This unique machine is available from Fichbein Company, 2700 30th Avenue, South, Minneapolis, MN 55406-1600, telephone 612-721-4806.

SHOPPING WISELY

It is often difficult to locate sources of mailroom equipment. Books listing industrial sources for all kinds of products devote little, if any, space to mailroom equipment. Consulting the *Yellow Pages* is a good start, but if you are off the beaten path or in a smaller community, they are often inadequate. These are some of the reasons why it is important for a busy mail manager, who wants to stay abreast of new developments, to receive several of the magazines devoted to office and mail management. The advertisements that appear in such magazines allow mail center managers to "browse and shop," to make some elementary decisions regarding the applicability of various types of equipment, and to identify new products that have the potential for reducing costs.

There are several other important sources, and they are listed in

Chapter 18.

If you have either too little time or too little budget, you can, for a relatively small fee, visit the exhibit halls of the *National Postal Forums* without taking part in the entire program. Other sponsors may also allow visits to exhibits. Taking a day trip can give you great flexibility when you find it is simply impossible to attend a conference but want to see the equipment on display. Exhibit halls available to mailers anywhere within a hundred miles or so of where the event is being held--or even farther if you stay in a hotel room for one night. That is not a big investment if you are appraising a piece of equipment worth five or ten thousand dollars.

The Postal Service encourages its *Postal Customer Councils* (PCCs) to include exhibits in conjunction with their meetings, and some PCCs have annual affairs that include well-attended exhibits as part of a mini-forum program.

The manufacturers and dealers of mailroom equipment often maintain mailing lists of potential customers to which they periodically mail new product information. Do not hesitate to add your name to their lists at every opportunity, for they offer a fine source of information and are very valuable to the professional mail manager.

There is still another important source of information on mail equipment. That is, advice from someone who already has something similar to what you need, or *networking*. There is an unlimited number of sources, and you could contact any organization that you think might have the type of equipment you need. Any businesses or organizations similar to yours, for example, would also be places you might ask to visit. Other sources for people using the equipment you are considering might be among the members of a PCC.

Proof Positive

As in any industry that is growing rapidly, along with a strong interest in electronics, there are occasionally a few wild claims and exaggerations. The shopper can become confused and skeptical, but there is a simple solution. *Just ask a few questions!*

- Where do you have an installation of this model?
- How long has it been installed there?
- May I have the name and telephone number of the manager?
- Do you have other installations nearby?
- Can you arrange for me to visit one of these installations?

Either the sales representative will have several installations that you may telephone to learn more about how well the equipment operates under actual business conditions or else he or she will dodge the issue. Most of the time you will get a completely honest report from an actual user, with even a few pet gripes perhaps about some operating detail. Then you will be in a much better position to evaluate just how well the piece of equipment might fit into your own operation. Prospective purchasers of mailroom equipment do not use this method of evaluation as often as they might, yet it is practically foolproof.

If you are located in a smaller community and do not have neighbors that utilize the type of equipment that you may be investigating, do not hesitate to call long distance to verify the satisfaction of a user. Obviously, the amount of investment in researching the satisfaction of other users must be in proportion to the cost of the equipment. But as the price goes up a trip by automobile to a city 100 miles away or even a round-trip airline ticket may be a wise expenditure.

Request a Proposal

As your search narrows down to the exact features and the specific model of equipment you believe will best suit your requirements, you should always require the manufacturer or dealer to provide you with a written proposal on the model you have selected. The proposal should include all of the benefits that the sales representative believes you will gain and the *specifications* of large, complex equipment. This is the time to get in writing all of the points the sales representative may have promised, particularly those having to do with service and warranties. If the sales representative has provided lease figures they should be included in the proposal as well.

Obviously, the proposal provides you with a written record of the terms and conditions of the sale and the features of the equipment, but it does more. It provides you with a valuable tool if you have to seek management's concurrence to buy or lease the equipment. More than likely, the sales representative has been especially trained to sell the equipment in question. In addition, he or she may have several years of experience, so it is doubtful that you could begin to "sell" the equipment as well. Consequently, not only will the proposal do a better job of selling than you might be able to do, you may consider taking the salesperson along if you must meet with your management to discuss the merits of the proposed equipment.

Request a Free Trial

Either before or after you have obtained the necessary approvals from your management and are relatively sure of the benefits of the new equipment, you may take one more precaution and that is to *request a free trial period*. While there are some types of equipment that do not lend themselves well to a trial period, a great many do. If the equipment does not require some customizing that would permanently affect it, a conscientious manufacturer or dealer will usually welcome the opportunity to place equipment on trial.

There are several advantages to a free trial. It will give you an opportunity to see how well your employees adapt to the equipment, how well it will process *your* forms, envelopes, or other material, and it may provide you with an opportunity to have your management people view the equipment in action. Many mail managers have reported that if they use a piece of equipment on trial they do *not* confide in the employees that it is only a trial. They feel very strongly that the employees respond more naturally and honestly to equipment when they think it is there to stay.

Investigate Leasing

Finally, after all the shopping around, the proposals, and the trials, when there is no question remaining about getting the new equipment, *you should investigate leasing.*

In the early sixties it took real sales effort to convince a mailer that it was profitable to lease a piece of equipment rather than buy it. The lease cost more on the face of the transaction, but the disbelievers soon realized that the value in having a piece of equipment wasn't in *owning* it, it was in *using* it.

The idea grew rapidly. By the late seventies, perhaps 35 percent of all office and mailroom equipment was *leased* to customers. Some manufacturers even established their own leasing companies (known as *captives)* to conveniently handle the leases their sales representatives write for customers. By the latter part of the eighties, leasing of equipment exceeded $100 billion.

The lease gives mailers a much greater opportunity to acquire all the equipment they want without taking actual ownership of the machines. The mailer selects the equipment, the manufacturer sells the equipment to a leasing organization, who in turn leases it to the mailer. It is an excellent way to improve any mail center operation without a large outlay of cash. You should understand, however, while some manufacturers "rent" equipment, often with 30-day cancellation options, a lease binds the lessee for a definite period, usually 36 or 60 months. The lessee is responsible for the full term of the lease, and most leasing companies will not consider cancelling any lease prior to its completion.

One of the reasons that financial people like to lease equipment is that, in most cases, the entire lease payment is a tax deductible business expense. But, there is another equally important reason to lease mail center equipment. In a world where there are often significant changes, in the quantities and types of mail, in new postal discount programs, and in new equipment, it is very rewarding to have some flexibility to make changes. If you *purchase* a piece of equipment and *own* it, you may be astounded at the low trade-in it will have in just three years. On the other hand, if that same piece of equipment is on a 36-month lease, you simply tell the leasing company to come get the equipment at the end of the lease term. Then you are free to select that newer, bigger, faster piece of equipment with up-to-date technology and far more benefits for your mail center.

Usage Amortization

In analyzing your needs, be careful that the price tag doesn't scare you half to death. The price tag is really of no consequence whatsoever. What *is* important is *what the machine will do for you and how it will benefit your organization.* That is the only consideration as you evaluate whether your organization should invest in any piece of equipment.

Furthermore, do not let the accountants lead you astray. Unless the price is many, many thousands of dollars, the length of time it will take for the organization to "write off" a piece of equipment is unimportant. It doesn't matter whether the tax experts recommend that you carry the expense of equipment for 5 years, 7 years, or 10 years. Just because you may still have several hundred dollars to write off on an old clunker is no reason to continue to keep an outdated machine you have outgrown.

Instead, the way to analyze your investment should be based on *usage amortization.* Never mind the *tax* amortization, the accountants will take care of that. What you want to do is study the piece of equipment on a basis of *usage,* because that's what will pay for it, not the tax write-off. Here is an example of how this works. If you are considering a piece of equipment that you know positively can be justified in work hours saved over a two-year period, your only concern might be based solely on whether that piece of equipment will operate well for those two years. At the end of that time, the machine will be paid for in dollars saved in labor. What you do with the equipment after that date should have no bearing whatsoever on the tax amortization because you know you paid for it with *usage amortization.*

Preventive Maintenance

After you have proven that the dollars invested in the new mailing equipment are a bargain, what are you going to do about preventive maintenance? Far too often the answer from the mail manager is, "We'll worry about that when the time comes." So, the initial investment is used and abused until one day it quits, long before its time, and ends up as a small trade-in on a new model. Often the same person who thoroughly studies the cost versus the benefits *before* a purchase or lease will ignore the need to protect the investment with proper service and maintenance *after* acquiring the equipment.

Professional mail managers will not lose sight of the inconvenience and waste in work hours that can be caused by improperly maintained equipment. Some of the records necessary to equipment maintenance are suggested in *Chapter 13.*

CHAPTER 17

MANAGING MAILROOM PERSONNEL

You may have the finest layout in your mail center and all of the latest equipment, but if you cannot effectively manage your personnel you will have one headache after another. It may often seem that you have to work as hard to motivate your people as to keep up-to-date on mailing equipment or the latest postal regulations. Yet, in some mail centers you find everyone is pulling together, everyone helps get each other's tasks completed on time, and there is a sense of urgency in the air. In other mailrooms, there is considerable bickering, everyone seems disorganized, and there seems to be one problem after another. What causes such extreme differences in the same basic kinds of work, the same general wages, and similar working conditions? Why does it often take one crew twice as long as an other to get similar tasks finished? Why are the attitudes in the two mail centers so radically different?

There can be many answers to those questions. But the greatest overall factor in the less productive mailroom is probably the kind of treatment the employees receive. If they are managed by a domineering tyrant in an organization that has no feeling for the employees, the employees are highly unlikely to put their best effort into their work. If they are treated poorly throughout the organization, have little self-respect, and believe they are trapped in a low-paying job, there will be little incentive to improve their skills.

But take those same people and treat them as if you care about them, encourage them to learn new skills, provide a pleasant environment for them to work in, and offer several levels of income that they may strive for, and you will have a totally new work force. Basically, you only need to treat them like you yourself would like to be treated, and you will see a new sense of cooperative spirit begin to develop which will invariably result in greater productivity. This chapter contains many more ideas for you to use to increase productivity but the most important are simply to show that you and your organization *care* and create a pleasant workplace with adequate compensation.

DEVELOPING JOB DESCRIPTIONS

Job descriptions are a blessing in disguise for everyone: the employee, the manager, and the organization as a whole. Without a job description only the employee knows what he or she does all day long. If no one else knows what work is accomplished, the employee is not likely to be fairly compensated for work that is completed. If the immediate manager does not know what the employee should do all day, it is impossible to determine whether or not the employee is completing the work assigned or is allowing the work to expand to fill the hours. And, finally, if management has no idea what any of the employees are *supposed* to do all day, there will be chaos.

To aid you in establishing your own realistic mailroom job descriptions, you can use the following methods to collect the data you need:

1. Observation of workers as they perform their tasks
2. Interview of workers to clarify and verify information
3. A questionnaire with multiple-choice or structured questions
4. Logs maintained by the workers indicating duties performed
5. Combinations of these data collection methods

After you have collected information to use in analyzing each position and you begin to create the actual job descriptions, the format shown in Figure 13 will serve as a guide. In establishing both the duties and the personal requirements, be very specific but be realistic so the personal attributes can actually be found within your organization or job market. Also, be sure the duties actually can be achieved. Goals should serve as a carrot for the worker, but they must be *attainable* if they are to be effective. Professional mail managers will make sure that the employees under their super-vision are provided with an adequate income, goals that are attainable, job satisfaction, and plain old-fashioned self-respect.

UTILIZING PERSONNEL

In addition to the general concepts of managing mailroom personnel that were mentioned at the beginning of this chapter, there are other ways you can obtain maximum productivity from your people. Some may not fit into your organization at present but may be useful later. These are not earth-shaking, but when grouped together they will greatly improve your overall mail operation.

Advantages of Early Birds

Since each individual is different and has different likes and dislikes, those basic differences can work to your advantage in managing the mail clerks' working hours. Some people are early morning people, others start more slowly in the morning but never seem to tire as evening approaches. Even as you are reading this, you know exactly who is likely to turn the lights on tomorrow morning in your mail center. Most people are creatures of habit, so that person probably comes in early *every morning* and enjoys arriving at that time of day. Perhaps you are fortunate in having several people who arrive before the others every day. If so, you may find that

---

POSITION TITLE: Manager, Incoming Mail   DATE: January 22, 1991

DIVISION: Office Services   POSITION INDEX NO.: MC-23

DEPARTMENT: Communications   PREPARED BY: Fred N. West

LOCATION: Headquarters   APPROVED BY: J. Hartley

RESPONSIBILITIES: Receives and processes all incoming organization mail; collects and redistributes all internal mail messages.

DEFINITION OF DUTIES: 1-Gives overall direction to receiving and processing all incoming mail.

2-Remains thoroughly familiar and up-to-date with entire organizational structure.

3-Establishes priorities for sorting and distributing all incoming mail.

4-Establishes distribution scheme for all incoming mail to assure delivery to ultimate destination.

5-Establishes and directs the distribution of all internal mail messages.

6-Performs actual sorting and distribution of both inbound and internal mail as necessary.

7-Works closely with Manager, Outgoing Mail; maintains working knowledge of all USPS mailing regulations and requirements. Performs other duties on outgoing mail as requested.

PERSONAL REQUIREMENTS

EDUCATION REQUIRED: High school education or equivalent; extensive knowledge of Domestic Mail Manual.

EXPERIENCE DESIRABLE: Two years' minimum actual work experience in mailroom or related mail processing.

PHYSICAL DEMANDS: General good health; capability of lifting 70# mail sacks is desirable.

LEADERSHIP: Must be able to communicate well, both orally and in writing. Responsible to Supervisor, Mail Services, for all Incoming Mail Handlers, currently authorized for three to four employees.

Figure 13 Typical format for mailroom job description.

they will welcome the opportunity to arrive extra early at a specific time, to open your mail center and get the day started. Of course there must be work for them to do, but such an arrangement is especially helpful if you can get your incoming mail very early in the morning. Then if you can arrange to let those people go home a half an hour or an hour before the others, you will have a staggered work crew without any great inconvenience to anyone and with no additional cost for overtime. In that way you will be able to provide mail service to the organization for a longer period each day.

Operating Two Shifts

All of the USPS mail "factories" operate on a 24-hour basis (except for Sunday evening) and there are three 8-hour shifts. While you may not need to provide such extended hours of mail service to your organization, the nature of your organization may make it highly desirable to have your mail center open considerably longer than eight hours.

For example, if you are able to pick up your mail early enough to begin sorting at 7:30 a.m., those sorters may be earning overtime after 4:30 p.m. But, shut down the mailroom in the average organization at 4:30 p.m., and you are likely to hear loud repercussions. In fact, with a couple of hard-driving executives around, you may be expected to get the last few pieces of mail about 6:00 p.m., or even later.

There are two ways to deal with this late mail, assuming you can get it deposited directly into an SCF, MSC, or division facility for processing that night. One is to use some reliable person or persons to arrive late and stay late, in conjunction with an "early bird." But, if relatively large volumes of outgoing mail consistently arrive late in the day, you may find it extremely advantageous to utilize two shifts. In that manner you can continue to process your incoming mail very early in the morning and yet have some mail clerks work until 6:00 p.m. or later. Using two shifts will give you greater flexibility (and probably make you a hero, or a heroine, upstairs). Remember, too, just because you are working two shifts does not mean that they must be equal in size. You may need more people to process your outgoing mail than it takes to handle incoming mail, so you may have 20 percent more people available in the latter part of the afternoon. Furthermore, you should personally visit the mailroom periodically during the early and late periods to see that everyone is gainfully employed.

Part-time and Temporary Employees

All kinds of businesses have peak loads from time to time that strain their capacity to complete work on time. Those businesses have the same problems that you do, they have an unexpected volume of work and a specific date when it must be finished.

The Postal Service consistently has large peaks of volume and has long employed *part-time workers* to assist in processing mail during peak periods. In fact, it employs what at first may sound like a contradiction of terms, *permanent part-time* employees. That is, employees who work only part-time, but do so continually, usually on a specific schedule.

There are many advantages to permanent part-time employees. They help you cope with large peaks of work such as annual dues, monthly statements, membership notices, or any type of mailing that is larger than usual. They may be equally valuable coping with the Monday or post-holiday mail, or following any promotion that generates incoming mail.

Permanent part-time employees are less expensive to employ than permanent employees because they usually do not participate in the various fringe benefits, such as vacation or sick pay, medical coverage, or retirement costs. Yet they can be a godsend when you experience peaks in mail volume.

There are many sources for permanent part-time employees. Retirees often enjoy a few hours of work and the additional income. Housewives with children in school are often available during school hours, and many businesses employ students from nearby colleges and universities. Most newspapers have a "part-time" column in the help-wanted sections.

At the same time, do not overlook the advantages of *temporary* workers, whether you build a file of interested people or call on an employment agency that provides temporary employees. The employment agencies usually screen their candidates relatively well, and many have considerable office skills.

If you think you may need a temporary worker at some time in the future, do not wait until the need is urgent. Instead, you should do your research *before* the crisis, so you will know exactly who to call, and they in turn will know what kind of people you require. The National Association of Temporary Services offers a free booklet, *How To Buy Temporary Help Services*, if you send a stamped, self-addressed envelope to them at 119 S. St. Asaph Street, Alexandria, VA 22314-3119.

Primary and Secondary Operators

If you walk into your office tomorrow morning and find that Joe, the inserting machine operator, has called in sick with the flu, who will get all of those statements out? Do you panic whenever key personnel are suddenly absent because of illness or some other emergency? It need not be that way. All you have to do is to assign *primary* and *secondary* operators to each piece of equipment, train each one to develop operational skills, and post the list on a permanent bulletin board. Such a system eliminates problems about who is going to do what, and it eliminates anxiety. The secondary operator may even need replacing on his or her usual machine assignment, but that is all right, the more time each operator spends on different machines the more proficient he or she becomes on each one. In this manner your systems and processes keep right on functioning. This cross-training is vital to a smoothly running operation for any mail center. It is an easy thing to put off, what with training new employees, attending meetings yourself, and a thousand other details. But the importance of this cross-training and use of primary and secondary operators may be right at the top of the list of urgent steps toward developing a smoother operation.

MANAGING THROUGH SUPERVISORS

If you chat awhile with a military person you are likely to hear that person say, "Oh, the sergeants take care of that!" It isn't that the sergeants do all of the work, but they are *responsible* for those who do. Mail management needs its sergeants too, to supervise. Even a very small mailroom needs to have someone in charge at all times. If nothing else, you need a supervisor to take over the responsibility when *you* are absent, on vacation, or attending meetings and mail conferences.

It is difficult to pinpoint exactly how large an operation needs a supervisor, beyond designating someone to fill in for your own absence. It depends a great deal on how complex the types of mail are in your mail center, but it is somewhere between 6 and 10 people. At that point you will find it increasingly difficult to train, observe, motivate, encourage, console and manage each one individually. As the number of people increases you need to devote careful attention to the ratio of supervisors to mail clerks. But because many mail clerks are often entry level personnel, they will definitely require considerable leadership and direction. Thus, the supervisors need to do more than simply manage in your absence, for they are a great deal more than a substitute for a manager. Here are some of the ways they can increase productivity in any mail center.

▪*Assist in Training*: When you are busy trying to do 10 things at once, who is going to train that new employee who started last week? Are you all thumbs when it comes to operating mechanical equipment? With a knowledgeable, well-developed supervisor you can be relieved of those chores and yet have confidence that the new employee will be well trained. If you cultivate those persons who are trainers, feed them every kind of information on material, machines, and postal regulations, they will become more and more valuable to you. You will be able to depend on them to a greater extent to carry out your wishes and instructions. This, in turn, frees you to chase down and resolve problems, to spend more time in maintaining and analyzing records, and to *manage* the work instead of *doing* the work.

There is another big plus for you when you develop a competent supervisor. More than one person has been held back because management believed, "There just isn't anyone who can do your job as well as you do, we can't spare you now." Whatever career path you choose to pursue, having a sharp assistant whom you have personally trained, ready to step into your job, will always be a plus for you.

■*Train in Greater Depth*:   With the kinds of job pressures the average professional mail manager experiences, personnel training will rarely be as thorough as that which a supervisor can do.   Every time you start to settle down and review postal cautions or important operating procedures for a piece of equipment, the phone will ring, or you will be called to a meeting with management.   You should be involved in management techniques involving postal regulations, machines, and people, and you rarely can devote sufficient time to adequately train newer employees.   So, a supervisor not only relieves you of some of the training responsibility but is able to do it better and more thoroughly.   You should remember, too, the better the training in the beginning, the fewer mistakes and problems later.

■*Oversee Processing Accuracy*:   In addition to carrying the burden of comprehensive training, a supervisor can watch over *all* of the many processes that take place in the average mail center.   Are the right people doing the right jobs?   Are the inserts being folded correctly to fit the window envelope accurately?   Has the date on the postage meter been changed?   Is the mailing machine sealing the mail properly?   The supervisor oversees these daily double-checks which prevent a major problem.   The more postal programs in which you participate, the more you will need to rely on someone to check behind those preparing the mail.

■*Carryout Management's Wishes*:   Whatever policies you and your management establish, whatever rules you set up to control productivity and the general working conditions in the mail center, the supervisor can help you implement them.   Properly managed, the supervisor wears two hats.   He or she becomes a sort of shop steward or representative of the others who work in the mailroom but understands what management expects and helps to carry out those wishes.   A sensitive supervisor may help smooth out ruffled feathers one instant and gently enforce a basic ground rule of behavior the next.

■*Provide Job Incentives*:   Carrying the concept of executing management's wishes one step further, if you appointed five or six supervisors, you probably should establish a supervisor for the supervisors.   This so-called *chain of command* serves two distinct and important purposes.   True, it is a valuable tool to aid you in managing all of your employees.   But, equally important, each position of *supervisor* is looked upon as an honor and therefore becomes a strong incentive for all of the employees.   It is even an incentive for the person who *already holds the position*.

BENEFITS OF SPECIALISTS

Whether you have three employees or 30, you will experience great benefits if you develop *specialists*.   If you will carefully cultivate specialists throughout your operation you will soon see that nothing beats the expertise of employees who pride themselves on being well informed.   This must be a continual process.   You provide the sources of information and then make sure to rely on that person for answers. Here are some of the kinds of specialists you should develop.

■*Machine Operators*: Not everyone is dexterous, not everyone is mechanically inclined, in fact half of the people can't program their own VCR! But, hopefully, you have found one or two who are excellent machine operators. When you do find such a person, you should make sure you assign him or her to your most complicated piece of equipment. That is the person to send to service training, that is the person you ask to help others less (mechanically) talented, and that is the person you make the guru of all equipment. As that specialist develops greater expertise in use of your equipment your mechanical problems will be few and far between.

■*Rates and Classification*: This specialist has to be chosen carefully; it will probably be a supervisor who takes pride in reading and understanding the *Domestic Mail Manual*. He or she will also need to develop a key contact at your local post office (an account rep or the manager of mailing requirements) in order to clarify questions that arise.

This specialist may not be easy to identify among your employees for the *DMM* is not a simple guide, to say the least. It is somewhat complex. So, you will have to select someone who will accept the challenge of carefully reading each issue of the *Postal Bulletin*, and who has a desire to learn his or her way around in the *DMM*.

This is the person you occasionally send out or take along to classification training classes sponsored by the USPS or others. This is the person who is responsible for maintaining your subscriptions to the *DMM* and the *Postal Bulletin*, and who maintains the *Postal Bulletin* files.

■*Presort or Other Programs*: This person needs to have somewhat the same personal drive as the rates and classification specialist. Motivated to have *every* mailing accepted perfectly at the post office, this person must learn every detail of each USPS program in which you participate. If you farm out your mail to a presort bureau, this specialist is responsible for having the proper meter stamp and legends on the mail and serves as the liaison with the presort bureau.

■*Special Services*: Can third-class mail be certified? Can a padded bag be registered? What exactly is special handling? Who knows? Your special services specialist will know and will save you from all kinds of wasted postage for unnecessary services or returned mail. The more varied your mail operation is, the more valuable this specialist will be to you.

■*International Mail*: This specialist is similar to the rates and classification specialist, only he or she works with the *International Mail Manual*, learns all the ins and outs of international mail, and keeps you advised of potential disasters.

■*Air Express*: This specialist works closely with all carriers who offer overnight air express for both domestic and international destinations. He or she should maintain an up-to-date library of the shipping guides from carriers with whom you do business and understand the special services available from overnight carriers. This specialist may also operate manifest systems for you on all rush shipments and can save you a great deal of money.

ADEQUATE COMPENSATION

This is a trying time for labor and management alike. In the last half of 1990, over one million people were laid off. By mid-'91, Sears alone expects to lay off over 20,000 employees. Profits are down in many companies, and many businesses are looking for ways to cut expenses.

Those facts, coupled with what has become a recognized recession, do not contribute to a growing, healthy income scale for the average mail center clerk. Whenever organizations want to reduce their payroll, they often look at dismissing those in entry-level positions. This can have a drastic impact on the success of any mail operation. Turnover in the mail center can be very detrimental to the quality of service you are trying to develop and maintain. Furthermore, turn-over coupled with inadequate compensation simply causes more aggravation.

One of the greatest contributions you can make toward stabilizing your operation is to continually work to convince your management that the pay scale in the mail center *must* be at least equal to that of all other beginning positions throughout the organization. The other essential ingredient is to provide a level of pay comparable to that for similar jobs in your area, whether it be downtown Chicago or a tiny town in Texas. If all of the fast food restaurants are paying $6 or $7 an hour, you are not likely to attract very many competent employees if your highest mailroom wage is only $4.25 an hour, or the current minimum wage. A number of experienced mail managers have reported that when they offered 10 to 20 percent *more* than surrounding employers, their turnover was almost eliminated.

These things are not easy to change, but you should remember that the wage level in your mail center must be comparable to wages for (1) similar positions elsewhere in the organization, and (2) similar positions in the surrounding community.

GRADUATED PAY SCALES

Regardless of the level of pay you are able to negotiate with management you will benefit by having a graduated pay scale. No one likes to work for two or three years for exactly the same income. Even if your organization provides an annual cost of living allowance, you should consider establishing several levels of compensation for each job category in your mailroom. Many managers will use a probationary period of about 90 days to evaluate a new employee, provide a small increase, and then begin annual increases of hourly pay. Such a setup is not a huge incentive but it does provide some inducement to improve basic skills. If you are able to establish graduated pay scales, be sure to identify each level on the corresponding job description.

MORALE AND MOTIVATION

When you consider that the mailroom often has the lowest paid jobs in any organization, and that only recently has the mailroom been recognized as deserving better than the basement, then it is no wonder that you can find low morale among many mail clerks. In one mail center you might find inadequate compensation, a dirty, crowded area, and poorly maintained equipment. In another you might find inadequate equipment, no career opportunities, no recognition of workers' feelings, and a management in which no one will listen.

Each of those problems affects the attitudes of the mail center employees, often causing mental stress, and generally reducing the morale of each one. But it does not have to be that way. It is not necessary to provide a richly outfitted, spacious area to process the mail. Employees do not have to receive outlandish pay checks. All they need are things that say, "Hey, we think you are very special." They simply need to know the organization cares.

Here are a few ideas that you might incorporate into your motivation program.

■*Cash Suggestion Program:* Always keep soliciting suggestions from your mail center people. Time- and money-saving ideas most often originate from those who do the work. You do not have to pay $500 for every idea, there are plenty of ideas that may be worth only $25, but you never know when you might hit the jackpot. Keep 'em thinking all the time!

■*Always Promote From Within:* Whenever you need a supervisor or a specialist, try to promote someone who is already working in your mailroom. Obviously, if you can hire someone with extensive experience you should do so. But if you let people from the print shop, the shipping department, or somewhere else in the organization come in as supervisors, it will disillusion the rest of your staff.

■*Year-end Bonuses:* Suppose you tackle a new USPS discount program during the year. Your people work hard at learning new procedures and together you save $32,000. Do you think your management would agree to year-end bonuses of $25 or $50? Probably, and they would be sure to get their money's worth in higher morale.

■*Small Cash Awards:* If Mary assumes the responsibility for implementing the new rates, does her homework carefully, and helps others become familiar with the changes, or Harry learns all about the new inserter and soon has it humming, they would both deserve some extra appreciation. Such instances are perfect opportunities for small cash awards. Carefully awarded, without the slightest favoritism, small cash awards are excellent methods of motivation.

■*"Earn a Day Off" Program:* When people put forth extra effort such as in the previous examples there is another method of rewarding them. With the blessings of management, when you can perceive a lighter work load, you can allow an employee to *earn a day off* as a reward for special industriousness. If you are able to let someone off without harming your processing, this incentive is "free," it doesn't cost a cent. It too is a strong motivator.

■*Off-Premise Training:* There are various kinds of training that can benefit the mail center and some types, such as machine operation or special Postal Service programs, are conducted outside of your office. Attendance at such seminars, off-premise, are usually highly regarded by an individual, somewhat of a compliment to his or her ability. Such training can often lead to a supervisor's position and, when promoted in that manner, can also be a valuable tool for motivation.

■*Special Smocks or Jackets:* At a recent mail management session, a large group of business mailers was discussing methods of motivation. The group leader mentioned providing special smocks for all mail center employees and one participant said he had 25 people who wouldn't be caught dead in a smock. Another manager promptly agreed and expressed an opinion that only jackets were acceptable. With that, the manager for incoming mail at one of the major TV networks reported that he had tried smocks only as a test and the employees simply refused to give them up.

Some type of outer smock or jacket helps identify mail center workers and distribution clerks. It adds a certain amount of distinction to the mail function. But just as that true story reflects, you will have to test to see what sort of reaction you get.

■*Personal Lockers:* Whenever you have employees that do not perform desk work and, consequently, have no desk at all, you may subject them to an unnecessary hardship if you do not provide them with a *personal locker.* Not only will the addition of personal lockers help the morale in your mail center, it will help keep all kinds of clutter out of sight. For more information about personal lockers, refer to the section on *Administrative Space* in *Chapter 15.*

You are not likely to appeal to *everyone* when offering the incentives mentioned here, although some will tell you that in any list of incentives, money is way ahead of what's in second place. Other managers may disagree and believe that any other sort of recognition is more worthwhile. You will have to experiment to see which ideas are best suited to your employees, and likely to be approved by your management.

OPERATING PROCEDURES

The section discussing supervisors briefly mentioned the need for someone to be *designated* as in charge whenever you must be out of the office, but you need to go beyond that.

For the mailroom to operate efficiently at all times, regardless of who is absent, you need to establish a definite line of authority. This should be a written list that provides at least three or four people in succession to assume responsibility for your mail center. This should be posted permanently somewhere in the mailroom (along with the list of primary and secondary machine operators). Then one cold damp morning when you wake up with the flu, and the next two people cannot get in to the office either, the mail operation will not drift like a rudderless ship.

You will also find it helpful to your staff (even if it consists of only two or three people) if you take the time to establish written procedures for routine mail processing. This doesn't have to be an encyclopedia, just 10 pages in a loose-leaf ring binder will do fine. But you need to take each operation, one at a time, and write up exactly what *should* happen, step by step. Along with all of your other concerns, you might do one phase a week until you have each mail processing function documented. Once you get those written down, don't forget to make changes as your processing changes, or if you incorporate new USPS programs.

When you get all of your processing documented, your operating procedures manual becomes a guide for all your employees, an excellent training tool, a testimony of your management skills for your boss, and a godsend for those who may follow in your footsteps.

IMPROVING MAILROOM SECURITY

If you review a long list of steps you can take to improve the security in your mail center, you may feel that individually they do not add much protection. But, taken as a group of actions, they will add an overall sense of security and generally improve overall productivity.

Many mail managers dismiss the subject of security in the mail center with the rationale that they simply do not process any negotiable documents or any other type of material worth stealing. That may be true, but there are other losses that can occur. For example, a wide open mail center invites "loitering and visiting" by other members of the organization looking for a niche in which to hide from their own work. It also provides easy access to the postage meter.

Here are some suggestions for strengthening security in any mail center, many of which were originated by the *Postal Inspectors* of the USPS who have extensive experience in this area.

■*Know Your Employees:* The larger your staff is the more difficult it may be, but you take a definite risk in being aloof from them. It may not be possible for you to know each one's intimate life, but you do need to take a few minutes with each from time to time to develop some understanding of their personalities. If you listen well (and don't talk too much) you can have some concept of how they feel about their families, their jobs and their lot in life. You must also try to recognize some of those feelings during the hiring interview, and from the history of previous jobs, which you should require. If you believe an employee has problems at home, serious financial problems, or an attitude that "the world owes me a living," you need to devote special understanding to that person or you are sure to have difficulty with him or her. When you sit and listen to such a person you may be the only one in the whole world who will!

■*Secure Your Mailroom:* You will find it helpful to have so-called *dutch doors*, a door cut in half about 36 inches from the floor with a 12-inch shelf mounted on top of the lower portion. This forms a barrier to strangers and helps discourage other members of the organization from "visiting" with your staff but allows you to close the upper half when you need to lock your area. If you are fortunate enough to have double doors, each may be fixed with a shelf and the two can be latched securely together when you close them.

■*Require a Sign-in Sheet:* It is likely that if anyone has a serious intent to defraud you a sign-in sheet might not deter that person, or he or she would not sign a correct name. But, a sign-in sheet keeps out the "visitors" and does provide you with a complete record of every person entering your mail center. Even if you only use it sporadically, it adds a sense of security to your entire operation.

■*Control Registered Mail:* As you may recall, every person in the Postal Service who handles a piece of registered mail must sign for it, and you should not do any less. If you receive large quantities of registered mail, it might be well to go to your nearest post office, explain your needs, and ask to see the protective wire cage where most post offices process registered mail. You also will need some type of forms to retain and track your registered mail, or to acquire a wand to read the registered OCR-readable labels (see *Accounting Systems* in *Chapter 16*).

If you only receive one or two pieces of registered mail a week, a simple bound book or custom-designed form can suffice as you hand carry each envelope to its addressee.

■*Control Metered Postage:* In many mailrooms there is a certain air of benevolence about using the organization's postage meter. At today's postage rates, that is a wasteful attitude. Many years ago mailers, occasionally received telephone calls from the post office inquiring if the owner or manager realized that personal mail was being stamped with their meter. But in these days of automation, no one has time to look at envelopes except to verify the postage, if at all. The control is all up to you. You are the one who must exercise control over your postage meter.

Consequently you need to see that mailing machines are locked whenever the mailroom is closed. (But keep executives who may work late or on weekends and holidays aware of how to obtain postage.) This security can easily be assigned to a supervisor.

That same supervisor might be the *designated record keeper* and made responsible for recording the figures from your meters or making sure that manifest systems produce the required records. At the same time, that supervisor can make periodic checks for misuse of meters.

Remember, you need to eliminate improper use of the postage meter, see that the mailing machine is locked when not in use, and employ only one person to do all of the record keeping.

■*Use Checks for Postage:* If you must keep some cash on hand, keep it in a secure place to be sure it is not a temptation for anyone. Better yet, eliminate it completely.

Whenever you are purchasing postage for your meter (if you are not fortunate enough to have a meter that can be set electronically over the telephone) *always pay by check*, never with cash. As an added precaution be sure your designated record keeper verifies that the amount of postage has been correctly set by the post office clerk.

■*Protect Valuable Merchandise:* This may seem an unnecessary caution, but it is not. Companies who send valuable, expensive merchandise often leave the doors to the mail centers wide open, allowing anyone to walk in without a challenge. You need to take special precautions against theft whenever you process valuables, precautions against other employees and strangers alike.

■*Prosecute Thieves:* The *Inspection Service* of the USPS will always tell you that if you catch a thief you should prosecute him or her to the fullest extent. It's believed that those who go unpunished will only survive to steal again another day. In addition, the *Inspection Service* reports that prosecution of the guilty is always a great detriment to others.

Incidentally, someone tampering with mail before it leaves or after it is delivered to your office is your problem. But if it appears to be a full blown *scheme*, the Postal Inspectors may assist you in your investigation.

CONTINUAL EDUCATION

In addition to being a strong motivating force, one of the most valuable benefits an organization can provide its workers is a continual source of education. This is true whether it be teaching the employee to read better, do simple arithmetic more accurately, learn mechanical skills, or learn about more sophisticated topics, such as computer expertise or advanced supervisory skills. The benefits for the organization may be as great in the area of mail handling as anywhere else in the organization.

When *Fortune* magazine recently quizzed the chief executive officers of America's largest companies, in the *Fortune 500 CEO Poll*, 91 percent said their companies were spending more on educating workers. In a related question, 64 percent said that improving education was the single most important step that American businesses could take to improve the quality of the U.S. work force. Another 11 percent stated the most important step would be *to expand training programs*. As you initiate and expand your own training and education programs you will be in good company.

DRUGS AND ALCOHOL

Our society is burdened with numerous problems, but the two most detrimental may be drug addiction and alcohol abuse. Both are widespread in the workplace, and both are very difficult with which to cope. Nevertheless, you must be alert to the symptoms of drug use and alcohol misuse. They have no respect for race, creed, color, or age, and that often makes their detection all the more difficult!

If you are alert to unexplained behavior and believe someone on your staff is involved with either drugs or alcohol, you should immediately report your suspicions to your immediate superior and consult with *professional organizations* that can provide you with advice on how to cope with these very serious and widespread problems.

Astute mail center management of personnel should be a combination of the Golden Rule, "Do unto others as you would have them do unto you," tempered by the reminder in P. T. Barnum's philosophy, "There's a sucker born every minute."

CHAPTER 18

HOW TO STAY UP-TO-DATE

If you did not believe that it is important to stay up-to-date you probably would not be reading this book. But, to reinforce that point, you should recall all of the many little details of postal regulations that may have changed in the past six months, all of the new mail center systems and equipment that have been announced in the past six months, and all of the changes in your own organization during the same period. It is likely that you could develop a long list of those changes, and many of them have had an impact on your own mail operation.

It is not easy to keep up with all of the changes that take place in the world of mail. There are so many demands for your time that it can become quite frustrating to realize how many changes are taking place. If you had a program set up to carry out just half of the suggestions and recommendations in this book, you would be very busy. Add new technology by several equipment manufacturers and a couple of changes in USPS regulations (such as the rules for *automation-compatible mail* that are scheduled to take effect in September of '91 and February of '92) and you may not know which way to turn next.

But you can minimize this pressure to stay up-to-date and take steps to assure that you become aware of all kinds of important changes as soon as they take place. Once you get this awareness program running smoothly you will be surprised to see how easy it is to keep abreast of all kinds of changes. You will also be surprised to see that the cost is relatively small.

ESTABLISHING A LIBRARY

The first step is to establish a *library* in your mail center. It will be helpful if you will obtain a book rack, perhaps 12 inches long, that can be located on a table or counter that will be convenient to everyone. This easy accessibility is very important if you expect your staff to use the information you will be accumulating. Put the books and manuals in a glass-front bookcase behind your desk, and no one will touch them!

Here's what you need to place in your library (with 1991 rates).

■*Memo to Mailers:* Requests for a *free* subscription should be sent to

Memo to Mailers, U.S. Postal Service, Headquarters - Room 5300, Washington, DC 20260-3100. Published monthly by the Postal Service, this publication contains many tips on postal products, USPS organizational information complete with telephone numbers, and changes in rates or classification. For maximum convenience and easy reference it should be filed in a loose-leaf ring binder.

■*National Five-Digit ZIP Code and Post Office Directory*: Available from any medium size post office for $12. (Look for a rebate coupon on the inside cover of your present directory.) Even if you have electronic access to ZIP Codes, this book is well worth the price for it contains so many other kinds of information.

■*Postal Bulletin*: Subscriptions should be ordered from Superintendent of Documents, U.S. Government Printing Office, 710 N. Capitol Street, NW, Washington, DC 20402-9371, or you may telephone 202-783-3238 as they accept Visa and MasterCard in addition to checks. Subscriptions are $56 per year for domestic addresses and $70 for international subscriptions. Single copies, as far back as 16 issues, are available for $2 to domestic addresses and $2.50 to international addresses.

Published every other Thursday, with supplemental issues when there are major changes, this publication is essential to any mailroom. It is used by the Postal Service to provide management direction for internal procedures to approximately 27,000 postmasters, so you will see many references that are meaningless to you. But, when the information *is* meaningful for you it is priceless, timely, and 100 percent accurate. In fact, when there is a major rate change, you will treasure the issue that contains *all* of the changes.

Postal Bulletins are difficult to file because many issues are too thick to be punched in an office-size hole punch. However, they can be maintained in chronological order in heavy pressboard file folders with expanding sides. The USPS publishes quarterly indexes, and you will want to add some type of tab to indicate the location of each one.

■*Domestic Mail Manual*: Subscriptions should be sent to the Superintendent of Documents, Government Printing Office, Washington, DC 20402-9371, or the *DMM* may be ordered over the telephone by calling 202-783-3238. Annual subscriptions of four issues are $19 to domestic addresses and $23.75 to foreign addresses. Fax orders may be sent to 202-275-0019. In addition to charge cards, the GPO will accept checks made payable to the Superintendent of Documents or, if you purchase other publications on a regular basis, you may keep a *GPO Deposit Account* to simplify ordering. The *DMM* is also available on magnetic tape and diskettes which may be ordered via 202-275-3329.

To repeat a suggestion in *Chapter 7,* the *DMM* should be considered an essential part of professional mail management in all but the very smallest mailroom. The Postal Service has worked hard to purge it of governmental gobbledygook and to write the regulations so that you can understand their intent. Perhaps more important, it not only states what you cannot do, it clearly states what you **can** do.

■*International Mail Manual:* Like the *DMM*, this is available from the Superintendent of Documents, Government Printing Office, Washington, DC 20402-9371, and may also be ordered over the telephone by calling 202-783-3238. Fax orders may be sent to 202-275-0019. Four annual issues are $14 to domestic subscribers and $17.50 to international addresses. As indicated previously, the Government Printing Office accepts Visa, MasterCard or checks made payable to the Superintendent of Documents.

You should consider the *International Mail Manual (IMM)* a necessity for your mail center even if you have only a small volume of international mail. If it helps you avoid only a few international mistakes, it will more than repay its small cost. The *International Mail Manual* can serve as a basic textbook for the beginner or an essential aid to the professional mail manager.

That library can provide you with an answer to every possible question you could ask about Postal Service rules and regulations, and continue to keep you up-to-date, day in and day out throughout the year. Admittedly, you might need a translation of some of the *DMM* occasionally, but understanding it is a great deal easier than interpreting the laws of most other government agencies. Furthermore, a review of *Chapter 2* (of this book) will tell you exactly who to call for clarification. You could never get that much information anywhere else at a total annual cost of only **$101**!

POSTAL SERVICE LITERATURE

The Postal Service publishes special informative folders, brochures, and booklets on practically every program they provide for businesses. So your next step is to begin to be a scavenger for every one of those publications you can obtain. Most can be punched on a standard three-hole punch and filed in the ring binder along with the *Memo to Mailers.* You might also use dividers to set up sections for each major USPS program. You should also ask your postmaster or account representative to provide you with a full selection of program literature. While many of the publications are designed to encourage business people to use the service being described, they usually include the ground rules that can provide a quick reference for your staff.

Here is a list of publications that were available in early '91:

A Guide to Business Mail Preparation, Publication 25, 44 pages
International Postal Rates and Fees, Publication 51, 36 pages
Express Mail Users Guide, Publication 161, 28 pages
Creative Solutions for Your Business Needs: (A series of pamphlets)
Accelerated Reply Mail, Notice 57

Address Information Systems, Publication 40
Addressing With Bar Codes, Notice 53
Addressing For Success, Notice 221
Business Reply Mail Accounting System, Notice 46
Metering, Notice 125
National Change of Address, Notice 47
Operation Mail, Notice 48
ZIP + 4 Code, Notice 186
Priority Mail, Publication 20
Express Mail: (A series of pamphlets)
   General Information, Notice 43
   Corporate Account Application, Notice 42
   Drop Ship Service, Notice 198
   Insurance, Notice 7
   Reship Service, Notice 22
   Same Day Airport Service, Notice 44-A
Postage Rates, Fees and Information, Poster 103, (17x22)
International Postal Rates and Fees, Poster 51, (17x22)

As you can imagine, the literature is updated from time to time, or as rates change, so they may not all be available. If you attend any conference where the Postal Service exhibits, you should always try to collect every publication that is available to add to your library.

In addition to all of those booklets and pamphlets, you should try to obtain a 77-page booklet titled *Glossary of Postal Terms (Publication 32).* It defines and explains more than 750 terms that are unique to the USPS or have special meanings within the postal community. It would be especially helpful to anyone who has recently become involved in mail management.

If your postmaster or account representative cannot obtain a copy for you, write to the Materiel Distribution Center, Route 206, V.A. Supply Depot, Somerville, NY 08877-0001, and enclose a check for $1 made payable to the USPS.

THE FEDERAL REGISTER

The nation's capital is always enchanted with *proposed* changes in rules and regulations, whether they are being considered by Congress, the IRS, or the Postal Service. New government regulations or proposals are often changed so much by the time they become law that you might not recognize the original. A professional mail manager should be so busy managing the present regulations that there is hardly time to pursue the impact of what *might* become law. Nevertheless, large mailers who wish to know the details of every proposal that the USPS is considering should subscribe to the *Federal Register*.

The *Federal Register* is a daily publication, published by the Office of the Federal Register, National Archives and Records Service, General Services Administration. It is the method by which all federal agencies first publish proposed rules and regulations for comment by the public before they are made final. If you wish to know the details of any upcoming USPS proposal, the *Federal Register* is the place it will appear first.

A subscription to the *Federal Register* may be obtained from the Superintendent of Documents, Government Printing Office, Washington, DC 20402-9371, and may also be ordered over the telephone by calling 202-783-3238, and fax orders may be sent to 202-275-0019. An annual subscription is $340, and six month subscriptions are available. Single copies are available for $1.50 per issue, telephone 202-523-5240. As indicated previously, the Government Printing Office accepts Visa, MasterCard or checks made payable to the Superintendent of Documents.

If a subscription is too great a strain on your budget, most public libraries maintain a subscription to the *Federal Register*. They will allow you to copy any specific proposal that you may have heard about through other sources or discussions.

POSTAL CUSTOMER COUNCILS

Ever since the Postal Service was first created in 1970, it has become more and more *customer* oriented, and the *Postal Customer Councils (PCCs)* were one of the very first efforts to work more closely with postal business customers. This was strange to some of the old-line Post Office Department managers who thought more in terms such as "mail user" and "patron." But in 21 years the USPS has made great strides, and currently there are over 200 active Postal Customer Councils throughout the U.S.

The PCCs are jointly managed by a co-chair from the Postal Service and a co-chair from industry. Depending on the size and activities of the PCC, there is usually a vice-chair from industry and a treasurer. In addition there may be a secretary who is responsible for maintaining a mailing list of active members and for publishing a newsletter. Membership is free because, as the sponsor of the PCC, the USPS prohibits mandatory dues in order to take part in the activities. However, a PCC will occasionally make a small profit on a meal or ask for contributions from its larger members.

The PCCs sponsor a wide variety of events for their members. They often have short breakfast meetings or morning coffees with panel discussions on postal know-how. Others feature a semi-annual luncheon meeting with a notable speaker preceded by an "attitude adjustment period." Larger PCCs will often invite senior executives from USPS headquarters or regional offices as the principal speakers. Other times there will be industry speakers, such as the manager of major training facilities or the editor of a prominent postal newsletter. Many PCCs also sponsor clinics featuring USPS experts in rates and classification matters.

There are a number of advantages to being an active member of a Postal Customer Council. First, you have an opportunity to meet all of your local postal managers. Most people will agree that it is easier to do business with people you have met face to face, and postal managers are no exception. It also helps to know whom to call when you need a question answered. Then you meet other industry managers who are likely to have the same problems you are experiencing. This *networking* can be a most rewarding experience when you are looking for someone who has experience with equipment you are investigating. A further advantage is the equipment exhibits that many of the larger PCCs feature as part of an all-day mini-forum with exhibits, panel discussions, and a knowledgeable luncheon speaker.

Some PCCs publish newsletters which can provide important details about using new USPS products and postal programs. As a PCC member, you can usually rely on receiving up-to-date information several times a year from your local postal facility.

If there is no Postal Customer Council in your area, you can easily start one. The PCC program is totally dependent on a partnership, equal work and support by both industry and the Postal Service. If interest waned in your area it may be that no one in industry felt he or she could contribute the time to make the PCC effective. On the other hand, the managers in the Postal Service may have become so inundated with mail processing concerns, changing personnel, and other business pressures that they simply put off reorganizing a PCC until it almost disbanded. But it is easy to revitalize a PCC, you only need one enthusiastic person from industry and one from the Postal Service.

NATIONAL BUSINESS SHOWS

Anytime you get three machine vendors together one of them will say, "Hey, let's have a business show." Or so it seems. You will have to stay alert for advertising featuring exhibits, but they can be valuable places to shop for whatever you are looking for or just to stay up-to-date. Many of the publications listed later on in this chapter publish a calendar of events, and they are excellent places to track down business shows. Typical shows held in larger cities are sponsored by the National Office Products Association (1-800-542-NOPA), the Association of Records Managers and Administrators (913-341-3808), and the National Office Machine Dealers Association (816-941-3100). Their shows will not concentrate solely on mailing equipment as other forums do but will exhibit other administrative supplies and machines that might assist you in managing your office.

However, there is one business show specifically targeted at the mailing industry. It is the *Mid-America Mailing and Shipping Conference* scheduled to be held November 13 and 14, 1991, in the Ramada Hotel

O'Hare in Chicago. With a small admission charge of less than $10, and over 60 exhibitors, perhaps it is an excellent opportunity to see on display the very equipment you are considering. For more information contact Advance Management of Wisconsin, Inc., 1019 Jonathon Drive, Madison, WI 53713-3228, or telephone 608-271-2764.

NATIONAL POSTAL FORUMS

Founded in 1967 to foster a closer working relationship between the former Post Office Department and its customers, the *National Postal Forum (NPF)* is a not-for-profit educational corporation. Its board of directors works closely with the Postal Service to sponsor meetings and conferences that provide opportunities for mailers, trade suppliers, and postal officials to freely exchange information and ideas.

Since 1988, the NPF has sponsored forums each year on both the east and west coasts, and in 1991 forums are scheduled for Chicago and Orlando. It has also sponsored new rate conferences, which have been very well attended by industry mailers. A typical forum will have over 40 panel sessions where you can hear postal and industry experts discuss mail programs and management techniques for three full days. The 1991 registration fee of $375 ($350 for early registration) includes all of the business sessions, admission to the exhibit hall, and several meal functions.

You may obtain additional information about the National Postal Forums by writing to P.O. Box 23450, Washington, DC 20026-3450, or telephone 202-268-2341.

OTHER NATIONAL CONFERENCES

The National Postal Forums have been so successful that you often find registration closed several weeks before the event, and the meeting rooms filled to capacity. This has caused other organizations to realize that many people beside the 3,500 who normally attend a Forum would like to hear similar discussions about mail management and be able to visit a well-stocked exhibit hall. Consequently, several organizations now sponsor similar conferences, and most feature exhibits as well.

MASA Mailer Strategies Conference

Directed mostly toward those involved in barcoding, presorting, and processing large amounts of First- and third-class mail, a Mailer Strategies Conference was held by the *Mail Advertising Service Association* (MASA) in February of '91, across the plaza from Postal Service Headquarters. With a registration fee of $450 ($350 for MASA members) the two-day session was typical of similar conferences which MASA has sponsored in the past in addition to its annual spring conference.

MASA is the trade association exclusively serving printers and mailers of advertising materials here and abroad and was founded in 1920. For more information write to Mail Advertising Service Association, 1421 Prince Street, Suite 200, Alexandria, VA 22314-2814, or telephone 703-836-9200. MASA publishes an annual *Who's Who, The MASA Buyers Guide to Blue Ribbon Mailing Services* consisting of over 170 pages.

MAST Expo

Held in New Orleans in March of '91, and sponsored by *Mast* magazine of Madison, WI, the *MAST Expo* consisted of two and one-half days of cost-conscious sessions with emphasis on shipping techniques. Supported by leaders from industry and the Postal Service, it featured over 100 exhibitors. Registration for recipients of *Mast* magazine was $225, but $250 to others.

Information on upcoming conferences is available from *Mast* magazine, 6000 Gisholt Drive, Suite 201, Madison, WI 53713-4616, or telephone 608-221-8730.

MAILCOM '91

The ninth annual conference and exhibition sponsored jointly by *The Mail Systems Management Association* (MSMA) and *MAIL: The Journal of Communication Distribution*, was scheduled for the spring of 1991, and featured two and one-half days of business sessions. Over 50 exhibitors supported *MAILCOM '91*, including Airborne Express, Federal Express, and United Parcel Service, whom you are not likely to see at a National Postal Forum! The early-bird registration was $295, and later registrants paid $325 (with a $50 discount for MSMA members).

You can contact the Mail Systems Management Association for information on future MAILCOM conferences at James A. Farley Building, P.O. Box 2155, New York, NY 10116-2155, or write to *MAIL* Magazine, Excelsior Publications, One Milstone Road, Milford, PA 18337-9607, or telephone 717-686-2111.

MAIL SHOW '91

Sponsored every other year by the publishers of *Postal World*, the *MAIL SHOW '91* conference is scheduled for September 9-11, 1991, at the Sheraton Washington Hotel in Washington, DC. Registration for the conference is $350, but you receive a $55 discount if you are a *Postal World* subscriber. The two and one-half day show will feature over 120 exhibitors, and will also include such companies as Airborne, DHL Express, Federal Express and United Parcel Service.

For more information, write to United Communications Group, 11300 Rockville Pike, Suite 1100, Rockville, MD 20852-3030, or telephone 1-800-487-4824, Ext. 684.

UTILIZING OTHER MAIL MANAGERS

One of the greatest benefits you may receive from attending a conference is the friendships you will develop with other mail managers. The attendance at all of these conferences is such that if you are managing the mail for an association you will meet other association people. If you are a banker you will meet other bankers. In fact, whatever type of organization you represent, you are likely to find someone from your industry. Not that you have to learn only from people in an organization like your own, but they are likely to understand your problems more thoroughly.

Once you have breakfast or lunch with someone, and talk about mail management solutions, you will be comfortable phoning, faxing, or writing to that person for other suggestions or ideas. Since the National Postal Forums have been running for more than 20 years, you will often see the same people together year after year, even though their offices may be a thousand miles apart.

The problems, solutions, and ideas that originate and are exchanged in these sessions are invaluable and may be equal to the knowledge you pick up in the business sessions.

An exchange of ideas is equally important back home, and that is one of the compelling reasons why you should become a "regular" member of your local Postal Customer Council. In larger PCCs, networking becomes a science as special industry-oriented clinics are often conducted in addition to the regular meetings.

SALES REPRESENTATIVES

A number of years ago, a rather crusty and abrupt vice president of a stationery business was busy going over his financial reports when one of his salesmen hesitantly stuck his head around the corner. "There is a manufacturer's rep downstairs who looks like he's down on his luck, but he wants to see the buyer. You don't want to talk to him do you?" The salesman couldn't believe his ears for the V-P smiled meekly and said, "I certainly do want to talk to him!" Later, the salesman couldn't wait to ask the V-P why he so quickly agreed to see the manufacturer's rep. When he finally was able to ask, the V-P gave a wise smile and said, "Look, I didn't know what on earth he was selling, but I couldn't afford not to listen. *He may have the greatest product in the world!*"

That is a true story. Think about it the next time you are tempted to chase a salesperson away without even listening to what he or she is offering. You can't tell, it may become the most valuable product in your mail center.

Instead, listen to what they offer, collect their literature and keep their business cards in a file. You may need exactly what they are offering when you least suspect it.

NEWSLETTERS

There is no substitute for an industry-oriented newsletter. Bankers rely on banking newsletters to keep up with all of the important details that may have an impact on banking. Investment brokers rely on investment newsletters to stay abreast of everyday changes in their business, and there is even a newsletter for editors of newsletters. The reason that all of these people rely on special newsletters is that only someone like a newsletter editor can keep you up-to-date about your *entire industry*. The Postal Service certainly isn't going to tell you about the new confirmation of delivery offered by United Parcel Service, nor is one of the over-night express companies likely to tell you about someone else's discount. But a newsletter will do exactly that. A newsletter editor has sources of information *throughout the industry* and, therefore, will provide you with information you probably cannot find anywhere else.

Both of the following editors have extensive contacts throughout the Postal Service and frequently meet and talk with everyone from the Postmaster General to mail carriers. Since they also have a wide assortment of other contacts throughout the mailing industry, you are assured of up-to-date reporting by both.

Business Mailers Review

A 20-year veteran of the mailing industry, *Van H. Seagraves* is the editor and publisher of *Business Mailers Review*. Van prides himself that his twice-monthly newsletter will help mailers get maximum performance out of their mailing programs because he has a unique "insider" understanding of how postal policies are developed and implemented. He guarantees that his readers will be completely satisfied or he will cancel their subscription and send a refund for all undelivered copies.

Subscription rates for *Business Mailers Review* are $198 for one year (24 issues) and $356 for a two-year subscription, with bulk rates on request. For more information, write to 1813 Shepherd Avenue, NW, Washington, DC 2001-5398, telephone 202-723-3397, or fax 202-723-0953.

Postal World

For over 15 years the editors of *Postal World* have been providing its subscribers with stories about slashing mail costs and solving thorny mail center problems. Its current editor, *Marcus J. Smith*, may be the most knowledgeable and well respected of all of those who preceded him. He, too, offers a 100 percent money-back guarantee if you do not think his money-saving ideas are worth every penny.

Subscription rates for *Postal World* are $337 annually (25 issues). For more information, write to 11300 Rockville Pike, Suite 1100, Rockville, MD 20852-3030, telephone 301-816-8950, or fax 301-816-8945.

THE POSTAL DIRECTORY

In addition to *Business Mailers Review,* Van Seagraves also publishes *The Postal Directory* every year in January. Advertised as *"The mailer's phone and fax guide to key persons in the Postal Service, Postal Rate Commission and Congress,"* the Directory shows how the USPS is organized with postal facilities listed by regions, in ZIP Code order. In addition to postal executives and managers in Washington and the five regional offices, *The Postal Directory* lists the staffing in the larger post offices. It also includes the names of classification specialists, transportation management specialists, and those operating the bulk mail centers. For the first time, the '91 issue lists the telephone numbers of postal logistic managers in the 73 divisions. They are the ones who now dictate when bulk mailings will be accepted at all destination postal facilities.

The 1991 cost of *The Postal Directory* is $25 for one copy, $40 for two, and 3-10 copies are $18 each, with bulk rates on request. They may be ordered from Business Mailers Review, 1813 Shepherd Street, NW, Washington, DC 20011-5398, telephone 202-723-3397, or fax 202-723-0953.

PERIODICAL PUBLICATIONS

Once your mail center library is established, you are well on your way toward keeping up-to-date. If you make sure publications such as the *DMM,* the *IMM,* and the *Memo to Mailers* are arriving in your office on a regular basis, you will be building the foundation for a steady stream of knowledge. But that knowledge will deal primarily with rules and regulations, and you need more than that. While they are no substitute for a newsletter other publications can also be very important to you. They provide a forum for advertisers to show you the latest in mailroom equipment and software and to explain their benefits. At the same time these publications publish articles written by many of the mailing industry leaders who can provide you with wise insights into all kinds of equipment, programs, and procedures. If you want to stay up-to-date, you also need a stream of this type of information arriving on a regular basis.

Direct Marketing

This monthly magazine has long been one of the primary sources of communication for those involved in all types of direct-response marketing, and especially direct mail. It may be drifting away from mail center management somewhat, but every monthly issue reports on many aspects of the mailing industry. *Direct Marketing* is published by Hoke Communications, 224 Seventh Street, Garden City, NY 11530, telephone 516-294-8141, or fax 516-294-8141.

Mailer's Review

You will not believe that it took over 50 years for someone to come up with a publication dedicated *primarily to mailroom equipment.* But it was not until December of 1988 when the first issue of the *Mailer's Review* was published. In May of '89, the magazine format was abandoned, and the present tabloid newspaper format was adopted. The 11½ x 17½ pages, coupled with occasional two-color printing, make excellent size photos of all kinds of mailroom equipment. The publisher, *Deborah A. Griffin*, and her staff go well beyond simply publishing advertisements of equipment by providing interesting reports about both new and time-proven equipment. While *Mailer's Review* does contain a few articles pertaining to rates and other pertinent information, it is primarily equipment oriented and a terrific source for up-to-date facts about all kinds of mailing equipment.

Subscriptions to *Mailer's Review* are $26 for one year (12 issues), and $24 for a two year subscription. For more information, write to 7850 SE Stark Street, Portland, OR 97215-2340, telephone 503-257-0764, or fax 503-257-7935.

Mailer's Review is unique because it is both a monthly *newspaper* and because it is devoted primarily to mailroom *equipment.* The following publications are all monthly *magazines.*

MAIL: The Journal of Communication Distribution

Guided by its robust publisher and chief editor, Francis Ruggiero, this magazine features a full range of articles to bring you the latest technology, news, and people in mail communications. It works very closely with the *Mail Systems Management Association* and jointly sponsors an annual conference and exhibition (See Mailcom '91).

Excelsior Publications, the publishers of *MAIL*, will cancel your subscription at any time you are dissatisfied and send you a refund for the unused portion. *MAIL* is published eight times a year (including a buyers' guide), and a subscription for one year is $27 and a subscription for 17 issues is $34. Subscriptions for *MAIL* should be sent to Gold Key Box 2425, Milford, PA 18337-9607. (See also Buyers' Guides).

MAST

This magazine is also 100 percent devoted to mail, mailing techniques and information on shipping. It also sponsors an annual conference and exhibition for the mailing and small parcel shipping industry. (See MAST EXPO.)

Subscriptions to *MAST* are $24 per year for six issues of the magazine ($45 for 12) plus six newsletters of current mailing information. Paid subscriptions also include the extensive buyers' guide. However, members of the mailing and/or shipping community can receive *free* bimonthly issues of *MAST* magazine.

Requests for either type of subscription should be sent to RB Publishing Company, 6000 Gisholt Drive, Suite 201, Madison, WI 53713-

4816, or telephone 608-221-8730. (See also *Buyers' Guides*.)

Modern Office Technology

This magazine is devoted to all types of business machines and systems, but often includes special articles about mail handling and equipment. Some of the types of equipment advertised, and some of the articles, are just as important to running a smooth mail center as those in publications that feature only mail-oriented articles and advertisements. Annual subscriptions to *Modern Office Technology* are $45 for one year and $75 for two years. However, *free* subscriptions are accepted from qualified management personnel. Requests for either type of subscription should be directed to Penton Publishers, 1100 Superior Avenue, Cleveland, OH 44197-8032, telephone 216-696-7000, or fax 216-696-7627.

Office Systems '91

This magazine may be somewhat unique in that it advertises, "the magazine for small and medium companies." So, if your organization is in that category, it may provide very relevant information. While it generally reports on *all* types of office products and systems, it devotes several issues annually to mailing processes.

Annual subscriptions are $36 for 12 issues, but subscriptions are *free* to *qualified* individuals. Requests for either type of subscription should be directed to *Office Systems '91*, 941 Danbury Road, Georgetown, CT 06829-0150, telephone 203-544-9526, or fax 203-544-8465.

The Office

This magazine is the granddaddy of *office* magazines, since its publisher, Office Publications, Inc., was founded in 1935. It has long been a favorite of office managers who wanted up-to-date facts on information systems and management. It also features articles and advertisements on a full line of office products, and provides several articles or issues on mailing know-how periodically.

Subscriptions to *The Office* are $40 for one year and $75 for two. However, you may obtain a *free* subscription if you and your organization meet their circulation audit requirements. Requests for either type of subscription should be sent to Office Publications, Inc., 1600 Summer Street, Stamford, CT 06905-5129, telephone 203-327-9670.

BUYERS' GUIDES

A *buyers guide* devoted to mailing equipment is quite unlike a publication such as the well-known *Consumer Reports*. Obviously, the market for refrigerators is far greater than that for a folding machine or a postal scale, so the expense of testing typical mailing equipment is beyond anyone's reach. Also, you can use a machine to slam the door on a refrigerator

25,000 times and report that it will last more than 15, years but it would take a carload of paper just to test one folding machine! Or, can you imagine testing four OCR barcode sorters, that might take an entire train load of paper.

The next best thing to *evaluating* equipment is to at least provide a matrix of the dimensions, operating features and other benefits of each machine. That is what many of the previously listed magazines frequently do on all types of equipment, mail oriented and others. Their reports become valuable sources of information for anyone in mail management, and (as previously suggested) you should consider clipping and saving such articles in a file devoted solely to equipment, or even file them by the specific type of equipment.

While there may be others, the two most well-known buyers' guides for mail center equipment and services are:

■*Official Mail Guide*: Published annually by *MAIL* magazine, a recent issue consisted of 142 pages of products and services. It is distributed at no additional charge to regular subscribers.

■*Mast Power Guide*: Published by *Mast* magazine, it is sent at no charge to *paid* subscribers, or may be purchased for $8.95. The 1991 edition was published in March and covered over 400 manufacturers.

TRAINING SEMINARS

Many people prefer to attend *live presentations* to learn the ins and outs of handling mail. Structured as a classroom environment with a knowledgeable instructor, a class or seminar is an excellent way to rapidly absorb a great deal of information about mail processing. Occasionally you may locate such classes at a community college, often sponsored by a Postal Customer Council, but they are elusive. If you would like to attend such a session to brush up on your knowledge, and to gain the most current methods to cut costs, you can attend either of the following.

Pitney Bowes Postal Education Center

In 1973, in Bethesda, MD, Pitney Bowes created the first facility specifically for teaching how to take advantage of all of the services of the Postal Service. That course also provided expertise in reducing costs and eliminating postage waste. Since then almost 10,000 people have attended the two-day course now located on a quiet wooded campus south of Atlanta.

Taught by Cliff Bennett, an acknowledged expert who appears on National Postal Forum panels and speaks to other groups all over the U.S., the courses are scheduled about 20 times a year. Fees for the program is $595 per person and includes tuition, all course materials, meals and accommodations.

For more information about these courses or information about training a group on your premises, contact Pitney Bowes, Postal Education

Center, 201 Aberdeen Parkway, Peachtree City, GA 30269-1422, telephone 404-487-3028, or fax 404-487-1063.

USPS Mailer Education Center

In 1987 the Postal Service began offering business mailers an opportunity for classroom training in the basement of a post office in lower Manhattan. Different seminars offered expertise in international mail, mailing procedures for second- and third-class mail, and mail center management by Postal Service experts. These fee-paid courses were so popular that the USPS soon moved the administration of its education program to Northeast Region Headquarters in Windsor, CT, and began to offer the courses in major cities throughout the U.S. To give you an idea of the frequency of these seminars, over 90 were scheduled during the first seven months of 1991.

The courses are relatively inexpensive, when you consider that the accuracy of the information you will receive regarding postal rules and regulations is practically guaranteed (since it comes from knowledgeable USPS employees), in contrast to an "outsider" attempting to "interpret" the *Domestic Mail Manual* or other official USPS regulations.

The half-day courses are $65, the one-day courses are only $125, and the two-day courses are $225, and they even accept Visa and MasterCard, or your check. Plus, multiple registrations from the same organizations are granted a discount. At that price, if a seminar is located in your city, you can afford to send staff "specialists" to make them experts in second- or third-class mailings, or other programs. The Postal Service will also conduct customized training seminars on your premises.

The seminars cover a wide variety of postal subjects and include:

- International Mail
- Marketing with Direct Mail
- Mailing Procedures for Administrative Personnel
- Designing Your Mail for Optimum Service
- Second-Class Mail
- Third-Class Bulk Mail
- Professional Mail Center Management

To obtain an 18-page brochure listing the dates and places of all upcoming seminars, write to *Mailer Education Center*, U.S. Postal Service, P.O. Box 836, Windsor, CT 06006-0836, or telephone 1-800-877-7843 (in CT 203-285-7030).

VIDEO CASSETTE TRAINING

It is unfortunate that the combination of television set and video cassette recorder (VCR) is not more commonly available as a one-piece unit. It is an excellent training method, especially when you consider the ability to reverse and review a previously seen section. The ability to *freeze* the image also makes it an excellent method of reviewing all kinds of check lists. If you do not have access to video equipment anywhere else in your organization, you might consider obtaining a TV and VCR specifically for training in your mail center, because most business educators believe there will be more and more cassettes available in the future. Think of it as a *live* training environment that doesn't require a moment of your time as an instructor. TV is a great teacher, and you don't have to be a parent to realize how much *Big Bird* has taught children!

USPS Video Training Series
The Postal Service offers two programs on video cassette that are unlike anything available elsewhere. The scripts to these video programs are well written, they include up-to-date managing techniques and are professionally produced. The two programs cover the following topics.

■*Mail Center Management Series*:
  Vol. 1 Managing Your Mail Center
  Vol. 2 Improving Mail Center Operations
  Vol. 3 Managing Your People
  Vol. 4 Cost Saving Solutions

■*International Mail*
  Vol. 1 International Mail Categories
  Vol. 2 International Priority Mail
  Vol. 3 International Surface Airlift
  Vol. 4 Express Mail International Service
  Vol. 5 Addressing Your Mail Properly

The video tapes are available in ½-inch VHS format, and each *series* is only $89.95. You may order these video tapes by telephoning 1-800-USPSVID, as they accept Visa and MasterCard. Or you may send a check to U.S. Postal Service, Mailer Education Center Video, P.O. Box 835, Windsor, CT 06006-0835.

POSTAL CONSULTANTS
If you follow any of the business magazines, you will read time and again that when a business is in serious financial trouble it often calls in a *consultant*. You can locate a number of different types of consultants in the *Yellow Pages*, and in Washington, DC, you can dial a wrong number and get a consultant! Unfortunately, consultants who have an in-depth knowledge of the Postal Service and are qualified to evaluate a mail operation are few and far between. There are thousands of letter shops that can accurately prepare third-class bulk mail and presort mail, but generally that is the limit of their competence in mail matters.

If you have mailing or management problems that seem beyond your own expertise, you may wish to call in a professional who has had *experience* in solving mail center problems. You need not have total confusion in your mailroom to seek the benefit of a consultant. One of the top brokerage offices in New York recently acknowledged a dozen major areas that were impeding their mail operation, all identified by a visit from a consultant.

There are undoubtedly a few others, but the following consultants have advertised their services:

Robert W. Belz, CMC
Time Critical Communications, Inc.
P.O. Box 810214
Boca Raton, FL 33481-0214

James C. Barlow, Jr.
Mail Systems Management
101 Margate Road
Lutherville, MD 21093-5838
301-321-8821

Harry Harden and Vera Squeri
Hardcopy Communications Consultants
2000 Powell Street, Suite 1200
Emeryville, CA 94608-1801
415-596-1769

Jacquelyn T. McPeak
Mail Management
691 Kennedy Road
Wayne, PA 19087-2036
215-688-3749

D. Gail Nickel
Nickel Resources
P.O. Box 14708
Madison, WI 53714-0708
608-251-4813

MANAGEMENT SERVICES

You might want to hire a consultant to help if you have a variety of problems, but if things seem hopeless you can simply throw in the towel. You can take all of the staffing problems, the training headaches, and the equipment shortcomings, and dump them in someone else's lap. You can have a professional mail management organization come in and provide complete facilities management including people and equipment. In other words, you simply contract out the entire function of the mail center exactly the way you might handle a cafeteria operation. Instead of paying extra for this service, many firms report savings over their previous operating costs of up to 10 percent.

One of the fastest growing organizations that can provide complete mail management is *Ameriscribe Management Services*. It has 39 branches across the U.S. plus regional offices in New York, Chicago, and Los Angeles. Americscribe manages mail operations for over 225 customers and its prestigious list of clients includes Price Waterhouse. It specializes in mail services for large law firms, which make up a large portion of their clientele. It also specializes in providing full-service, on-site copier and duplicating service to its clients. Ameriscribe Management Services has its headquarters at 75 Varick Street, New York, NY 10013-1917, telephone 1-800-669-0800.

Another organization that can manage your entire mail operation is *Archer Management Services*, 855 Avenue of the Americas, New York, NY 10001-4198. Archer offers a *free* five-minute self-analysis kit to rate your own support services. It can be obtained by calling 212-502-2100, or outside of NY call 1-800-ARCHER-1, Ext. 2100.

Archer can also provide *temporary personnel* that are trained to work in mail centers and are ready to work when they arrive in your office. The telephone numbers for Archer temporaries are New York, 212-563-8790; Washington, 202-682-4362; and Chicago, 312-939-5656.

ASSOCIATIONS

There are several associations that monitor events that can affect mail service, offer training on mail and parcel preparation, and generally keep their members well informed on what is happening in official postal circles in Washington. Some of these have been mentioned elsewhere in this book, but it may be especially helpful to have all of their addresses in this chapter for they will certainly help you stay up-to-date.

Direct Marketing Association
1101 17th Street, NW, Suite 900
Washington, DC 20006-4704
Telephone: 202-347-1222

Mail Advertising Service Association
1421 Prince Street, Suite 200
Alexandria, VA 22314-2814
Telephone: 703-836-9200

Parcel Shippers Association
1211 Connecticut Avenue, Suite 406
Washington, DC 20036-2701
Telephone: 202-296-3690

Third Class Mail Association
1333 F Street, NW, Suite 710
Washington, DC 20004-1108
Telephone: 202-347-0055

In addition to those associations, the Mail Systems Management Association (MSMA) provides for the professional development of its members. Organized in 1981, MSMA offers an accreditation and certification program for professionals in the mail systems arena. It also co-sponsors the *MAILCOM* conferences with *MAIL* magazine. For full information about the MSMA certification program write to the Mail Systems Management Association, JAF Building, Box 2155, New York, NY 10116-2155.

CHAPTER 19

HOW TO GET STARTED TODAY
TOWARD BETTER MAIL SERVICE

By now you have read hundreds and hundreds of suggestions, cautions, and ideas about how to efficiently manage a large mail center or a small mailroom. It is time to organize all of these loosely connected items into one cohesive plan which will help you to reach your objectives on improving your entire mail operation.

But you may feel like you just rushed into your living room to find that a spark has jumped out of the fireplace, set the sofa on fire, and now the curtains are burning! If you try to put it out by yourself, it may get out of hand, and you will definitely need help. If you and your next door neighbor are not able to put it out, you are going to need the fire department. What should you do first? *You do the things that are most vital to assure success.* You call the fire department, rush next door to get your friend, and *then* try to put the fire out. However hastily it was designed, you actually had a plan. You took care of long-range planning when you called the fire department, a more immediate concern when you went next door, and relieved an urgent problem when you began to try to put the fire out. Without a plan you could have had a major fire.

You may feel like you have a fire in your mail center, and here's how to put it out. First, as in struggling with the fire, you need to design a *plan* to revive your mail operation. For any plan to be successful, it is wise to review the *objectives* that the plan is expected to achieve. Each of the following should be important to your operation:

[ ] Eliminate postage and shipping cost waste

[ ] Reduce operating, shipping, and postage costs

[ ] Effectively utilize all of your available space

[ ] Effectively utilize and develop mail center personnel

[ ] Effectively utilize up-to-date mailroom equipment

[ ] Provide detailed and current postal information to employees

[ ] Develop a close working relationship with the Postal Service

[ ] Understand management's concepts of the mail operation

[ ] Understand how mail impacts other departments

CREATING AN ACTION PLAN

Now take that list and number each objective in the order of its importance *to your own particular needs.* That will be your first step, to set your sights on the *most important problem area,* and so on, to the least important area of concern. Like calling the fire department, what can you do that will take the least time but have the greatest long-range impact?

Next, make a copy of the list of objectives and have it typed in the order of importance in *your* mail operation. Leave about five lines under each objective so that you might further describe the nature of your concerns. In other words, list those problems or concerns that first caused you to put a high priority on that particular objective. Then find a quiet place and patiently list each concern on your new plan. Here's what it might look like:

Effectively utilize all of your available space
    1. No established mail flow
    2. Aisles too wide, wasted space
    3. Excess incoming sorting bins
    4. Need space to tray outgoing mail
    5. Surplus desks in alcove

Effectively utilize and develop mail center personnel
    1. Staff totally disorganized
    2. Need to appoint a supervisor
    3. Need to designate primary/secondary operators
    4. Need to establish training program
    5. Need to motivate, quickly

Understand management's concepts of the mail operation
    1. Meet with my manager to probe for problem areas
    2. Explain my objectives in asking questions
    3. Obtain approval to meet with other managers
    4. Design and circulate internal mail survey
    5. Arrange meeting with V.P. Administrative Services

This is what happened. You surveyed the mail center, you talked with your six employees, and you observed them at work. When you were introduced as the new manager of mail services in the cafeteria, you heard numerous derogatory wise cracks about the organization's mail services, including two by senior managers. With that baptism of fire you decided that you had inherited a poorly arranged mail center with a group of improperly trained employees who seemed devoid of any motivation and that management thought the mail operation was somewhat hopeless. (Perhaps the very opinions of management had contributed to the disintegration of service.)

You realized that since it was a little early to throw money at the problem you would:

- Redesign the mailroom to establish better mail flow, and clean and rearrange all equipment in three weeks.

- Immediately appoint a supervisor on trial for 90 days, privately interview each employee to get acquainted, order smocks for everyone, and determine the best choice for primary machine operators.

- Keep asking questions to determine past problems, study needs of other departments for mail services, gently work your way toward top management to learn their opinions of mail service needs, and survey entire organization on mail services.

With those plans established as an outline, you must then research each area and establish a *written plan of action* detailing each step of the plan. You might well "disappear" for two or three days while you research and write out your detailed plan. When you return you should know exactly what steps you will be taking for the next two to three months. If you are unable to devote an entire day to your reconstruction plan because of day-to-day work obligations, simply make sure you work on your plan at least an hour or two every day. *Do not let the small daily fires distract you from the main conflagration.*

So much for the immediate future. But do not relax yet. Choose the next three most important objectives. Itemize the five largest related problems in each area and follow the same steps that you did earlier. Then establish a time schedule to successfully reach those goals, and continue the same steps until you have revitalized or achieved each one of the objectives you have selected..

There is no magic formula for getting started toward better mail service. It is simply a slow, some say tortuous, path taken step by step to reach established objectives within a specified time frame. One word of caution however, do not set your sights so high that your goals cannot be reached on schedule. It is far better to have a smaller list of goals and reach every one on time than to set too lofty an objective and be disappointed in your own performance. Unrealistic goals may look inspiring at the beginning but as dates come and go and they are not achieved the plan will not look so rosy.

You may not have "inherited" the present problems you are experiencing in your mail center or mailroom. A crushing work load, a skimpy budget, or other factors almost beyond your control can all contribute to a mail operation that needs to be improved. Just imagine you are walking into your office for the first time and ask yourself:

■What can I fix that will have the most impact on my overall operation?

■What can I fix with the least effort?

■What can I fix with the least cost?

After you answer those three questions, simply follow the earlier suggestions in this chapter.

One more suggestion. Regardless of how long you have been in your present position, before you do anything else, examine the kinds of postal information you have arriving on a regular basis. Shortcomings in that area can be fixed in two hours or less. Admittedly it is a long-range program when you take time to order the *Domestic Mail Manual* or a newsletter, but it is much like calling the fire department first!

Getting Started

You can write the most optimistic plan in the world but it is worthless until you *get started*. Don't put it off another day. You CAN get started *today toward better mail service*. You CAN get *the best mail service at the least cost*. You are holding all the tools you need right in your hands!

BIBLIOGRAPHY

Akers, Herbert W. *Modern Mailroom Management.* McGraw-Hill, New York, 1979.

Bovard, James. *Slower Is Better: The New Postal Service.* Policy Analysis, Issue 146. Cato Institute, Washington, DC, 1991.

Cahn, William. *The Story of Pitney Bowes.* Harper Brothers, New York, 1961.

Pitney-Bowes. *Annual Report.* 1990.

Postmaster General. *Annual Report of the Postmaster General*, Fiscal Year 1987. Washington, DC, 1988.

_____. *Annual Report of the Postmaster General*, Fiscal Year 1988. Washington, DC, 1989.

_____. *Annual Report of the Postmaster General*, Fiscal Year 1989. Washington, DC, 1990.

_____. *Annual Report of the Postmaster General*, Fiscal Year 1990. Washington, DC, 1991.

Scheele, Carl H. *Neither Snow, Nor Rain.* Smithsonian Institution Press, Washington, DC, 1970.

United Parcel Service. *Report to Shareowners.* 1990.

U.S. Congress. House of Representatives, Committee on Government Operations, Report on Hearing: *Slower First-Class Mail Delivery Standards.* Washington, DC, September 1990.

U.S. Postal Service. *Comprehensive Statement on Postal Operations*, Fiscal Year 1989. Washington, DC, 1990.

U.S. Postal Service. *Comprehensive Statement on Postal Operations*, Fiscal Year 1990. Washington, DC, 1991.

U.S. Postal Service (Moroney, Rita L). *History of the U.S. Postal Service.* Washington, DC, 1984.

TRADEMARK ACKNOWLEDGEMENTS

The following are registered trademarks of the United States Postal Service: Express Mail, Express Mail Custom Designed Service, Express Mail Next Day Service, Express Mail Same Day Airport Service, First-Class Mail, U. S. Mail, United States Postal Service, ZIP, ZIP CODE, and ZIP+4.

IBM is a registered trademark of International Business Machines Corporation.

Tyvek is a registered trademark of DuPont Company.

Rigur is a registered trademark of Poly Pak America, Inc.

Cro-nel is a registered trademark of The Crowell Corporation.

3M Polygun, Jet-melt System, Labelgard, and Scotch Pouch Tape Pads are registered trademarks of 3M Company.

Eco-Foam is a registered trademark of the American Excelsior Company.

Astro-Green is a registered trademark of Astro-Valcour, Inc.

BagTagger is a registered trademark of Whittier Mailing Products.

Visa is a registered trademark of VISA U.S.A.

MasterCard is a registered trademark of MasterCard International, Inc.

PIP is a registered trademark of Parcel Insurance Plan.

UPSCODE is a registered trademark of United Parcel Service.

APSS is a registered trademark of Aristo Computers, Inc.

LIBRA II is a registered trademark of Airborne Express.

LaserNet is a registered trademark of DHL Worldwide Express.

EMCON is a registered trademark of Emery Worldwide.

COSMOS is a registered trademark of Federal Express.

FAXLYNK is a registered trademark of DHL Worldwide Express.

EPG Automated Dispatch System is a registered trademark of Essex Products Group.

Zipnet Printer is a registered trademark of Loch Ness, Inc.

ZBC-10000 is a registered trademark of M.A.I.L. code, Inc.

Mailmobile is a registered trademark of Bell & Howell Mailmobile Company.

Transcar is a registered trademark of TransLogic Corporation.

Dispensa-Matic is a registered trademark of Commercial Mailing Accessories, Inc.

Postage on Call is a registered trademark of Friden Alcatel.

Tele Meter Setting is a registered trademark of International Mailing Systems, Inc.

Postage By Phone is a registered trademark of Pitney Bowes.

Quick Seal is a registered trademark of Mail Solutions, Inc.

EZ Seal is a registered trademark of Pitney Bowes.

Seal-Tight is a registered trademark of Postmatic, Inc.

Note: The publisher has made every attempt to supply trademark information about company names, products, and services mentioned in this book. The trademarks indicated above were derived from many sources. The publisher cannot attest to the accuracy of this information.

This book was created using *Microsoft Works* software on an *Epson Equity I+* personal computer. The text is printed in *Times Roman* fonts. The camera-ready copy was printed on an *Hewlett Packard LaserJet IIP*.

INDEX